READINGS ON AMERICAN CULTURE AND SOCIETY

读本中的美国文化与社会

王爱华 / 主编

北京大学出版社
PEKING UNIVERSITY PRESS

图书在版编目(CIP)数据

读本中的美国文化与社会/王爱华主编. —北京：北京大学出版社,2021.7
ISBN 978-7-301-32259-8

Ⅰ.①读…　Ⅱ.①王…　Ⅲ.①英语－高等学校－教材②美国－概况　Ⅳ.①H319.39

中国版本图书馆CIP数据核字(2021)第126338号

书　　名	读本中的美国文化与社会	
	DUBEN ZHONG DE MEIGUO WENHUA YU SHEHUI	
著作责任者	王爱华　主编	
责 任 编 辑	朱丽娜	
标 准 书 号	ISBN 978-7-301-32259-8	
出 版 发 行	北京大学出版社	
地　　址	北京市海淀区成府路205号　100871	
网　　址	http://www.pup.cn　新浪微博:@北京大学出版社	
电 子 信 箱	zln0120@163.com	
电　　话	邮购部010-62752015　发行部010-62750672　编辑部010-62759634	
印 　刷 　者	北京溢漾印刷有限公司	
经 　销 　者	新华书店	
	787毫米×1092毫米　16开本　15.5印张　450千字	
	2021年7月第1版　2021年7月第1次印刷	
定　　价	58.00元	

未经许可，不得以任何方式复制或抄袭本书之部分或全部内容。
版权所有，侵权必究
举报电话：010-62752024　电子信箱：fd@pup.pku.edu.cn
图书如有印装质量问题，请与出版部联系，电话：010-62756370

前　言

著名美国文化专家Ray Browne认为流行文化就像一面镜子。举起这面镜子，你就可以看到自己。因此学习流行文化有助于我们更好地了解自己。美国文化对整个世界的影响毋庸置疑，学习美国文化有助于我们了解世界。

20世纪80年代以来，世界发生了巨大的变化。世界已然成了地球村，世界各国的联系与交流日益密切。整个世界的趋势是和平发展，要发展就必须互相学习、互相借鉴。"知己知彼，百战不殆。"在当今世界，为了中美两国人民的利益，我们需要互相学习，需要建立新型大国关系，我们也需要了解美国文化。

从英语教育的角度来看，我们也需要了解美国文化。人文教育论有三个基本原则：语言教育应与人文教育紧密结合；语言能力包含思辨能力和跨文化能力；语言教学是一个合作参与的社会文化建构过程。根据此原则，本教材旨在通过语言与知识的融合式学习，同步提高语言能力、思辨能力、跨文化能力和人文素养。在了解美国文化过程中注意培养学习者文化批评能力。同时通过文化学习语言，提高英语水平和跨文化交际能力。

本教材从各类关于美国文化与社会的经典读本及其他原版读物中撷取关于美国文化与社会的代表性文章，配合相关注释与练习，帮助学习者学习了解美国社会与文化概貌、开阔视野。

本教材共有11个单元，内容涉及美国国家象征，美国地理，美国历史，美国政治体系，宗教信仰，美国教育体系，美国国民喜爱的运动，大众传媒与美国流行音乐。每单元第一部分主要是从各种关于美国文化与社会的经典读本中选取的经典篇章，用于学习从美国人的视角来看待美国社会与文化。每篇文章后面附有注释，简要解释文中重要人物、重大事件及典故，还包括单词释义及表达法释义。这些注释帮助学习者从字面了解文章内容。注释之后附有阅读理解练习。第一个理解练习对文章中有深意之处提出问题，帮助学习者从深层次了解文章内容。第二个理解练习是从文中提炼出能表达文章主要观点的句子让学习者选词填空,用以加深学习者对文章主要观点的理解。阅读理解后的结构练习提供一些有用的表达,供学习者进行语言学习与操练。

本教材每单元第二部分为文化背景注释,是笔者在阅读了各种关于美国文化与社会的原版读物之后汇编而成。主要内容出自原文,保证语言的原汁原味。此部分内容可以帮助学习者比较全面系统地了解美国文化与社会的方方面面。在此板块之后配有和各个专题相关的有用词汇与表达,帮助学习者学习关于美国文化与社会的表达方法。

笔者在北京大学开设了十几年美国文化课程,此教材是在这门课程所用材料基础上编写而成,有一定的积累与编写基础。此教材全文也经过美国杨百翰大学前商务传媒系主任Robyn Bergstrom教授仔细审阅推敲,在此深表谢意。

感谢本书选篇的各位原作者。虽然其中相当一部分作者已经作古,但是他们为我们在美国文化与社会领域的研究所留下的丰厚遗产是永不磨灭的;还有一些作者是当代研究美国文化与社会的新锐,他们的写作为我们打开了很多研究美国社会与文化的新窗口、开拓了我们研究美国文化与社会的新思路。由于种种原因,有些作者实在未能取得联系,我们也借此机会希望看到这本书的原作者与我们联系,我们在此诚挚致谢。

本书的编写和出版得到了北京大学2018年度教材建设立项的资助以及责任编辑朱丽娜老师的大力支持,在此表示衷心感谢。由于编写仓促,缺点在所难免,笔者诚挚地希望使用本教材的师生和读者提出批评和意见,以便今后改进和完善。

王爱华
2021年7月于燕园

Catalogue

Unit 1	Star-Spangled Banter	1
Unit 2	Our Wall	18
Unit 3	The Historian and His Facts	34
Unit 4	The Historian and His Facts (Part II)	59
Unit 5	The Historian and His Facts (Part III)	82
Unit 6	A Nation of Welfare Families	101
Unit 7	Toward a Hidden God	120
Unit 8	The Feel-Good Trap	146
Unit 9	Jockpop: Popular Sports and Politics	163
Unit 10	The Way We Are	189
Unit 11	Music	211
Answer Key		227

Unit 1   Star–Spangled Banter

Hendrik Hertzberg

Ted Turner set off a firecracker of his own this Fourth of July [1997]. Speaking in front of Independence Hall, in Philadelphia, he argued that it's time to dump "The Star-Spangled Banner." Over the years, Mr. Turner has had many capital ideas — CNN, Turner Classic Movies, and interrupting Jane Fonda's career as a serial monogamist, to name three. Now he has come up with another, and one cannot but agree with him. By all means, let us ease the old chestnut into well-deserved retirement. But not for the reason he offers and not to make way for the alternative he recommends.

Mr. T notes that the national anthem is warlike, whereas the age we live in is (relatively) peaceful. He is right on both counts, but his second point makes his first less compelling. Just as gun control is more urgent in Detroit than in Lausanne, bellicose songs are more worrying in bellicose times than in times of tranquility. "The Star-Spangled Banner" is warlike, yes. But so are a lot of first-rate national anthems. ("The Marseillaise," with its ghoulish call to "drench our fields" in "impure blood," makes its American counterpart sound like a Joni Mitchell ditty.) In any case, there are plenty of better reasons for getting rid of "The Star-Spangled Banner." Its tonal range corresponds to that of the electric guitar, as Jimi Hendrix proved, but not to that of the human voice. The lyrics include some fine phrases — "the twilight's last gleaming," "the ramparts we watched" — that are a reliable source of titles for the type of potboiler novel that goes in for raised lettering on the jacket, but on the whole the words don't convey what politicians call core American values. Francis Scott Key's poem was written to immortalize the siege of Fort McHenry, Maryland, during the War of 1812— a silly war, a minor war, a war that ended in what was at best a tie. (The British torched the White House and smashed our hopes of gobbling up Canada. We got to keep our independence.) The poem lends itself to mishearing, from the traditional "José, can you see" opening, through "O, sadists that stars spank," to the closing "Orlando D. Free and Homer D. Brave."

Congress designated "The Star-Spangled Banner" our national anthem during the Hoover administration, when the country's judgment was impaired by clinical depression. The relevant bill — whose sponsor hoped to promote the tourist trade in his district, which included Fort McHenry — was rejected three times by the House before it finally passed, on a slow day. It was supported by the "Americanism" busybodies of the Daughters of the American Revolution and the American Legion but opposed by music teachers — an important group at a time when pianos were more common than phonographs. The complaints then were identical to the complaints now: too martial, too irritating, too hard to sing.

What's the alternative? Mr. T suggests "America the Beautiful" — the music teachers' choice back in 1930, by the way. It's nice, but, like so many nice things, it's also wimpy. The best that can be said for it is that it's more singable than the incumbent. A third contender — "America (My Country, 'Tis of Thee)" — has O.K. words, but the tune is the same as that of "God Save the Queen." This would make for an unusually severe "Is there an echo in here?" problem during joint appearances by Bill Clinton and Tony Blair. How about "This Land Is Your Land"? Plenty of progressive-school pupils already think Woody Guthrie's populist jingle is the national anthem, but the tune is a little too Barney the Dinosaurish, and the lyrics have a musty, Popular Front feeling about them.

Our country has at hand what is perhaps the greatest patriotic hymn ever written: "The Battle Hymn of the Republic." But secularists would object that it is too God-filled, and Southerners— white Southerners, at least — would complain that the vineyards it advocates trampling were their vineyards. ("The Star-Spangled Banner" was also popular with the Union Army, but never mind.) Perhaps "The Battle Hymn of the Republic" could be twined with "Dixie," as in the Elvis Presley version, but "Dixie" has its own problems. Anyhow, serious countries do not have national medleys.

This space would like to offer a recommendation of its own: "Lift Ev'ry Voice and Sing." James Weldon Johnson, a poet of the Harlem Renaissance, wrote it, in 1990, for a Lincoln's Birthday celebration. It is already a national anthem of sorts; its alternative title, in fact, is "The Negro National Anthem." Its tune (by J. Rosamond Johnson, the poet's brother) is stirring, and so are its words. The opening verse, the one that would be sung at ballgames, goes, in part:

> Lift ev'ry voice and sing,
> Till earth and heaven sing.
> Ring with the harmonies of liberty…

Sing a song full of the faith that the dark past has taught us,

Sing a song full of the hope that the present has brought us;

Facing the rising sun of our new day begun,

Let us march on till victory is won.

No bombast, no boasting, no wimpishness — just good, solid values that are both American and universal. How about it, Ted?

→ Notes

1. **Ted Turner:** Robert Edward Turner III (1938—) is an American media mogul and philanthropist. As a businessman, he is known as founder of the Cable News Network (CNN), the first 24-hour cable news channel.

2. **Jane Fonda:** Jane Seymour Fonda (1937—) is an American actress, writer, political activist, former fashion model and fitness guru.

3. **Lausanne:** a city in the French-speaking part of Switzerland. It is the smallest city in the world to have a rapid transit system.

4. **The Marseillaise:** the national anthem of France.

5. **Joni Mitchell:** a Canadian singer-songwriter and painter. Her lyrics are noted for their developed poetics, addressing social and environmental ideals alongside personal feelings of romantic longing, confusion, disillusion, and joy.

6. **Jimi Hendrix:** James Marshall "Jimi" Hendrix (1942—1970) was an American rock guitarist, singer, and songwriter. Although his mainstream career spanned only four years, he is widely regarded as one of the most influential electric guitarists in the history of popular music, and one of the most celebrated musicians of the 20th century.

7. **Francis Scott Key:** an American lawyer and poet who wrote the lyrics to the United States' national anthem, "The Star-Spangled Banner."

8. **The War of 1812:** a military conflict that lasted from June 18, 1812 to February 18, 1815, fought between the United States of America and the United Kingdom.

9. **The Daughters of the American Revolution (DAR):** a lineage-based membership service organization for women who are directly descended from a person involved in the United States' efforts towards independence. A non-profit group, they promote historic preservation, education, and patriotism. The organization's membership is limited to direct lineal descendants of soldiers or others of the Revolutionary period who aided the cause of independence.

10. **The American Legion:** a U.S. war veterans organization headquartered in Indianapolis, Indiana.

11. **"America the Beautiful":** an American patriotic song.

12. **"My Country, 'Tis of Thee":** also known as "America," is an American patriotic song. The melody used is the same as that of the national anthem of the United Kingdom, "God Save the Queen." The song served as one of the *de facto* national anthems of the United States (along with songs like "Hail, Columbia") before the adoption of "The Star-Spangled Banner" as the official U.S. national anthem in 1931.

13. **Bill Clinton:** William Jefferson Clinton (1946—) is an American politician who served as the 42nd President of the United States from January 20, 1993 to January 20, 2001.

14. **Tony Blair:** Anthony Charles Lynton Blair (1953—) is a British politician who served as Prime Minister of the United Kingdom from 1997 to 2007 and Leader of the Labour Party from 1994 to 2007.

15. **"This Land Is Your Land":** one of the United States' most famous folk songs. Its lyrics were written by American folk singer Woody Guthrie in 1940, based on an existing melody, a Carter Family tune called "When the World's on Fire," in critical response to Irving Berlin's "God Bless America." When Guthrie was tired of hearing Kate Smith sing "God Bless America" on the radio in the late 1930s, he sarcastically wrote "God Blessed America for Me" before renaming it "This Land Is Your Land."

16. **Woody Guthrie:** Woodrow Wilson Guthrie (1912—1967) was an American singer-songwriter, one of the most significant figures in American folk music; his music, including songs, such as "This Land Is Your Land," has inspired several generations both politically and musically.

17. **Barney the Dinosaur:** a character from *Barney & Friends*. *Barney & Friends* is an American children's television series aimed at children from ages one to eight. It premiered on PBS on April 6, 1992. The series features the title character Barney, a purple anthropomorphic *Tyrannosaurus Rex* who conveys educational messages through songs and small dance routines with a friendly, optimistic attitude.

18. **Popular Front:** is a broad coalition of different political groupings, usually made up of leftists and centrists. In addition to the general definition, the term "popular front" also has a specific meaning in the history of Europe and the United States during the 1930s, and in the history of Communism and the Communist Party.

19. **The "Battle Hymn of the Republic":** also known as "Mine Eyes Have Seen the Glory," outside of the United States, is a lyric by the American writer Julia Ward Howe using the

music from the song "John Brown's Body." The song links the judgment of the wicked at the end of the age with the American Civil War. Since that time, it has become an extremely popular and well-known American patriotic song.

20. **"Dixie":** also known as "Dixie's Land," "I Wish I Was in Dixie," and other titles, is a popular song in the Southern United States. It is one of the most distinctively Southern musical products of the 19th century and probably the best-known song to have come out of blackface minstrelsy.

21. **Elvis Aaron Presley (1935—1977):** an American singer and actor. Regarded as one of the most significant cultural icons of the 20th century, he is often referred to as the "King of Rock and Roll" or simply the "King."

22. Following is the full text of James Weldon Johnson's poem, **"Lift Ev'ry Voice and Sing,"** which was quoted in Hendrik Hertzberg's article, "Star-Spangled Banter."

Lift Ev'ry Voice and Sing
Lift Ev're Voice and Sing,
Till earth and heaven ring,
Ring with the harmonies of Liberty;
Let our rejoicing rise
High as the list'ning skies,
Let it resound loud as the rolling sea.
Sing a song full of the faith that the dark past has taught us,
Sing a song full of the hope that the present has brought us;
Facing the rising sun of our new day begun,
Let us march on till victory is won.

Stony the road we trod,
Bitter the chast'ning rod,
Felt in the days when hope unborn had died;
Yet with a steady beat,
Have not our weary feet
Come to the place for which our fathers sighed?
We have come over a way that with tears has been watered,
We have come, treading our path through the blood of the slaughtered,
Out from the gloom past,

Till now we stand at last

Where the white gleam of our bright star is cast.

God of our weary years,

God of our silent tears,

Thou who hast brought us thus far on the way;

Thou who hast by Thy might,

Led us into the light,

Keep us forever in the path, we pray.

Lest our feet stray from the places, our God, where we met Thee,

Lest our hearts, drunk with the wine of the world, we forget Thee;

Shadowing beneath Thy hand,

May we forever stand,

True to our God,

True to our native land.

James Weldon Johnson (1900)

Vocabulary

1. banter ['bæntə]: *n.* friendly conversation in which people make a lot of jokes with and amusing remarks about each other   戏谑

2. dump [dʌmp]: *vt.* to get rid of something that you don't want   摆脱，扔弃

3. capital ['kæpɪt(ə)l]: *adj.* (*old-fashioned*) excellent   极好的

4. monogamist [mə'nɑgəmist]: *n.* a person that is married to only one person at a particular time   一夫一妻论者

5. chestnut ['tʃesnʌt]: *n.* (*informal*) an old joke or story that has been told so many times that it is no longer amusing or interesting   老掉牙的故事

6. bellicose ['belɪkəus]: *adj.* behaving in a way that is likely to start an argument or fight   好战的

7. ghoul [guːl]: *n.* an evil spirit in stories that takes bodies from graves and eats them   （东方神话中的）食尸鬼 /ghoulish: *adj.*

8. ditty ['dɪtɪ]: *n.* a short simple poem or song, used humorously   小曲

9. rampart ['ræmpɑrt]: *n.* a wide pile of earth or a stone wall built to protect a castle or city in the past   壁垒

10. potboiler ['pɒtbɔɪlə]: *n.* a book or film that is produced quickly to make money and which is not of very high quality, especially one that is exciting or romantic 粗制滥造的文艺作品

11. sadist ['sedɪst]: *n.* someone who enjoys hurting other people or making them suffer 虐待狂

12. impair [ɪm'pɛr]: *vt.* to change something or make something worse 损害；削弱

13. busybody ['bizi 'bɑdi]: *n.* a person who is too interested in what other people are doing 好管闲事的人

14. wimp [wɪmp]: *n.* a man who is thin and physically weak 懦弱的人 /wimpy: *adj.*

15. incumbent [ɪn'kʌmb(ə)nt]: *n.* someone who has been elected to an official position, especially in politics, and who is doing that job at the present time 现任者

16. populist ['pɒpjʊlɪst]: *n.* people who believe in a type of politics that claims to represent the opinions and wishes of ordinary people 平民政治；民意论

17. jingle ['dʒɪŋgl]: *n.* a short song or tune that is easy to remember and is used in advertising on radio or television（收音机或电视广告中容易记的）短歌，短曲

18. musty ['mʌstɪ]: *adj.* a musty room, house, or object has an unpleasant smell, because it is old and has not had any fresh air for a long time 发霉的

19. medley ['medlɪ]: *n.* a group of songs or tunes sung or played one after the other as a single piece of music 混合物

20. bombast ['bɒmbæst]: *n.* important-sounding insincere words with little meaning 夸大的言辞

Expressions

1. Ted Turner <u>set off</u> a firecracker of his own this Fourth of July.
   set off: to start a process or series of events 引发；激起

2. Now he has <u>come up with</u> another, and one cannot but agree with him.
   come up with (something): to find or produce an answer 找到（答案）

3. <u>By all means</u>, let us ease <u>the old chestnut</u> into well-deserved retirement.
   by all means: definitely or certainly 一定，务必；尽一切办法
   the old chestnut: an old joke or story that has been told so many times that is no longer amusing or interesting 老掉牙的故事

4. He is right <u>on both counts</u>…
   on all /several/ both, etc. counts: in every way, in several ways, etc. 从所有方面说；在两方面

5. The lyrics include some fine phrases that are a reliable source of titles for the type of potboiler novel that <u>goes in for</u> raised lettering on the jacket.

   go in for: to take an exam or enter a competition 参加考试（或竞赛）

6. The British torched the White House and smashed our hopes of <u>gobbling up</u> Canada.

   gobble up: to take control of 贪婪地抓住

7. This would <u>make for</u> an unusually severe "Is there an echo in here?" problem during joint appearances by Bill Clinton and Tony Blair.

   make for: to help make something possible 促成

8. Our country has <u>at hand</u> what is perhaps the greatest patriotic hymn ever written.

   at hand: very near in place or time 在手边

Comprehension

I. Discuss the Main Point and the Meanings.

1. Why did Ted Turner argue it's time to dump "The Star-Spangled Banner"?
2. What are the author's reasons for getting rid of the national anthem?
3. What are the problems with the three suggested alternatives for the national anthem in paragraph four?
4. Why does the author jokingly suggest a medley for the national anthem in paragraph five?
5. What is the solid reason for the author to recommend "Lift Ev'ry Voice and Sing" by James Weldon Johnson as the national anthem (paragraph six)?

II. Fill in the blanks with the appropriate words or expressions in the box.

core American values	that of the human voice	the Battle Hymn of the Republic
too hard to sing	solid	

1. The tonal range of the national anthem corresponds to that of the electric guitar, but not to _____.

2. The lyrics of the national anthem are a reliable source of titles for the type of potboiler novel, but on the whole the words don't convey _____.

3. Music teachers don't like "The Star-Spangled Banner" because it is too martial, too irritating, _____.

4. "_____" is perhaps the greatest patriotic hymn ever written.

5. "Lift Ev'ry Voice and Sing" conveys good, _____ values that are both American and universal.

8

→ Structure

I. Find out how the words and expressions in bold are used in the following sentences.

1. Ted Turner **set off** a firecracker of his own this Fourth of July.

2. **Over the years**, Mr. Turner has had many capital ideas — CNN, Turner Classic Movies, and interrupting Jane Fonda's career as a serial monogamist, **to name three**.

3. Now he has **come up with** another, and one **cannot but** agree with him.

4. **By all means**, let us ease the old chestnut into well-deserved retirement.

5. But not for the reason he offers and not to **make way for** the alternative he recommends.

6. "The Marseillaise," … makes its American **counterpart** sound like a Joni Mitchell ditty.

7. **In any case**, there are plenty of better reasons for getting rid of "The Star-Spangled Banner."

8. Its tonal range **corresponds** to that of the electric guitar, as Jimi Hendrix proved, but not to that of the human voice.

9. **On the whole** the words don't convey what politicians call core American values.

10. The War of 1812 ended in what was **at best** a tie.

11. **Is there an echo in here**?

12. Our country has **at hand** what is perhaps the greatest patriotic hymn ever written.

13. But secularists would **object** that it is too God-filled.

14. The opening verse, the one that would be sung at ballgames, goes, **in part**…

II. Complete the following sentences with some of the above words or expressions in bold.

1. Many local people _____ to the building of the new airport.

2. We can't get there before two _____.

3. Panic on the stock market _____ a wave of selling.

4. The British job of Lecturer _____ roughly to the US Associate Professor.

5. The women's shoe, like its male _____, is specifically designed for the serious tennis player.

6. She _____ a brilliant idea to raise the fund.

7. Several houses have to be pulled down to _____ the new theatre.

8. He'd heard her complaints _____ but didn't take them that seriously.

9. He is so brilliant. I _____ admire him.

10. I'm not a Republican, and I don't drink Scotch. So you are wrong _____.

11. There's no point complaining now—we're leaving tomorrow _____.

12. _____, I'm in favor of this idea.

National Symbols

I. Flag of the United States

Flag of the United States, popularly called the American flag, the official national flag of the United States. It consists of 13 horizontal stripes, 7 red alternating with 6 white, and in the upper corner near the staff, a rectangular blue field, or canton, containing 50 five-pointed white stars. The stripes symbolize the 13 colonies that originally constituted the United States of America. The stars represent the 50 states of the Union. In the language of the Continental Congress, which defined the symbolic meanings of the colors red, white, and blue, as used in the flag, "White signifies Purity and Innocence; Red, Hardiness and Valor; and Blue, Vigilance, Perseverance and Justice." Because of its stars, stripes, and colors, the American flag is frequently called the Star-Spangled Banner, the Stars and Stripes, or the Red, White, and Blue. Another popular, patriotic designation, Old Glory, is of uncertain origin.

II. National Anthem

Star-Spangled Banner, national anthem of the United States, approved by act of Congress on March 3, 1931. The text was written by the American lawyer and poet Francis Scott Key on board a British frigate during the British bombardment of Fort McHenry in Baltimore, Maryland, in 1814. Key had boarded the ship under a flag of truce to arrange for the release of a prisoner held by the British during the War of 1812 and had been temporarily detained during the attack. The sight of the flag still flying on the following morning inspired Key to write the poem. First printed in a handbill and then in a Baltimore newspaper, it soon became a popular song, sung to the tune of the drinking song "To Anacreon in Heaven," which was attributed to the British composer John Stafford Smith.

Unit 1   Star–Spangled Banter

The Lyrics of the National Anthem:

O say can you see, by the dawn's early light,

What so proudly we hailed at the twilight's last gleaming,

Whose broad stripes and bright stars through the perilous fight,

O'er the ramparts we watched, were so gallantly streaming?

And the rockets' red glare, the bombs bursting in air,

Gave proof through the night that our flag was still there;

O say does that star-spangled banner yet wave

O'er the land of the free and the home of the brave?

On the shore dimly seen through the mists of the deep,

Where the foe's haughty host in dread silence reposes,

What is that which the breeze, o'er the towering steep,

As it fitfully blows, half conceals, half discloses?

Now it catches the gleam of the morning's first beam,

In full glory reflected now shines in the stream:

'Tis the star-spangled banner, O long may it wave

O'er the land of the free and the home of the brave.

And where is that band who so vauntingly swore

That the havoc of war and the battle's confusion,

A home and a country, should leave us no more?

Their blood has washed out their foul footsteps' pollution.

No refuge could save the hireling and slave

From the terror of flight, or the gloom of the grave:

And the star-spangled banner in triumph doth wave,

O'er the land of the free and the home of the brave.

O thus be it ever, when freemen shall stand

Between their loved homes and the war's desolation.

Blest with vict'ry and peace, may the Heav'n rescued land

Praise the Power that hath made and preserved us a nation!

Then conquer we must, when our cause it is just,

And this be our motto: 'In God is our trust.'

And the star-spangled banner in triumph shall wave
O'er the land of the free and the home of the brave!

III. The Seal

The Seal pictures an American bald eagle holding a ribbon in its beak; the ribbon has the motto of the USA, "E PLURIBUS UNUM," meaning "Out of many, one." The eagle is clutching an olive branch (with 13 olives and 13 leaves) in one foot (symbolizing peace) and 13 arrows in the other (the 13 stands for the original 13 colonies and the arrows symbolize the acceptance of the need to go to war to protect the country).

A shield is in front of the eagle; the shield has 13 red and white stripes (representing the original 13 colonies) with a blue bar above it (it symbolizes the uniting of the 13 colonies and represents congress). Above the eagle are rays, a circle of clouds, and 13 white stars.

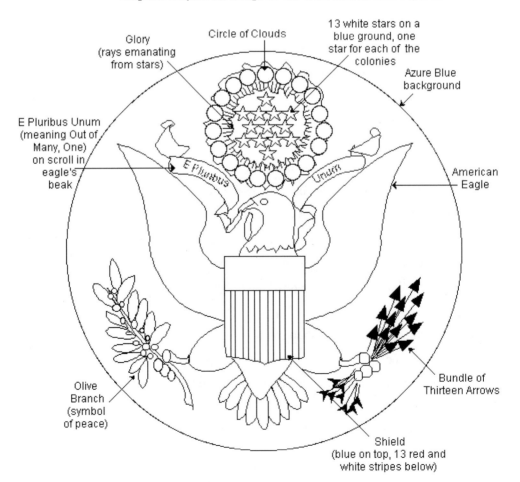

IV. The Statue of Liberty

The Statue of Liberty, national monument proclaimed in 1924. It is located on Liberty Island in the waters of New York City. This monumental sculpture has come to symbolize freedom throughout the world. Its formal name is Liberty Enlightening the World. The statue depicts a woman escaping the chains of tyranny, which lie at her feet. Her right hand holds aloft a burning torch that represents liberty. Her left hand holds a tablet inscribed with the date "July 4, 1776" (in Roman numerals), the day the United States declared its independence. She is wearing flowing robes and the seven rays of her spiked crown symbolize the seven seas and continents.

The Statue of Liberty is 46 m (151 ft) high. Its base and pedestal increase the height of the monument to 93 m (305 ft). The surface of the statue is composed of hammered copper sheets 2.4 mm (0.01 in) thick that are riveted to an iron framework. The iron frame was devised by French engineer Alexandre-Gustave Eiffel, who also built the Eiffel Tower in Paris. The statue rests upon a concrete-and-granite pedestal designed by American architect Richard Morris Hunt. A star-shaped wall surrounds the 47-m (154-ft) pedestal.

V. The Liberty Bell

The Liberty Bell is an iconic symbol of American Independence, located in Philadelphia, Pennsylvania. Bells were rung to mark the reading of the Declaration of Independence on July 4, 1776, and while there is no contemporary account of the Liberty Bell ringing, most historians believe it was one of the bells rung.

VI. Mount Rushmore

Mount Rushmore National Memorial is the national memorial authorized in 1925. Located in southwestern South Dakota, in the Black Hills, the memorial features the heads of United States presidents George Washington, Thomas Jefferson, Abraham Lincoln, and Theodore

Roosevelt carved into a granite bluff. Each face is about eighteen meters high. Sculptor Gutzon Borglum was chosen to create the Mount Rushmore memorial. It was completed in 1941, after 14 years.

Each president represents important values in America. George Washington led the cause for independence. Thomas Jefferson represented the belief in equality. Abraham Lincoln ended slavery and saved the Union. And Theodore Roosevelt was a conservationist and symbol of the progressive spirit of America.

VII. Uncle Sam

Uncle Sam is the nickname and cartoon image used to personify the U.S. government. It is derived from the initials U.S. and was first popularized on supply containers during the War of 1812. The first visual representation or caricature of an Uncle Sam figure, attired in stars and stripes, appeared in political cartoons in 1832. The character came to be seen as a shrewd Yankee, possibly after the character Brother Jonathan in the play *The Contrast* (1787) by Royall Tyler. In the 20th century Uncle Sam has usually been depicted with a short beard, high hat, and tailed coat. In 1961 the U.S. Congress adopted the figure as a national symbol.

VIII. The Bald Eagle

The bald eagle was chosen on June 20, 1782, as the emblem of the United States of America because of its long life, great strength and majestic looks, and also because it was then believed to exist only on this continent. It is a symbol of freedom, strength and courage.

Vocabulary of National Symbols

1. The Statue of Liberty is **the national monument** proclaimed in 1924.

2. The Statue of Liberty is probably **the single most iconic landmark** in all of the United States.

3. For decades, immigrants coming to New York first passed by the Statue before reaching the city, making this **a historic landmark and much-visited attraction**.

4. The Liberty Bell is **an iconic symbol of** American Independence, **located in** Philadelphia, Pennsylvania.

5. The bald eagle was chosen on June 20, 1782, as the **emblem** of the United States of America.

6. The statue **depicts** a woman escaping the chains of tyranny, which lie at her feet.

7. Mount Rushmore National Memorial, **features** the heads of United States presidents George Washington, Thomas Jefferson, Abraham Lincoln, and Theodore Roosevelt carved into a granite bluff.

8. The seal **pictures** an American bald eagle holding a ribbon in its beak; the ribbon has the motto of the USA, "E PLURIBUS UNUM," **meaning** "Out of many, one."

9. The 13 stripes **symbolize** the 13 colonies that originally constituted the United States of America.

10. The 50 stars **represent** the 50 states of America.

11. Thirteen **stands for** the original 13 colonies.

12. White **signifies** Purity and Innocence.

13. Uncle Sam is the nickname and cartoon image used to **personify** the U.S. government.

14. The Star-Spangled Banner, national anthem of the United States, was **approved** by an act of Congress on March 3, 1931.

15. The Statue of Liberty is a national monument **proclaimed** in 1924.

16. Mount Rushmore National Memorial is a national memorial **authorized** in 1925.

17. In 1961 the U.S. Congress **adopted** the figure as a national symbol.

18. Congress **designated** "The Star-Spangled Banner" our national anthem during the Hoover administration.

Unit 2 Our Wall

Charles Bowden

In the spring of 1929, a man named Patrick Murphy left a bar in Bisbee, Arizona, to bomb the Mexican border town of Naco, a bunny hop of about ten miles. He stuffed dynamite, scrap iron, nails, and bolts into suitcases and dropped the weapons off the side of his crop duster as part of a deal with Mexican rebels battling for control of Naco, Sonora. When his flight ended, it turned out he'd hit the wrong Naco, managing to destroy property mainly on the U. S. side, including a garage and a local mining company. Some say he was drunk, some say he was sober, but everyone agrees he was one of the first people to bomb the United States from the air.

Borders everywhere attract violence, violence prompts fences, and eventually fences can mutate into walls. Then everyone pays attention because a wall turns a legal distinction into a visual slap in the face. We seem to love walls, but are embarrassed by them because they say something unpleasant about the neighbors — and us. They flow from two sources: fear and the desire for control. Just as our houses have doors and locks, so do borders call forth garrisons, customs officials, and, now and then, big walls. They give us divided feelings because we do not like to admit we need them.

Now as the United States debates fortifying its border with Mexico, walls have a new vogue. At various spots along the dusty, 1,952-mile boundary, fences, walls, and vehicles barriers have been constructed since the 1900s to slow the surge in illegal immigration. In San Diego, nine miles of a double-layered fence have been erected. In Arizona, the state most overrun with illegal crossings, 65 miles of barriers have been constructed already. Depending on the direction of the ongoing immigration debate, there may soon be hundreds more miles of walls.

The 800 or so residents of Naco, Arizona, where Patrick Murphy is part of the local lore, have been living in the shadow of a 14-foot-high steel wall for the past decade. National Guard

Unit 2 Our Wall

units are helping to extend the 4.6-mile barrier 25 miles deeper into the desert. The Border Patrol station is the biggest building in the tiny town; the copper roof glistens under the blistering sun. In 2005, a pioneering bit of guerrilla theater took place here when the Minutemen, a citizen group devoted to securing the border, staked out 20 miles of the line and patrolled it. Today about 8,000 people live in Naco, Sonora, on the Mexico side of the metal wall that slashes the two communities.

Only a dirt parking lot separates the Gay 90s bar from the Naco wall. Inside, the patrons are largely bilingual and have family ties on both sides of the line. Janet Warner, one of the bartenders, has lived here for years and is one of those fortunate souls who has found her place in the sun. But thanks to the racks of stadium lights along the wall, she has lost her nights, and laments the erasure of the brilliant stars that once hung over her life. She notes that sometimes Mexicans jump the new steel wall, come in for a beer, then jump back into Mexico. The bar began in the late 1920s as a casino and with the end of Prohibition added alcohol. The gambling continued until 1961, when a new country sheriff decided to clean up things. On the back wall are photographs of Ronald and Nancy Reagan when they'd stop by on their way to a nearby Mexican ranch.

The bar is one of only a handful of businesses left. The commercial street leading to the border is lined with defunct establishments, all dead because the U.S. Government sealed the entry to Mexico after 9/11 and rerouted it to the east. Leonel Urcadez, 54, a handsome man who has owned the bar for decades, has mixed feelings about the wall. "You get used to it," he says. "When they first built it, it was not a bad idea — cars were crossing illegally from Mexico and the Border Patrol would chase them. But it's so ugly."

The two Nacos came into being in 1897 around a border crossing that connected copper mines in both nations. By 1901 a railroad linked the mines. A big miners' strike in 1906, one cherished by Mexicans as foreshadowing the revolution in 1910, saw troops from both nations facing each other down at the line. The town of Naco on the Mexican side changed hands many times during the actual revolution — at first the prize was revenue from the customs house. Later, when Arizona voted itself dry in 1915, the income came from the saloons. Almost every old house in Naco, Arizona, has holes from the gun battles. The Naco hotel, with its three-foot mud walls, advertised its bulletproof rooms.

The boundary between Mexico and the United States has always been zealously insisted upon by both countries. But initially Mexicans moved north at will. The U.S. patrols of the border that began in 1904 were mainly to keep out illegal Asian immigrants. Almost 900,000 Mexicans legally entered the United States to flee the violence of the revolution. Low population in both nations and the need for labor in the American Southwest made this

19

migration a non-event for decades. The flow of illegal immigrants exploded after the passage of the North American Free Trade Agreement in the early 1990s, a pact that was supposed to end illegal immigrants but wound up dislocating millions of Mexican peasant farmers and many small industrial workers.

The result: Naco was overrun by immigrants on their way north. At night, dozens, sometimes, hundreds, of immigrants would crowd into hotel rooms and storage rental sheds along the highway. The local desert was stomped into a powder of dust. Naco residents found their homes broken into by desperate migrants. Then came the wall in 1996, and the flow of people spread into the high desert outside the town.

The Border Patrol credits the wall, along with better surveillance technology, with cutting the number of illegal immigrants captured near Naco's 33-mile border by half in the past year. Before this new heightening of enforcement, the number caught each week, hiding in arroyos thick with mesquite and yucca, often exceeded the town's population. At the moment, the area is relatively quiet as "coyotes," or people smugglers, pause to feel out the new reality, and the National Guard has been sent in to assist the Border Patrol. At the nearby abandoned U.S. Army camp, the roofs are collapsing and the adobe bricks dribble mud onto the floor. Scattered about are Mexican water bottles — illegals still hole up here after climbing the wall.

Residents register a hodgepodge of feelings about the wall. Even those who have let passing illegal immigrants use their phones or given them a ride say the exodus has to stop. And even those sick of finding trash in their yards understand why the immigrants keep coming.

"Sometimes I feel sorry for the Mexicans," says Bryan Tomlinson, 45, a custodial engineer for the Bisbee school district. His brother Don chimes in, "But the wall's a good thing."

A border wall seems to violate a deep sense of identity most Americans cherish. We see ourselves as a nation of immigrants with our own goddess, the Statue of Liberty, a potent symbol as the visual representation of our yearning for freedom.

Walls are curious statements of human needs. Sometimes they are built to keep restive population from fleeing. The Berlin Wall was designed to keep citizens from escaping from East Germany. But most walls are for keeping people out. They all work for a while, until human appetites or sheer numbers overwhelm them. The Great Wall of China, built mostly after the mid-14th century, kept northern tribes at bay until 17th century. Hadrian's Wall, standing about 15 feet high, 9 feet wide, and 74 miles long, kept the crazed tribes of what is now Scotland from running amok in Roman Britain — from A.D. 122 until it was overrun in 367. Then you have the Maginot Line, a series of connected forts built by France after World War I to keep the German army from invading. It was a success, except for one flaw: The troops of the Third Reich simply went around its northwestern end and invaded France through the Netherlands and Belgium. Now tourists visit its labyrinth of tunnels and underground barracks.

In 1859 a rancher named Thomas Austin released 24 rabbits in Australia because, he noted, "the introduction of a few rabbits could do little harm and might provide a touch of home, in addition to a spot of hunting." By that simple act, he launched one of the most extensive barriers ever erected by human beings: the rabbit fences of Australia, which eventually reached 2,023 miles. Within 35 years, the rabbits had overrun the continent, a place lacking sufficient and dedicated rabbit predators. For a century and a half, the Australian government has tried various solutions: imported fleas, poisons, trappers. Nothing has dented the new immigrants. The fences themselves failed almost instantly — rabbits expanded faster than the barriers could be built, careless people left gates open, holes appeared, and, of course, the rabbits simply dug under them.

In Naco all the walls of the world are present in one compact bundle. You have Hadrian's Wall or the Great Wall of China because the barrier is intended to keep people out. You have the Maginot Line because a 15-minute walk takes you to the end of the existing steel wall. You have the rabbit fences of Australia because people still come north illegally, as do the drugs.

Perhaps the closest thing to the wall going up on the U.S.-Mexico border is the separation wall being built by Israel in the West Bank. Like the new American wall, it is designed to control the movement of people, but it faces the problem of all walls — rockets can go over it, tunnels can go under it. It offends people, it comforts people, it fails to deliver security. And it keeps expanding.

Rodolfo Santos Esquer puts out *El Mirador*, a weekly newspaper in Naco, Sonora, and he finds the wall hateful. He stands in his cramped office — a space he shares with a small shop peddling underwear — and says, "It looks like the Berlin Wall. It is horrible. It is ugly. You feel more racism now. It is a racist wall. If people get close to the wall, the Border Patrol calls the Mexican police, and they go and question people."

And then he lightens up because he is a sunny man, and he says it actually hasn't changed his life or the lives of most people in town. Except that the coyotes now drive to the end of the wall before crossing. And as the wall grows in length, the coyotes raise their rates. Santos figures half the town is living off migrants going north — either feeding them and housing them or guiding them into the U.S. Passage to Phoenix, about 200 miles away, is now $1,500 and rising. He notes that after the wall went up in 1996, the migration mushroomed. He wonders if there is a connection, if the wall magically beckons migrants. Besides, he says, people just climb over it with ropes.

Santos fires up his computer and shows an image he snapped in the cemetery of a nearby town. There, there, he points as he enlarges a section of the photo. Slowly a skull-shaped blur floats into view against the black of the night — a ghost, he believes. The border is haunted by ghosts — the hundreds who die each year from heat and cold, the ones killed in car wrecks as the packed vans of migrants flee the Border Patrol, and the increasing violence erupting between smugglers and the agents of Homeland Security. Whenever heat is applied to one part of the border, the migration simply moves to another part. The walls in southern California drove immigrants into the Arizona desert and, in some cases, to their deaths. We think of walls as statements of foreign policy, and we forget the intricate lives of the people we wall in and out.

Emanuel Castillo Erúnez, 23, takes crime and car wreck photos for *El Mirador*. He went north illegally when he was 17, walked a few days, then he was picked up and returned to Mexico. He sits on a bench in the plaza, shielded by a New York Yankee cap, and sums up the local feeling about the wall simply: "Some are fine with it, some are not." He thinks of going north again, but then he thinks of getting caught again. And so he waits.

There is a small-town languor about Naco, Sonora, and the wall becomes unnoticeable in this calm. The Minuteman and National Guard terrify people. At the Hospedaje Santa Maria, four people wait for a chance to go over the wall and illegally enter the wealth of the United States. It is a run-down, two-story building, one of many boarding houses for migrants in Naco. Salvado Rivera, a solid man in his early 30s, has been here about a year. He worked in Washington State, but, when his mother fell ill, he returned home to Nararit, Mexico, and is now having trouble getting past the increased security. He left behind an American girlfriend he can no longer reach.

"For so many years, we Mexicans have gone to the U.S. to work. I don't understand why they put up a wall to turn us away. It's not like we're robbing anybody over there, and they don't pay us very much."

But talk of the wall almost has to be prompted. Except for those engaged in smuggling drugs or people, border crossers in Naco, Sonora, continue to enter through the main gate, as they always have. They visit relatives on the other side, as they always have. What has changed is this physical statement, a big wall lined with bright lights, that says, yes, we are two nations.

Jesús Gastelum Ramírez lives next to the wall, makes neon signs, and looks like Willie Nelson. He watches people climb the wall and he understands a reality forgotten by most U.S. lawmakers — that simply to go through the wire instantly raises a person's income tenfold. Gastelum knows many of his neighbors smuggle people, and he understands.

Unit 2 Our Wall

Until recently, a volleyball team from the Mexican Naco and a team from the U.S. Naco used to meet once a year at the point where the wall ends on the west side of town, put up a net on the line, bring kegs of beer, and play a volleyball game. People from both Nacos would stream out to the site and watch. And then the wall would no longer exist for a spell. But it always confronts the eye.

Dan Duley, 50, operates heavy equipment and is a native of the Naco area. He was living in Germany after serving in the Air Force when the Berlin Wall came down, and he thought that was a fine thing. But here he figures something has to be done. "We need help," he says. "We're being invaded. They've taken our jobs, our security. I'm just a blue-collar man living in a small town. And I just wish the government cared about a man who was blue."

But then, as in many conversations on the border, the rhetoric calms down. Duley, along with many other Naco residents, believes the real solution has to be economic, that jobs must be created in Mexico. There is an iron law on this border: The closer one gets to the line, the more rational the talk becomes because everyone has personal ties to people on the other side. Everyone realizes the wall is a police solution to an economic problem. The Mexicans will go over it, under it, or try to tear holes in it. Or, as is often the case, enter legally with temporary visiting papers and then melt into American communities. Of the millions of illegal immigrants living in the United States, few would have come if there wasn't a job waiting for them.

Over in Naco, Sonora, the final night of a fiesta is in full roar. Men drinking beer move by on horseback, groups of girls in high heels prance past. Nearby, folks play bingo, and in the band shell a group does a sound check for the big dance. Looming over the whole party is a giant statue of Father Hidalgo with his bald head and wild eyes. He launched the Mexican Wars of Independence in 1810. Two blocks away, the steel wall glows under a battery of lights.

In the Gay 90s bar in Naco, Arizona, a *quinceañera*, the 15th-birthday celebration that introduces a young girl to the world, is firing up. There are 200 people in the saloon's back room, half from Mexico and half from the U.S. The boys wear rented tuxedo vests, the girls are dressed like goddesses. One man walks in with a baby in a black polka-dot dress with pink trim.

The birthday girl, Alyssa, stands with her family for an official portrait.

Walls come and go, but *quinceañeras* are forever, I say to the man with the baby. He nods his head and smiles.

The steel barrier is maybe a hundred feet away. Outside in the darkness, Mexicans are moving north, and the Border Patrol agents are hunting them down. Tomorrow, work will continue on the construction of the wall as it slowly creeps east and west from the town. Tourists already come to look at it.

I have no doubt someday archaeologists will do excavations here and write learned treatises about the Great Wall of the United States. Perhaps one of them will be the descendant of a Mexican stealing north this moment in the midnight hour.

Notes

1. **Prohibition:** a nationwide constitutional ban on the production, importation, transportation, and sale of alcoholic beverages from 1920 to 1933.
2. **Ronald Reagan:** Ronald Wilson Reagan (1911—2004) was an American Politician who served as the 40th president of the United States from 1981 to 1989.
3. **The Berlin Wall:** a guarded concrete barrier that divided Berlin from 1961 to 1989.
4. **Hadrian's Wall:** also called the Roman Wall, Picts' Wall, was a defensive fortification in the Roman province of Britannia, begun in 122 A.D. in the reign of the emperor Hadrian. It is the most popular tourist attraction in Northern England and was designated as a UNESCO World Heritage Site in 1987.
5. **The Maginot Line:** named after the French Minister of War André Maginot, was a line of concrete fortifications, obstacles and weapon installations that France constructed on the French side of its borders with Switzerland, Germany and Luxembourg during the 1930s. The line was a response to France's experience in World War I and was constructed during the run-up to World War II.
6. **Willie Nelson:** an American musician, singer, songwriter, author, poet, actor, and activist.
7. **Bingo:** a game of chance played with different randomly drawn numbers which players match against numbers that have been pre-printed on 5×5 cards. The cards may be printed on paper or card stock, or electronically represented, and are referred to as cards. Many versions conclude the game when the first person achieves a specified pattern from the drawn numbers. The winner is usually required to call out the word "Bingo!", which alerts the other players and caller of a possible win. All wins are checked to make sure the person has not made a mistake before the win is officially confirmed at which time the prize is secured and a new game is begun.
8. **Father Hidalgo:** Don Miguel Gregorio Antonio Ignacio Hidalgo-Costilla y Gallaga Mandarte Villaseñor (1753—1811), more commonly known as *Don Miguel Hidalgo y Costilla* or simply *Miguel Hidalgo*, was a Mexican Roman Catholic priest and a leader of the Mexican War of Independence.

Unit 2 Our Wall

Vocabulary

1. garrison ['gærɪs(ə)n]: *n.* the buildings which the soldiers live in   卫戍地

2. blistering ['blɪstərɪŋ]: *adj.* blistering heat is very great heat   酷热的

3. defunct [dɪ'fʌŋ(k)t]: *adj.* no longer exists or has stopped functioning or operating   已废止的

4. arroyo [ə'rɔɪo]: *n.* a stream or brook   小河；河谷；干涸沟壑

5. mesquite ['meskiːt; me'skiːt]: *n.* any of several small spiny trees or shrubs of the genus Prosopis having small flowers in axillary cylindrical spikes followed by large pods rich in sugar   豆科灌木（产于美国西南部和墨西哥）

6. yucca ['jʌkə]: *n.* any of several evergreen plants of the genus Yucca having usually tall stout stems and a terminal cluster of white flowers; warmer regions of North America   丝兰

7. coyote [kaɪ'oti, 'kaɪˌot]: *n.* a North American wild animal of the dog family   丛林狼；草原狼；此处指引外国人从墨西哥偷渡进入美国的不法分子

8. adobe ['ədobɪ]: *n.* mud that id dried in the sun, mixed with straw and used as a building material   （建筑用）黏土

9. hodgepodge ['hɒdʒpɒdʒ]: *n.* a number of things mixed together without any particular order or reason   杂乱无章的一堆东西

10. restive ['restɪv]: *adj.* impatient, bored, or dissatisfied   不宁的；焦躁的

11. barrack ['bærək]: *n.* a building or group of buildings where soldiers or other members of the armed forces live and work   军营

12. predator ['predətə]: *n.* an animal that kills and eats other animals   食肉动物

13. dent [dent]: *v.* to do nonphysical, usually minor damage to something   削弱

14. languor ['læŋgə]: *n.* A dreamy, lazy mood or quality   倦怠

15. fiesta [fɪ'ɛstə]: *n.* a public event when people celebrate and are entertained with music and dancing, usually connected with a religious festival in countries where the people speak Spanish   （通常指说西班牙语国家的）宗教节日，节日

16. prance [prɑːns]: *v.* walk or move around with exaggerated movements, usually because they want people to look at them and admire them   昂首阔步

17. polka-dot: 圆点花样的布料

18. excavation [ekskə'veɪʃ(ə)n]: *n.* the act or process of digging, removing earth, hollowing something out, or excavating an archaeological site   挖掘

25

Expressions

1. …the Minutemen…<u>staked out</u> 20 miles of the line and patrolled it.

   stake out: to establish the boundaries of an area intended to be used or controlled 立桩为界

2. Scattered about are Mexican water bottles — illegals still <u>hole up</u> here after climbing the wall.

   hole up: you hide or shut yourself somewhere, usually so that people cannot find you or disturb you 躲藏

3. His brother <u>chimes in</u>, "But he wall's a good thing."

   chime in: to join or interrupt a conversation 插嘴；打断谈话

4. Santos <u>fires up</u> his computer…

   fire up: If you fire up a machine, you switch it on 启动

5. The Great Wall of China… <u>kept</u> northern tribes <u>at bay</u> until 17th century.

   keep somebody at bay: to prevent an enemy from coming close 使无法近身

6. Hadrian's Wall…kept the crazed tribes of what is now Scotland from <u>running amok</u> in Roman Britain.

   run amok: to suddenly become very angry or excited and start behaving violently, especially in a public place （尤指在公共场所）发狂

Comprehension

I. Discuss the Main Point and the Meanings.

1. According to the passage, what are people's feelings toward border walls in general?

2. What is the United States predicted to do to fortify its border with Mexico?

3. What do American people feel about the wall along the border with Mexico?

4. What are walls built for in general? What is the function of the several walls mentioned in the passage respectively?

5. Why are all the walls present in Naco?

6. What do Mexicans feel about the border wall?

7. What is the author's opinion of the border wall?

Unit 2 Our Wall

II. Fill in the blanks with the appropriate words or expressions in the box.

a legal distinction	a police solution	borders	fear
feelings	fleeing	foreign policy	human needs
immigrants	the desire for control	walls	we are two nations

1. Borders everywhere attract violence, violence prompts fences, and eventually fences can mutate into _____. Then everyone pays attention because a wall turns _____ into a visual slap in the face.

2. We seem to love walls, but are embarrassed by them because they say something unpleasant about the neighbors — and us. They flow from two sources: _____ and _____.

3. Just as our houses have doors and locks, so do _____ call forth garrisons, customs officials, and, now and then, big walls.

4. Residents register a hodgepodge of _____ about the wall.

5. A border wall seems to violate a deep sense of identity most Americans cherish. We see ourselves as a nation of _____ with our own goddess, the Statue of Liberty, a potent symbol as the visual representation of our yearning for freedom.

6. Walls are curious statements of _____. Sometimes they are built to keep restive population from _____. But most walls are for keeping people out.

7. We think of walls as statements of _____, and we forget the intricate lives of the people we wall in and out.

8. What has changed is this physical statement, a big wall lined with bright lights, that says, yes, _____.

9. Everyone realizes the wall is _____ to an economic problem.

10. _____ come and go, but quinceañeras are forever…

→ Structure

I. Find out how the words and expressions in bold are used in the following sentences.

1. When his flight ended, it **turned out** he'd hit the wrong Naco, managing to destroy property mainly on the U. S. side…

2. Just as our houses have doors and locks, so do borders **call forth** garrisons, customs officials, and, now and then, big walls.

3. The gambling continued until 1961, when a new country sheriff decided to **clean up** things.

4. The two Nacos **came into being** in 1897 around a border crossing that connected copper mines in both nations.

5. The town of Naco on the Mexican side **changed hands** many times during the actual revolution.

6. The boundary between Mexico and the United States has always been zealously **insisted upon** by both countries. But initially Mexicans moved north **at will**.

7. …a pact that was supposed to end illegal immigrants but **wound up** dislocating millions of Mexican peasant farmers and many small industrial workers.

8. At night, dozens, sometimes, hundreds, of immigrants would **crowd** into hotel rooms and storage rental sheds along the highway.

9. Naco residents found their homes **broken into** by desperate migrants.

10. At the moment, the area is relatively quiet as "coyotes," or people smugglers, pause to **feel out** the new reality…

11. Residents **register** a hodgepodge of feelings about the wall.

12. …the introduction of a few rabbits could do little harm and might provide **a touch of home**…

13. And then he **lightens up** because he is a sunny man.

14. Santos figures half the town is **living off** migrants going north…

15. He notes that after the wall **went up** in 1996, the migration mushroomed.

16. He sits on a bench in the plaza, shielded by a New York Yankee cap, and **sums up** the local feeling about the wall simply: "Some are fine with it, some are not."

17. I don't understand why they **put up** a wall to turn us away.

18. Or, **as is often the case**, enter legally with temporary visiting papers and then melt into American communities.

II. Complete the following sentences with some of the above words or expressions in bold.

1. She _____ when she found out it wasn't so bad after all.

2. Voters wish to _____ their dissatisfaction with the ruling party.

3. They _____ in an unhappy marriage.

4. This company _____ many times over the years.

5. His predictions _____ to be quite wrong.

6. The immigrants were able to come and go _____ before the wall.

7. You can hear _____ sarcasm in her voice.

8. It has no industry, and about two-thirds of the population _____ the government.

Unit 2   Our Wall

9. A new social class _____ because of this change in the society.

10. His speech _____ an angry response.

11. They _____ a refund of the full amount.

12. He _____ a fence between his property and his neighbour's.

13. How many new houses _____ this year?

14. Someone _____ my car and stole my bag.

15. Robert will open the debate and I will _____.

→ U.S. Geography

I. The location and size of the United States

The United States is the third or fourth biggest country in the world. Only Russia and Canada are bigger. If you do not count the area of the Great Lakes, China is also bigger. It has an area of 9,826,630 sq km (3,794,083 sq mi). Over a quarter million square miles of U.S. territory consists of bodies of water such as the Great Lakes, and the Chesapeake Bay. The estimated U.S. population for the year 2005 is 295,734,130, third in the world behind China and India.

America consists of 50 states. And except for Hawaii which is out in the middle of the Pacific Ocean, every state is located on the Continental North America. The "Lower Forty-Eight" states cover much of the North American Continent. They are bordered by the Nations of Canada on the north and Mexico to the South.

The 50 U.S. states vary widely in size and population. The largest states in area are Alaska at 1,717,854 sq km (663,267 sq mi), followed by Texas, and California. The smallest state is Rhode Island, with an area of 4,002 sq km (1,545 sq mi). The state with the largest population is California (35,893,799, 2004 estimate), followed by Texas, and Florida. Only 506,529 people (2004 estimate) live on the plateaus and rugged mountains of Wyoming, the least populous state.

In addition to the 50 states, the United States includes a number of outlying areas, such as the Commonwealth of Puerto Rico and the Virgin Islands of the United States, which are located on the Caribbean Sea, and the islands of American Samoa and Guam located in the Pacific Ocean.

II. The Appalachian Mountains

The Appalachian Mountains are a large group of North American mountains which stretch from Alabama to the Canadian border and beyond, running parallel to the east coast. They are old mountains with many coal-rich valleys between them, and are set back from the Atlantic by a large piece of coastal lowland. While this coastal region does not contain remarkable scenery, or mineral wealth, it was here that the American nation was planted and took root in the 17th century.

The system is 2,400 km (1,500 mi) long and varies from 160 to more than 480 km (100 to more than 300 mi) in width. Its altitude varies between 460 and nearly 2,040 m (1,500 and nearly 6,700 ft). The highest is Mt. Mitchell in North Carolina (6,684 ft or 2,037m).

III. The Rocky Mountains

The Rocky Mountains are often considered to be "the backbone of the continent." The Rockies are high, rough, and irregular. The western United States around the Rockies, unlike the east, has no coastal plain. It is a peculiar and wonderful place—a land of impressive scenery, considerable environmental variety, and great mineral wealth.

It is the longest mountain chain in North America and the third longest in the world. It stretches from the northernmost part of British Columbia, in western Canada, to New Mexico, in the southwestern United States. The Rocky Mountains are more than 3,000 miles long (4,800 kilometers). The highest point in the Rocky Mountains is Mt. Elbert. Mt. Elbert is 14,433 ft tall.

IV. The Great Plains

The Great Plains are a vast grassland region of central North America extending from the Canadian provinces of Alberta, Saskatchewan, and Manitoba southward to Texas. They slope gently eastward from the foothills of the Rocky Mts. at an elevation of 6,000 ft (1,829 m) to merge into the interior lowlands at an elevation of roughly 1,500 ft (457 m).

Perhaps the most defining feature of the entire region is its relatively flat land, varying from low rolling hills in some parts to vast areas of perfectly flat landscape, almost treeless, where you can see for miles. The combination of flat lands, rich top soil and adequate rainfall and hot temperatures has made agriculture flourish throughout the region. Much of the area is used for cattle and wheat ranching. It is often referred to as the heartland, not only for its central location, but also because of its great importance in feeding and supplying the needs of the nation.

The region's continental climate creates an environment of extremes: excessive heat and cold, and violent weather patterns.

In the 1930s, areas of the Great Plains were known collectively as the Dust Bowl. Poor agricultural practices led to depletion of topsoil, which was blown away in huge dust storms.

V. The Mississippi River

Mississippi, river in the central United States, is the largest and most important river in

North America. The Indians called it the Mississippi: "Father of Waters." It is also affectionately called "Old Man River."

The Mississippi flows from near the northern border of the United States south into the Gulf of Mexico. It is 2,348 miles long; it is the second longest river in the United States behind the Missouri (2,466 miles).

The Mississippi River and its network of tributaries, which includes the Ohio, Missouri, Tennessee, Arkansas, Red, and Illinois rivers, drains most of the central United States. The waters of the Mississippi have been a vital element in forging modern America. More than half of the freight transported on inland waterways in the United States travels on the Mississippi.

Many cities and towns began along the Mississippi and continue to depend on the river for their economic base. St. Louis, known as the Gateway to the West, is located near the junction of the Missouri and grew as a port linking the Mississippi with the Great Plains.

In the 19th century, during the height of Manifest Destiny, the Mississippi and several western tributaries, most notably the Missouri, formed pathways for pioneers partaking in the western expansion of the United States.

The Mississippi is not merely a useful river; it also serves as a potent geographic symbol—the traditional dividing line in America between "East" and "West."

Mark Twain's most famous work, *Adventures of Huckleberry Finn*, is largely a journey down the river. The novel works as an episodic meditation on American culture with the river having multiple different meanings including independence, escape, freedom, and adventure.

VI. The Great Lakes

The Great Lakes are five large lakes in east-central North America. They hold 21% of the world's surface fresh water. All together, by volume, they are the largest group of fresh water lakes in the world.

All but one of the Great Lakes has a name from Native American languages: Michigan, Huron, Erie and Ontario. The biggest lake, Superior, was named by the French. Lake Superior is the largest freshwater lake in the world. Lake Michigan is the only one of the lakes that is located entirely in the United States. The other four lakes lie on the border between the United States and Canada.

Today, almost 20 percent of the U.S. population lives along the shores of the Great Lakes, concentrated in five large cities: Chicago, Illinois; Milwaukee, Wisconsin; Detroit, Michigan; Cleveland, Ohio; and Buffalo, New York. These urban centers benefit greatly because of the movement and manufacture of goods throughout the Great Lakes region.

Readings on American Culture and Society

The Rust Belt

Starting in the 1950s, the areas around the Great Lakes and in the Northeast, which had been major manufacturing centers, lost jobs as industries moved overseas or to other parts of the country. This trend accelerated in the 1970s. The area around the Great Lakes became known as the Rust Belt because of its closed, deteriorating factories. Some of the region's major 19th-century industrial towns—Detroit, Michigan; Gary, Indiana; Akron, Ohio; Cleveland, Ohio; Erie, Pennsylvania; and Buffalo, New York—lost significant population.

➡ *Vocabulary of Geography*

1. America **consists of** 50 states.

2. In addition to the 50 states, the United States **includes** a number of outlying areas…

3. While this coastal region **contains** no very remarkable scenery…

4. It **has an area of** 9,826,630 sq km (3,794,083 sq mi).

5. The United States **encompasses** some 3,794,000 square miles.

6. The "Lower Forty-Eight" states **cover** much of the North American Continent.

7. They are **bordered** by the Nations of Canada on the north and Mexico to the South.

8. Each of the these 48 states **shares a border with** at least with one other state.

9. It **shares its eastern boundary with** Canada.

10. The Gulf of Mexico **marks the border with** Mexico.

11. The Great Lakes **establish much of the border with** Canada.

12. The Appalachian Mountains **stretch** from Alabama to the Canadian border and beyond, running parallel to the east coast.

13. A major mountain system **extends** more than 4,827 km from northwest Alaska to the Mexican border.

14. In Canada the Rockies **rise to** 3,956.5 m at Mount Robson.

15. The system **is** 2,400 km (1,500 mi) **long** and varies from 160 to more than 480 km (100 to more than 300 mi) **in width**.

16. Its **altitude** varies between 460 and nearly 2,040 m (1,500 and nearly 6,700 ft).

17. The Mississippi **flows** from near the northern border of the United States south into the Gulf of Mexico.

18. The Mississippi River and its network of **tributaries, drains** most of the central United States.

19. St. Louis, known as the Gateway to the West, is located near the **junction** of the Missouri.

20. It **discharges** three times as much water as St. Lawrence.

21. The Great Lakes **hold** 21% of the world's surface fresh water.
22. Much of the region **was home to** American Bison herds.
23. When European settlers arrived, they found rivers **teeming with** wild lives.
24. The Appalachians **are rich in** coal.
25. The scenic ranges also **abound in** resorts and recreation areas.

Unit 3: The Historian and His Facts

Edward Hallett Carr

What is history? Lest anyone think the question meaningless or superfluous, I will take as my text two passages relating respectively to the first and second incarnations of The *Cambridge Modern History*. Here is Acton in his report of October 1896 to the Syndics of the Cambridge University Press on the work which he had undertaken to edit:

> It is a unique opportunity of recording, in the way most useful to the greatest number, the fullness of the knowledge which the nineteenth century is about to bequeath.... By the judicious division of labor we should be able to do it, and to bring home to every man the last document, and the ripest conclusions of international research.
>
> Ultimate history we cannot have in this generation; but we can dispose of conventional history, and show the point we have reached on the road from one to the other, now that all information is within reach, and every problem has become capable of solution.

And almost exactly sixty years later Professor Sir George Clark, in his general introduction to the second *Cambridge Modern History*, commented on this belief of Acton and his collaborators that it would one day be possible to produce "ultimate history," and went on:

> Historians of a later generation do not look forward to any such prospect. They expect their work to be superseded again and again. They consider that knowledge of the past has come down through one or more human minds, has been "processed" by them, and therefore cannot consist of elemental and impersonal atoms which nothing can alter.... The exploration seems to be endless, and some impatient scholars take refuge in skepticism, or at

least in the doctrine that, since all historical judgments involve persons and points of view, one is as good as another and there is no "objective" historical truth.

Where the pundits contradict each other so flagrantly the field is open to enquiry. I hope that I am sufficiently up-to-date to recognize that anything written in the 1890's must be nonsense. But I am not yet advanced enough to be committed to the view that anything written in the 1950's necessarily makes sense. Indeed, it may already have occurred to you that this enquiry is liable to stray into something even broader than the nature of history. The clash between Acton and Sir George Clark is a reflection of the change in our total outlook on society over the interval between these two pronouncements. Acton speaks out of the positive belief, the clear-eyed self-confidence of the later Victorian age; Sir George Clark echoes the bewilderment and distracted skepticism of the beat generation. When we attempt to answer the question, What is history? Our answer, consciously or unconsciously, reflects our own position in time, and forms part of our answer to the broader question, what view we take of the society in which we live. I have no fear that my subject may, on close inspection, seem trivial. I am afraid only that I may seem presumptuous to have broached a question so vast and so important.

    The nineteenth century was a great age for facts. "What I want," said Mr. Gradgrind in *Hard Times*, "is Fact.... Facts alone are wanted in life." Nineteenth-century historians on the whole agreed with him. When Ranke in the 1830's, in legitimate protest against moralizing history, remarked that the task of the historian was "simply to show how it really was [*wie es eigentlich gewesen*]," this not very profound aphorism had an astonishing success. Three generations of German, British, and even French historians marched into battle intoning the magic words, "*wie es eigentlich gewesen*" like an incantation — designed, like most incantations, to save them from the tiresome obligation to think for themselves. The Positivists, anxious to stake out their claim for history as a science, contributed the weight of their influence to this cult of facts. First ascertain the facts, said the positivists, then draw your conclusions from them. In Great Britain, this view of history fitted in perfectly with the empiricist tradition which was the dominant strain in British philosophy from Locke to Bertrand Russel. The empirical theory of knowledge presupposes a complete separation between subject and object. Facts, like sense-impressions, impinge on the observer from the outside, and are independent of his consciousness. The process of reception is passive: having received the data, he then acts on them. *The Shorter Oxford English Dictionary*, a useful but tendentious work of the empirical school, clearly marks the separateness of the two processes by defining a fact as "a datum of experience as distinct from conclusions." This is what may be called the common-sense view of history. History consists of a corpus of ascertained facts. The facts are available to the historian in documents, inscriptions, and so on, like fish on the fishmonger's slab. The historian collects them, takes them home, and cooks and serves them in whatever style appeals to him. Acton, whose culinary tastes were austere, wanted them served plain. In his letter of instructions to contributors to the first Cambridge Modern History he announced the requirement "that our Waterloo must be one that satisfies French and English, German and Dutch alike; that nobody can tell, without examining the list of authors where the Bishop of Oxford laid down the pen, and whether Fairbaim or Gasquet, Liebermann or Harrison took it up." Even Sir George Clark, critical as he was of Acton's attitude, himself contrasted the "hard core of facts" in history with the "surrounding pulp of disputable interpretations" — forgetting perhaps that the pulpy part of the fruit is more rewarding than the hard core. First get your facts straight, then plunge at your peril into the shifting sands of interpretation — that is the ultimate wisdom of the empirical, common-sense school of history. It recalls the favorite dictum of the great liberal journalist C. P. Scott: "Facts are sacred, opinion is free."

Now this clearly will not do. I shall not embark on a philosophical discussion of the nature of our knowledge of the past. Let us assume for present purposes that the fact that Caesar crossed the Rubicon and the fact that there is a table in the middle of the room are facts of the same or of a comparable order, that both these facts enter our consciousness in the same or in a comparable manner, and that both have the same objective character in relation to the person who knows them. But, even on this bold and not very plausible assumption, our argument at once runs into the difficulty that not all facts about the past are historical facts, or are treated as such by the historian. What is the criterion which distinguished the facts of history from other facts about the past?

What is a historical fact? This is a crucial question into which we must look a little more closely. According to the common-sense view, there are certain basic facts which are the same for all historians and which form, so to speak, the backbone of history—the fact, for example, that the Battle of Hastings was fought in 1066. But this view calls for two observations. In the first place, it is not with facts like these that the historian is primarily concerned. It is no doubt important to know that the great battle was fought in 1066 and not in 1065 or 1067. The historian must not get these things wrong. But when points of this kind are raised, I am reminded of Housman's remark that "accuracy is a duty, not a virtue." To praise a historian for his accuracy is like praising an architect for using well-seasoned timber or properly mixed concrete in his building. It is a necessary condition of his work, but not his essential function. It is precisely for matters of this kind that the historian is entitled to rely on what have been called the "auxiliary sciences" of history—archaeology, epigraphy, numismatics, chronology, and so forth. The historian is not required to have the special skills which enable the expert to determine the origin and period of a fragment of pottery or marble, or decipher an obscure inscription, or to make the elaborate astronomical calculations necessary to establish a precise data. These so-called basic facts which are the same for all historians commonly belong to the category of the raw materials of the historian rather than of history itself. The second observation is that the necessity to establish these basic facts rests not on any quality in the fact themselves, but on a priori decision of the historian. In spite of C. P. Scott's motto, every journalist knows today that the most effective way to influence opinion is by the selection and arrangement of the appropriate facts. It used to be said that facts speak for themselves. This is of course, untrue. The facts speak only when the historian calls on them: It is he who decides to which facts to give the floor, and in what order or context. It was, I think, one of Pirandello's characters who said that a fact is like a sack—it won't stand up till you've put something in it. The only reason why we are interested to know that the battle was fought at Hastings in 1066 is that historians regard it as major historical event. It is the historian who has decided for his own reasons that Caesar's crossing of that petty stream, the Rubicon, is a fact of history, whereas the crossing of the Rubicon by millions of other people before or since interests nobody at all. The fact that you arrived in this building half an hour ago on foot, or on a bicycle, or in a car, is just as much a fact about the past as the fact that Caesar crossed the Rubicon. But it will probably be ignored by historians. Professor Talcott Parsons once called science "a selective system of cognitive orientations to reality." It might perhaps have been put more simply. But history is, among other things, that. The historian is necessarily selective. The belief in a hard core of historical facts existing objectively and independently of the interpretation of the historian is a preposterous fallacy, but one which it is very hard to eradicate.

  Let us take a look at the process by which a mere fact about the past is transformed into a fact of history. At Stalybridge Wakes in 1850, a vendor of gingerbread, as the result of some petty dispute, was deliberately kicked to death by an angry mob. Is this a fact of history? A year ago I should unhesitatingly have said "no." It was recorded by an eye-witness in some little-known memoirs; but I had never seen it judged worthy of mention by any historian. A year ago Dr. Kitson Clark cited it in his Ford lectures in Oxford. Does this make it into a historical fact? Not, I think, yet. Its present status, I suggest, is that it has been proposed for membership of the select club of historical facts. It now awaits a seconder and sponsors. It may be that in the course of the next few years we shall see this fact appearing first in footnotes, then in the text, of articles and books about nineteenth-century England, and that in twenty or thirty years' time it may be a well established historical fact. Alternatively, nobody may take it up, in which case it will relapse into the limbo of unhistorical facts about the past from which Dr. Kitson Clark has gallantly attempted to rescue it. What will decide which of these two things will happen? It will depend, I think, on whether the thesis or interpretation in support of which Dr. Kitson Clark cited this incident is accepted by other historians as valid and significant. Its status as a historical fact will turn on a question of interpretation. This element of interpretation enters into every fact of history. (*to be continued*)

Notes

1. **Edward Hallett Carr** (1892—1982): an English historian, diplomat, journalist and international relations theorist, and an opponent of empiricism within historiography. Carr was best known for his 14-volume history of the Soviet Union, in which he provided an account of Soviet history from 1917 to 1929, for his writings on international relations, particularly *The Twenty Years' Crisis*, and for his book *What Is History*? in which he laid out historiographical principles rejecting traditional historical methods and practices.

2. **Acton:** John Emerich Edward Dalberg-Acton, 1st Baron Acton (1834—1902), was an English Catholic historian, politician, and writer.

3. **Sir George Clark** (1890—1979): an English historian, academic and British Army officer. He was the Chichele Professor of Economic History at the University of Oxford from 1931 to 1943 and the Regius Professor of Modern History at The University of Cambridge from 1943 to 1947. He served as Provost of Oriel College, Oxford from 1947 to 1957.

4. **The Beat Generation:** The Beat Generation was a literary movement started by a group of authors whose work explored and influenced American culture and politics in the post-World War II era. Central elements of Beat culture are rejection of standard narrative values, spiritual quest, exploration of American and Eastern religions, rejection of materialism, explicit portrayals of the human condition, experimentation with psychedelic drugs, and sexual liberation and exploration.

5. ***Hard Times***: a novel written by Charles Dickens.

6. **Ranke:** Leopold von Ranke (1795—1886) was a German historian and a founder of modern source-based history. According to Caroline Hoefferle, "Ranke was probably the most important historian to shape [the] historical profession as it emerged in Europe and the United States in the late 19th century." He was able to implement the seminar teaching method in his classroom and focused on archival research and analysis of historical documents. Building on the methods of the Göttingen School of History, Ranke set the standards for much of later historical writing, introducing such ideas as

reliance on primary sources (empiricism), an emphasis on narrative history and especially international politics.

7. **Positivism:** a philosophy of science. According to this philosophy, information derived from logical and mathematical treatments and reports of sensory experience is the exclusive source of all authoritative knowledge, and that there is valid knowledge (truth) only in this derived knowledge. Verified data received from the senses are known as empirical evidence. Positivism holds that society, like the physical world, operates according to general laws. Introspective and intuitive knowledge is rejected, as is metaphysics and theology. Although the positivist approach has been a recurrent theme in the history of western thought, the modern sense of the approach was developed by the philosopher Auguste Comte in the early 19th century. Comte argued that, much as the physical world operates according to gravity and other absolute laws, so does society.

8. **Locke:** John Locke (1632—1704) was an English philosopher and physician, widely regarded as one of the most influential of Enlightenment thinkers and commonly known as the "Father of Liberalism."

9. **Bertrand Russel:** Bertrand Arthur William Russell (1872—1970) was a British philosopher, logician, mathematician, historian, writer, social critic, political activist, and Nobel laureate.

10. **C. P. Scott:** Charles Prestwich Scott (1846—1932), usually cited as C. P. Scott, was a British journalist, publisher and politician.

11. **Caesar:** Gaius Julius Caesar (100 BC—44 BC) was a Roman politician and military general who played a critical role in the events that led to the demise of the Roman Republic and the rise of the Roman Empire.

12. **Housman:** Alfred Edward Housman (1859—1936), usually known as A. E. Housman, was an English classical scholar and poet.

13. **Pirandello:** Luigi Pirandello (1867—1936) was an Italian dramatist, novelist, poet, and short story writer whose greatest contributions were his plays. He was awarded the 1934 Nobel Prize in Literature for "his almost magical power to turn psychological analysis into good theatre."

14. **Talcott Parsons** (1902—1979), a U.S. sociologist of the classical tradition, best known for his social action theory and structural functionalism. Parsons is considered one of the most influential figures in sociology in the twentieth century. Parsons viewed voluntaristic action through the lens of the cultural values and social structures that constrain choices and ultimately determine all social actions, as opposed to actions that are determined based on internal psychological processes.

15. Kitson Clark: George Sidney Roberts Kitson Clark (1900—1975) was an English historian, specialising in the nineteenth century.

Vocabulary

1. superfluous [suːˈpɜːfluəs; sjuː-]: *adj.* more than is needed or wanted   多余的

2. incarnation [ˌinkɑːˈneiʃən]: *n.* a new personification of a familiar idea   化身

3. syndic [ˈsɪndɪk]: *n.* one appointed to represent a city or university or corporation in business transactions   理事；评审员；公司代理人

4. bequeath [bɪˈkwiːð]: *v.* to pass knowledge, customs etc. to people who come after you or live after you   把……传下去

5. judicious [dʒuˈdɪʃəs]: *adj.* careful and sensible; showing good judgement   审慎的；有见地的

6. ulitimate [ˈʌltəmɪt]: *adj.* happening at the end of a long process   终极的

7. conventional [kənˈvɛnʃənl]: *adj.* (often disapproving) tending to follow what is done or considered acceptable by society in general; normal and ordinary   墨守成规的；普通平凡的

8. supersede [ˌsupɚˈsiːd]: *v.* to take the place of something or somebody that is considered to be old-fashioned or no longer the best available   取代，替代（已非最佳选择或已过时的事物）

9. elemental [ˌɛlɪˈmɛntl]: adj. basic and important   基本的；重要的

10. scepticism [ˈskɛptɪsɪz(ə)m]: *n.* an attitude of doubting that claims or statements are true or that something will happen   怀疑主义

11. pundit [ˈpʌndɪt]: *n.* someone who is often asked to give their opinion publicly of a situation or subject   博学者

12. flagrantly [ˈflegrəntli]: *adv.* extremely bad or shocking in a very obvious way   公然的；明目张胆的

13. presumptuous [prɪˈzʌm(p)tʃʊəs]: *adj.* doing something that you have no right to do and that seems rude   冒昧的

14. broach [brotʃ]: *v.* to begin talking about a subject that is difficult to discuss, especially because it is embarrassing or because people disagree about it   开始谈论（尤指令人尴尬或有异议的话题）

15. aphorism [ˈæfərɪz(ə)m]: *n.* a short phrase that contains a wise idea   格言；警句

16. intone [ɪnˈtəʊn]: *v.* to say something in a slow and serious voice without much expression   缓慢庄重地说

Unit 3　The Historian and His Facts

17. incantation [ˌɪnkæn'teʃən]: *n.* special words that are spoken or sung to have a magic effect　符咒

18. ascertain ['æsɚ'ten]: *v.* to find out the true or correct information about something　查明

19. empiricist [ɛm'pɪrəsɪst]: *adj.* believing in the use of experiments or experience as the basis for your ideas　实证论的；经验主义者的

20. impinge [ɪm'pɪndʒ]: *v.* to have a noticeable effect on something or somebody, especially a bad one　对……有明显影响

21. tendentious [ten'denʃəs]: *adj.* a tendentious speech, remark, book etc. expresses a strong opinion that is intended to influence people　宣传性的

22. corpus ['kɔrpəs]: *n.* a collection of written or spoken texts　文集；语料库

23. inscription [ɪn'skrɪpʃən]: *n.* words written in the front of a book or cut in stone or metal　铭刻；碑文

24. fishmonger ['fɪʃmʌŋgə]: *n.* someone who sells fish　鱼贩

25. slab [slæb]: *n.* a thick flat piece of a hard material such as stone　厚板

26. culinary ['kʌlɪnɛri]: *adj.* connected with food or cooking　烹饪的

27. austere [ɔ'stɪr]: *adj.* simple and plain　朴素的；简陋的

28. pulp [pʌlp]: *n.* the soft part inside some fruit and vegetables　（瓜果等的）肉质部分

29. plausible ['plɔzəbl]: *adj.* reasonable or likely to be true　可信的

30. epigraphy [ɪ'pɪgrəfɪ; e-]: *n.* the study of ancient inscription　铭文学

31. numismatics [ˌnjuːmɪz'mætɪks]: *n.* the collection and study of money (and coins in particular)　钱币学

32. chronology [krə'nɑlədʒi]: *n.* the order in which a series of events happened; a list of these events in order　年表

33. cognitive ['kɑgnətɪv]: *adj.* connected with mental processes of understanding　认知的

34. preposterous [prɪ'pɒst(ə)rəs]: *adj.* completely unreasonable or silly　荒谬的

35. fallacy ['fæləsi]: *n.* a false idea that many people believe is true　谬误

36. eradicate [ɪ'rædɪkeɪt]: *v.* to destroy or get rid of something completely, especially something bad　根除；杜绝

37. relapse [rɪ'læps]: *v.* to go back into a previous condition or into a worse state after making an improvement　退回原状

38. limbo ['lɪmbəʊ]: *n.* a situation in which nothing happens or changes for a long period of time, and it is difficult to make decisions or know what to do, often because you are waiting for something else to happen first　处于中间的或不定的状态

Expressions

1. Ultimate history we cannot have in this generation; but we can <u>dispose of</u> conventional history...

   dispose of: to get rid of or destroy　清除；去掉

2. Indeed, it may already have occurred to you that this enquiry <u>is liable to</u> stray into something even broader than the nature of history.

   be liable to do something: be likely to do something　可能做某事

3. The Positivists, anxious to <u>stake out</u> their claim for history as a science, contributed the weight of their influence to this cult of facts.

   stake out a claim: to say publicly that you think you have a right to have or own something　立桩标出

4. Facts, like sense-impressions, <u>impinge on</u> the observer from the outside, and are independent of his consciousness.

   impinge on something/somebody: to have a noticeable effect on something/somebody, especially a bad one　对……有明显作用（或影响）

5. I shall not <u>embark on</u> a philosophical discussion of the nature of our knowledge of the past.

   embark on something: to start to do something new or difficult　着手，开始（新的或艰难的事情）

6. The second observation is that the necessity to establish these basic facts rests not on any quality in the fact themselves, but on <u>a priori</u> decision of the historian.

   a priori: using facts or principles that are known to be true in order to decide what the probable effects or results or something will be　从事实推断结果；由因及果

7. Its status as a historical fact will <u>turn on</u> a question of interpretation.

   turn on: to depend on　依赖；视……而定

Comprehension

I. Discuss the Main Point and the Meanings.

1. What is the difference between ultimate history and conventional history?
2. What did Acton believe that historians could do?
3. According to Professor Sir George Clark, what do some impatient scholar tend to believe?
4. What is the common-sense view of history?

5. Do facts speak for themselves?

6. What is a historical fact? Does it exist objectively and independently of the interpretation of the historian?

II. Fill in the blanks with the appropriate words or expressions in the box.

a corpus of ascertained facts	accuracy	certain basic facts	essential function
facts	historical facts	interpretation	objective
selective	speak for themselves	the raw materials	

1. Some scholars think since all historical judgments involve persons and points of view, one is as good as another and there is no "_____" historical truth.

2. History consists of _____. This is what may be called the common-sense view of history.

3. First get your _____ straight, then plunge at your peril into the shifting sands of _____—that is the ultimate wisdom of the empirical, common-sense school of history.

4. It recalls the favorite dictum of the great liberal journalist C. P. Scott: "_____ are sacred, opinion is free."

5. According to the common-sense view, there are _____ which are the same for all historians and which form, so to speak, the backbone of history.

6. But when points of this kind are raised, I am reminded of Housman's remark that "_____ is a duty, not a virtue." To praise a historian for his accuracy is like praising an architect for using well-seasoned timber or properly mixed concrete in his building. It is a necessary condition of his work, but not his _____.

7. These so-called basic facts which are the same for all historians commonly belong to the category of _____ of the historian rather than of history itself.

8. It used to be said that facts _____. This is of course, untrue. The facts speak only when the historian calls on them: It is he who decides to which facts to give the floor, and in what order or context.

9. The historian is necessarily _____. The belief in a hard core of _____ existing objectively and independently of the interpretation of the historian is a preposterous fallacy, but one which it is very hard to eradicate.

10. The elements of _____ enters into every fact of history.

Readings on American Culture and Society

→ Structure

I. Find out how the words and expressions in bold are used in the following sentences.

1. It is a unique opportunity of recording the fullness of the knowledge which the nineteenth century **is about to** bequeath.

2. Here is Acton in his report of October 1896 to the Syndics of the Cambridge University Press on the work which he had **undertaken** to edit.

3. Historians of a later generation do not **look forward to** any such prospect.

4. But I am not yet advanced enough to be committed to the view that anything written in the 1950's necessarily **makes sense**.

5. Indeed, **it may already have occurred to** you that this enquiry **is liable to** stray into something even broader than the nature of history.

6. In Great Britain, this view of history **fitted in** perfectly **with** the empiricist tradition.

7. The process of reception is passive: having received the data, he then **acts on** them.

8. The historian collects them, takes them home, and cooks and serves them in whatever style **appeals to** him.

9. Nobody can tell, without examining the list of authors where the Bishop of Oxford **laid down** the pen, and whether Fairbaim or Gasquet, Liebermann or Harrison **took** it **up**.

10. According to the common-sense view, there are certain basic facts which are the same for all historians and which form, **so to speak**, the backbone of history.

11. But this view **calls for** two observations.

12. It is precisely for matters of this kind that the historian **is entitled to rely on** what have been called the "auxiliary sciences" of history.

13. The second observation is that the necessity to establish these basic facts **rests** not **on** any quality in the fact themselves, but on a priori decision of the historian.

14. The facts speak only when the historian **calls on** them.

15. It might perhaps have been put more simply. But history is, **among other things**, that...

16. I had never seen it judged **worthy of** mention by any historian.

II. Complete the following sentences with some of the above words or expressions in bold.

1. You have no experience to _____; you have never seen anything like this.

2. Anxiety about climate change may have, _____, gone off the boil in Washington, where the Democrats show no appetite to decisive action.

3. It doesn't _____ for you to work for 40 years in a job you hate.

4. College professors are supposed to both teach and _____ research at the same time.

5. I _____ seeing you again soon.

6. Has it ever _____ you that he might have lied to you?

7. The painting _____ all ages and social groups.

8. The situation _____ prompt action.

9. They _____ start when it rained.

10. Their ideas did not quite _____ our plans.

→ *A Brief Introduction to American History (1)*

The beginnings of English Colonization

The English permanent settlements in North America began in the seventeenth century when Western Europe was undergoing great changes. The first new force was the development of capitalism. The second major force that brought about the modern development of Europe was the Renaissance which pushed the development of technology. The third influential force was the Religious Reformation, a religious reform movement that started from Germany. In 1517, Martin Luther, a German professor of theology, protested against the Catholic Church. The Reformation came to be called the Protestant Reformation. Soon after Martin Luther began his revolt, John Calvin, a Frenchman, who had fled to Switzerland, started his reform movement. In England, King Henry VIII, because of the political disputes with the Roman Catholic Church and because of his personal marital problems, broke away from the Roman Catholic Church and set up the Church of England, and he became the head of the Church of England himself. The religious reforms had much in common. They all challenged the authority of the Pope and the Catholic Church which controlled people's religious beliefs and interfered in political affairs of the nation states. The individual Christian believers who supported the Reformation believed that human beings could be saved only by faith, by establishing a direct contact with God, not through the church or its priests.

Jamestown, Virginia

The first English permanent colony was founded in 1607 in Jamestown, Virginia. This was organized by the London Company with a charter from the English King James I. The company sent three small ships with 144 English men to Virginia. During the long voyage across the Atlantic Ocean, 44 people died. After the colonists settled on a peninsula on the James River, they named the settlement Jamestown. Life was hard for them, because they were not fit for such work. The settlers were mostly aristocrats and artisans who did not know how to farm, fish or hunt. If not for the help of the Indians, they would be starved to death. The settlement didn't go as planned, but it still began English rule in America.

Pilgrims

The other early English settlements in North America were much to the north of Virginia, in the present state of Massachusetts. The people who settled there left England for different reasons than those who settled in Jamestown. The Virginia settlers were looking for ways to earn money for English businesses. The settlers in Massachusetts were seeking religious freedom.

King Henry the Eighth of England had separated from the Roman Catholic Church. His daughter, Queen Elizabeth, established the Protestant religion in England. It was called the Church of England, or the Anglican Church. The Anglican Church, however, was similar to that of the Roman Catholic Church.

Not all Protestants liked this. Some wanted to leave the Anglican Church and form religious groups of their own. In 1606, members of one such group in the town of Scrooby did separate from the Anglican Church. About 125 people left England for Holland. They found problems there too, so they decided to move again to the New World.

These people were called pilgrims, because that is the name given to people who travel for religious purposes. They came to America on a ship call Mayflower in 1620. They established the Plymouth Colony in today's Massachusetts.

Puritans

Other English settlers began arriving in the area now called New England. One large group was called the Puritans. Like the pilgrims, the Puritans did not agree with the Anglican Church. But they did not want to separate from it. The Puritans wanted to change it to make it more holy. Their desire for this change made them unwelcome in England.

The first ship carrying Puritans left England for America in 1630. By the end of that summer, one thousand Puritans had landed in the northeastern part of the new country. The new English King, Charles, had given permission for them to settle the Massachusetts Bay area.

Puritans thought their religions was the only true religion and everyone should believe in it. They also believed that church leaders should lead the local government, and all people in the colony should pay to support the Puritan church. The Puritans thought it was the job of the government leaders to tell people what to believe.

Rhode Island

Some people did not agree with the Puritans who had become leaders of the colony. One of those who disagreed was a Puritan minister named Roger Williams.

Roger Williams believed, as all Puritans did that other European religions were wrong. He thought the Native Indian religions were wrong too. But he did not believe in trying to force others to agree with him. He thought that it was a sin to punish or kill anyone in the name of Christianity, and he thought that only church members should pay to support their church.

The Puritan leaders of the Massachusetts Bay Colony forced Roger Williams to leave the colony in 1636. He traveled south. He bought land from local Indians and started a city, Providence. The Parliament in England gave him permission to establish a new colony, Rhode Island, with Providence as its capital. As a colony, Rhode Island accepted people of all religious beliefs, including Catholics, Quakers, Jews and even people who denied the existence of God.

Roger Williams also believed that governments should have no connection to a church. This idea of separating church and state was very new. Later it became one of the most important of all America's governing ideas.

Quakers

One religious group that was not welcome in England was the Quakers. Quakers call themselves Friends. They believe that each person has an inner light that leads them to God. Quakers believe they do not need a religious leader to tell them what is right. So, they had no clergy.

Quakers believe that all people are equal. The Quakers in England refused to recognize the king as more important than anyone else. They also refused to pay taxes to support the Anglican Church. Quakers believe that it is always wrong to kill. So they would not fight even when they were forced to join the army. They also refused to promise loyalty to a king or government or flag or anyone but God.

The English did not like the Quakers for all these reasons. Many Quakers wanted to leave England, but were not welcome in most American colonies. One Quaker changed this. His name was William Penn.

In 1681, the king gave William Penn land which the King's Council named Pennsylvania, meaning Penn's woods.

The Quakers now had their own colony. It was between the Puritans in the north and the Anglicans in the south. William Penn said the colony should be a place where everyone could live by Quaker ideas.

That meant treating all people as equals and honoring all religions. It also meant that anyone could be elected. In most other colonies, people could believe any religion, but they could not vote or hold office unless they were a member of the majority church. In Pennsylvania, all religions were equal.

French and Indian War

During the eighteenth century, Spain, France and Britain controlled land in North America. Spain controlled Florida. France was powerful in the northern and central areas. Britain controlled the east. All three nations knew they could not exist together peacefully in North America. The situation could only be settled by war.

The French and Indian War was fought to decide if Britain or France would be the strong power in North America. France and its colonists and Indian allies fought against Britain, its colonists and Indian allies.

Britain and France signed a treaty to end it in Paris in 1773. The British had won.

After that Britain claimed all the land from the east coast of North America to the Mississippi River. Everything west of that river belonged to Spain. France gave all its western lands to Spain to keep the British out. Indians still controlled most of the western lands, except for some Spanish colonies in Texas and New Mexico.

American Revolution

After the French and Indian War, Britain imposed a series of direct taxes, adopting the policy that the colonies should pay a token proportion of the costs associated with defending them. The taxes together with other laws proved extremely unpopular in America despite the level of taxation being only 1/26 that paid by British taxpayers. Because the colonies lacked elected representation in the governing British Parliament, many colonists considered the laws to be illegitimate and a violation of their rights as Englishmen. **Taxation without representation** led to growing anger in the American colonies. It was one of the most important reasons for the American Revolution.

Boston Massacre

The road to revolution lasted several years. The most serious events began in 1770.

Relations between Britain and its American colonists were most tense in the colony of Massachusetts. There were protests against the British policy of taxing the colonies without giving them representation in Parliament. To prevent trouble, thousands of British soldiers were sent to Boston, the biggest city in Massachusetts. On March 5, 1770, tension led to violence. Five colonists were killed. The incident became known as the Boston Massacre.

The Boston Tea Party

To protect the interests of the East India Company, the British government decided to permit it to sell tea directly to the American colonies. The colonies would still have to pay a tea tax to Britain. The Americans did not like the new plan. They felt they were being forced to buy their tea from only one company. Officials in the colonies of Pennsylvania and New York sent the East India Company's ships back to Britain. In Massachusetts, things were different. The British governor there wanted to collect the tea tax and enforce the law. When the ships arrived in Boston, some colonists tried to block their way. The ships remained just outside the harbor without unloading their goods. On the night of December 16, 1773, a group of colonists went out in a small boat. They got on a British ship and threw all the tea into the water. The colonists were dressed as American Indians so the British would not recognize them, but the people of Boston knew who they were. A crowd gathered to cheer them. That incident — the night when British tea was thrown into Boston harbor — became known as the Boston Tea Party.

First Continental Congress

In June, 1774, the colony of Massachusetts called for a meeting of delegates from all the other colonies to consider joint action against Britain. This meeting of colonial delegates was called the First Continental Congress. It was held in the city of Philadelphia, Pennsylvania, in September, 1774. All the colonies except one was represented. The southern colony of Georgia did not send a delegate. Some say by then the American revolution started at that time.

Battle at Lexington and Concord — The Fighting Begins

By 1775, the colonists were prepared for war. Groups of armed men were doing military exercises in towns all around Massachusetts and in other colonies, too. And the colonists had been gathering weapons in the town of Concord, about 30 kilometers west of Boston. On April 19, 1775, the British forces were ordered to seize the weapons. But the colonists knew they were coming and were prepared. When the British reached the town of Lexington, they found it protected by about 70 colonial troops. These troops were called "Minute Men" because they had been trained to fight with only a minute's warning. Guns were fired. Eight colonists were killed. From Lexington, the British marched to Concord, where they destroyed whatever supplies the colonists had not been able to save. Other colonial troops rushed to the area. A battle at Concord's north bridge forced the British to march back to Boston. They were the first military engagements of the American Revolution War.

Common Sense

At the beginning, the Continental Army lost many early battles because it was full of volunteers who were inexperienced. However, morale did increase. People read Thomas Paine's pamphlet "Common Sense" where he confirmed them the only cause was independence and America cannot be controlled by Great Britain. In addition, the Americans proclaimed their liberty and independence by the Declaration of Independence.

Declaration of Independence

On July 4, 1776, representatives from each of the original 13 states voted unanimously in the Second Continental Congress to adopt a Declaration of Independence, which now rejected the British monarchy in addition to its Parliament, and established the sovereignty of the new nation. The Declaration established the United States, which was originally governed as a loose confederation through a representative democracy selected by state legislatures.

The Treaty of Paris

The Battle at Saratoga was the turning point of the war. After the battle, France joined the war on America's side. Also, the British public had stopped supporting the long and costly war. Finally the British Army surrendered in Yorktown, 1781.

Great Britain abandoned any claims of the United States with the Treaty of Paris in 1783. The independence of the United States was recognized. Western and northern borders were set.

The Articles of Confederation

America's first national government reflected widespread fears of centralized authority and its potential for corruption. In 1776 John Dickinson drafted a proposal for a national government, which he called the Articles of Confederation. Congress adopted a weakened version of the Articles and sent it to the states for ratification in 1777. The Articles finally became law in March 1781.

The Articles explicitly reserved to each state "its sovereignty, freedom and independence" and established a form of government in which Americans were citizens of their own state first and of the United States second.

The Articles of Confederation did not organize a central government. They did not create courts or decide laws. They did not provide an executive to carry out the laws. All the Articles of Confederation did was to create a Congress. But it was a Congress with little power.

The Constitution

The weakness of the system under the Articles of Confederation became clear soon after the war for independence ended. In 1787, 55 delegates met in Philadelphia as part of the Constitutional Convention. After much debate, James Madison wrote a new constitution.

On September 17, 1787, the Constitution of the United States was approved. It successfully reconciled the conflicting interests of the large and small states. Out of hard bargaining among different states' representatives emerged the Constitution's delicate balance between the desire of nearly all delegates for a stronger national government and their fear that governments tended to grow despotic. The Constitution augmented national authority in several ways. It vested in Congress to lay and collect taxes, to regulate interstate commerce, and to conduct diplomacy. All state officials had to swear to uphold the Constitution, even against acts of their own states. The national government could use military force against any state.

Although leaving much authority to the states, the Constitution established a national government clearly superior to the states in several spheres, and it utterly abandoned the notion of a federation of virtually independent states.

The Constitution became the law of the land on June 21, 1788, when the ninth state, New Hampshire, ratified by the close vote of 57—47.

The Federalists and Republicans

In 1789, George Washington was inaugurated as the first president of the United States. By the end of Washington's second term, politically conscious Americans had split into two hostile parties, Federalists and Republicans. The leader of the Federalists was Treasury Secretary Alexander Hamilton. The leader of the Republicans was Secretary of State Thomas Jefferson. Each group represented the political beliefs of its leader.

Hamilton and the Federalists wanted a strong national government with a powerful president and courts. They supported policies that helped bankers and wealthy businessmen. They urged close economic and diplomatic ties with Britain. They did not like democracy, which they described as mob rule.

The Federalists were extremely powerful. They controlled the Congress during the presidency of George Washington. And they almost controlled Washington himself, through his dependence on Alexander Hamilton.

Thomas Jefferson and the Republicans supported the Constitution as a plan of government. But they did not think the Constitution gave the national government unlimited powers.

They supported policies that helped the nation's farmers and small businessmen. They urged closer ties with the French people, who were rebelling against their king. And they demanded more rights and more democracy, for the people of the United States.

War of 1812

The Federalists as a national political force was eliminated after the war of 1812. The War of 1812 was a military conflict fought between the forces of the United States of America and those of the British Empire. The Americans declared war in 1812 for several reasons, including trade restrictions because of Britain's ongoing war with France, impressment of American merchant sailors into the Royal Navy, British support of American Indian tribes against American expansion, and over national honor after humiliations on the high seas.

During the war, British troops burned the presidential mansion along with other public buildings in Washington. Whitewash cleared the smoke damage to the presidential mansion; thereafter, it became known as the White House. The British attack on Fort McHenry, guarding Baltimore, prompted a young observer, Francis Scott Key, to compose "The Star-Spangled Banner." The final treaty, signed on Christmas Eve 1814, restored the status quo ante bellum: the United States neither gained nor lost territory.

The Monroe Doctrine

During the first quarter of the nineteenth century, besides Mexico almost every other important economy in Latin America gained independence from its mother country in Europe. However, as this occurred, certain powerful monarchies in Europe threatened to stamp out representative governments if they developed in the old colonies. That was the reason that in 1823 President James Monroe issued his now famous statement called the Monroe Doctrine. The message announced three key principles: that unless American interests were involved, the United States' policy was to abstain from European wars; that the "American continents" were not "subjects for future colonization by any European power"; and that the United States would construe any attempt at European colonization in the New World as an "unfriendly act." It was a uni-lateral declaration against European interference in the New World. The idea spelt out in Monroe Doctrine were very important and continued to shape American foreign policy to this very day.

Civil War

The publication in 1852 of Harriet Beecher Stowe's novel *Uncle Tom's Cabin* aroused wide northern sympathy for fugitive slaves.The 1850s were an increasingly tense time in the United States. The biggest legal question facing America was slavery.

Different belief systems and economies caused a rift between the northern and southern states. The north opposed the spread of slavery into states where slavery didn't already exist. Meanwhile, southern economy was largely based on plantations run by slave labor. So that region fought anti-slavery. They looked for compromises. Congress had passed a series of agreements, seeking to keep a balance between slave and free states. But when Abraham Lincoln was elected president in 1860, his opposition to slavery was seen as a threat to the economic interests of the Southern states.

On December 20, 1860, a South Carolina convention voted unanimously for secession; and by February 1, 1861, Alabama, Mississippi, Florida, Georgia, Louisiana, and Texas had followed South Carolina's lead. On February 4, 1861 delegates from these seven states met in Montgomery, Alabama and established the Confederate State of America. Jefferson Davis was inaugurated in February 1861 as the first president of the Confederacy.

To gain the dubious military advantage of attacking Fort Sumter, South Carolina, Confederate batteries began to bombard the fort shortly before dawn on April 12, 1861. It was the beginning of war.

When President Lincoln requested volunteer armies from each state, it caused four more states to secede and join the Confederacy. That meant eleven Confederate states versus 23 union states.

On January 1, 1863, Lincoln issued the Emancipation Proclamation. This document declared freedom for three quarters of the country's slaves and made slavery a priority of the war. It changed the dynamic of the war. The Union Army became a force for liberation. Black American soldiers rushed to enlist for the Union.

After four years of warfare, mostly within the Southern states, the Confederacy surrendered and slavery was outlawed everywhere in the nation. Southern influence in the U.S. had weakened.

Civil War remains the deadliest war in American history. The 620,000 American soldiers who lost their lives between 1861 and 1865 nearly equaled the number of American soldiers killed in all the nation's earlier and later wars combined.

Reconstruction Era of the United States

The Reconstruction period followed the Civil War. "Reconstruction Era" refers to the transformation of the Southern United States from 1863 to 1877, with the reconstruction of state and society in the former Confederacy. In battles between the president and Congress, the president prevailed until the election of 1866, which enabled the radical Republicans to take control of policy. A Republican coalition came to power in the southern states and set out to radically transform the society, with support from the Army and the Freedman's

Bureau. They removed from power the ex-Confederates, and enfranchised the Freedmen (freed slaves).

They introduced various reconstruction programs, including the founding of public schools in most states for the first time, and the establishment of charitable institutions. They raised taxes, which historically had been low as planters preferred to make private investments for their own purposes; offered massive aid to support railroads to improve transportation and shipping.

But conservative white Democrats calling themselves "Redeemers" regained control state by state, sometimes using fraud and violence to control state elections. A deep national economic depression following the Panic of 1873 led to major Democratic gains in the North, the collapse of many railroad schemes in the South, and a growing sense of frustration in the North. To keep the country together, Congress passed the Compromise of 1877, and withdrew the federal troops from the south. Republican control collapsed in the last three state governments in the South. This was followed by a period that white Southerners labeled Redemption, in which white-dominated state legislatures enacted Jim Crow laws and (after 1890) disfranchised most blacks and many poor whites through a combination of constitutional amendments and electoral laws. The Democratic Party monopolized the "New South" into the 1960s, when the civil rights and voting rights of African Americans were finally protected and enforced under new federal laws passed by the US Congress.

Jim Crow

Jim Crow, the system of laws and customs that enforced racial segregation and discrimination throughout the United States, especially the South, from the late 19th century to the 1960s.

Jim Crow was the name of a character in minstrelsy (in which white performers in blackface used African American stereotypes in their songs and dances); it is not clear how the term came to describe American segregation and discrimination.

Ku Klux Klan

The organized persecution of black Americans started right after the Civil War. In the spring of 1866, six young Confederate war veterans in Tennessee formed a social club, the Ku Klux Klan. Distinguished by elaborate rituals, hooded costumes, and secret passwords, the Klan's goals were to suppress black voting, reestablish white supremacy, and topple the Reconstruction governments. By 1872 the federal government had effectively suppressed the Klan.

Unit 3 The Historian and His Facts

In November 1915, a group of hooded men gathered at Stone Mountain, Georgia, and revived it. The Klan's promise to restore the nation to an imagined purity—ethnic, moral, and religious — appealed powerfully to ill-educated, deeply religious, and economically marginal Americans threatened by a rapidly changing society. The Klan collapsed with shocking suddenness.

But the Klan did not die, and after World War II again surfaced as a malignant influence in American life.

The Gilded Age

After the Civil War and Reconstruction, the era of rapid economic and population growth in the United States was dubbed "The Gilded Age." The term "Gilded Age" was coined by Mark Twain and Charles Dudley Warner in their book *The Gilded Age: A Tale of Today*.

The Gilded Age is most famous for the creation of a modern industrial economy. During the 1870s and 1880s, the U.S. economy grew at the fastest rate in its history, with real wages, wealth, GDP, and capital formation all increasing rapidly. Large corporations spread across the country.

But this period of growth also included corruption and inequality. Big businesses used their growing profit and power to destroy competitors and formed monopolies in the railroad, coal, steel and oil industries. Working conditions in mines and factories were harsh and dangerous. And as people flooded into cities in search of work, the problems of crowded housing and poor sanitation increased. Corrupted city leaders accepted bribes and gave contracts and jobs to their political allies.

At that time, some of the industrialists and financiers such as John D. Rockefeller, Andrew W. Mellon, Andrew Carnegie, Henry Flagler, Henry H. Rogers, J. P. Morgan, Cornelius Vanderbilt of the Vanderbilt family, and the prominent Astor family rose to position of great power in business. They were attacked as "robber barons" by critics, who believed they cheated to get their money and lorded it over the common people.

But the political system lagged behind in addressing the social problems of an increasingly urbanized and industrialized nation.

Progressive Era

The reform movement of progressivism arose to combat the greed, corruption and other problems the industrialization had created.

The Progressive Era in the United States was a period of social activism and political reform that flourished from the 1890s to the 1920s. Initially the movement operated chiefly at

55

local levels; later it expanded to state and national levels. The progressives viewed government as a major ally in the reform cause. And far from glorifying the individual or withdrawing from society, they saw organizations and social engagement as essential to reform.

One main goal of the Progressive movement was purification of government. Many reformers also insisted that restoring democracy required stricter regulation of business. Other reformers, emphasizing the humanitarian theme, called for laws to protect workers and urban poor. Finally, some reformers, viewing immigration, urban immorality, and incipient social disorder as the central problems, fought for immigration restriction, the abolition of prostitution and saloons, and other social-control strategies. All this contributed to the mosaic of progressive reform.

Progressive writers wrote fictional stories and poetry that revealed the hardships faced by many people living in American cities. Progressive journalists used biting articles and cartoons in newspapers and magazines to expose the corruption of city bosses and business leaders. These writers were called the "muckrakers" because they dug into the dirty deeds of those they wished to expose.

Teddy Roosevelt was America's first progressive president. Between 1901 and 1908, Roosevelt used his position to break up many trusts. These were huge combinations of companies that used their economic power to take advantage of their competitors and workers. Roosevelt's "square deal" was designed to give all Americans an equal chance to succeed.

Progressives also hoped to win the right for women to vote. Female activists had been fighting for the votes since the 1840s. Finally under President Woodrow Wilson, reformers convinced Congress to pass the 19th Amendment to the Constitution. Now women were guaranteed the right to vote.

Vocabulary of History/American History

1. It is a unique opportunity of **recording** the fullness of knowledge.

2. **Historians** of a later generation do not look forward to any such prospect.

3. Since all **historical judgments** involve persons and points of view, one is as good as another and there is no "**objective**" **historical truth**.

4. History consists of a corpus of ascertained **facts**.

5. Not all facts about the past are **historical facts**.

6. The element of **interpretation** enters into every fact of history.

7. The first English permanent **colony** was **founded** in 1607 in Jamestown, Virginia.

8. The other early English **settlements** in North America were much to the north of Virginia.

9. The Virginia **settlers** were looking for ways to earn money for English businesses.

10. These people were called **pilgrims**, because that is the name given to people who travel for religious purposes.

11. Like the Pilgrims, the **Puritans** did not agree with the Anglican Church.

12. **Quakers** believe that all people are equal.

13. After the French and Indian War, Britain **imposed** a series of direct taxes.

14. The British governor there wanted to collect the tea tax and **enforce** the law.

15. There were **protests** against the British policy of taxing the colonies without giving them representation in Parliament.

16. The road to revolution lasted several years. **The most serious events** began in seventeen seventy.

17. Five **colonists** were killed. The **incident** became known as the Boston Massacre.

18. In June, 1774, the colony of Massachusetts called for a meeting of **delegates** from all the other colonies to consider joint action against Britain.

19. In 1776, representatives from each of the original 13 states **voted** unanimously in the Second Continental Congress to adopt a Declaration of Independence.

20. The Declaration **established** the United States.

21. In 1776 John Dickinson **drafted** a proposal for a national government, which he called the Articles of Confederation.

22. The Articles finally became law in March 1781.

23. On September 17, 1787, the Constitution of the United States was **approved**.

24. The Americans **declared war** in 1812 for several reasons.

25. The final **treaty**, signed on Christmas Eve 1814, restored the status quo ante bellum: the United States neither gained nor lost **territory**.

27. The largest question affecting western lands was slavery, so they looked for **compromises**.

28. On December 20, 1860, a South Carolina convention voted unanimously for **secession**.

29. Jefferson Davis was inaugurated in February 1861 as the first president of the **Confederacy**.

30. "Reconstruction Era" refers to the **transformation** of the Southern United States from 1863 to 1877.

31. Congress **passed** the Reconstruction Act of 1867 and Johnson **vetoed** it.

32. This was followed by a period that white Southerners labeled Redemption, in which white-dominated state legislatures **enacted** Jim Crow laws…

33. It is not clear how Jim Crow came to describe American **segregation** and **discrimination**.

34. The goals of Ku Klux Klan were to suppress black voting, reestablish **white supremacy**, and topple the Reconstruction governments.

35. The super-rich industrialists and financiers in the Gilded Age were attacked as "**robber barons**" by critics.

36. Progressive journalists used biting articles and cartoons in newspapers and magazines to expose the corruption of city bosses and business leaders. They were called the "**muckrakers**."

Unit 4 The Historian and His Facts (Part II)

Edward Hallett Carr

May I be allowed a personal reminiscence? When I studied ancient history in this university many years ago, I had as a special subject "Greece in the period of the Persian Wars." I collected fifteen or twenty volumes on my shelves and took it for granted that there, recorded in these volumes, I had all the facts relating to my subject. Let us assume—it was very nearly true—that those volumes contained all the facts about it that were then known, or could be known. It never occurred to me to enquire by what accident or process of attrition that minute selection of facts, out of all the myriad facts that must have once been known to somebody, had survived to become the facts of history. I suspect that even today one of the fascinations of ancient and mediaeval history is that it gives us the illusion of having all the facts at our disposal within a manageable compass: the nagging distinction between the facts of history and other facts about the past vanishes because the few known facts are all facts of history. As Bury, who had worked in both periods, said, "the records of ancient and mediaeval history are starred with lacunae." History has been called an enormous jig-saw with a lot of missing parts. But the main trouble does not consist of the lacunae. Our picture of Greece in the fifth century B.C. is defective not primarily because so many of the bits have been accidentally lost, but because it is, by and large, the picture formed by a tiny group of people in the city of Athens. We know a lot about what fifth-century Greece looked like to an Athenian citizen; but hardly anything about what it looked like to a Spartan, a Corinthian, or a Theban—not to mention a Persian, or a slave or other non-citizen resident in Athens. Our picture has been preselected and predetermined for us, not so much by accident as by people who were consciously or unconsciously imbued with a particular view and thought the facts which supported that view worth preserving. In the same way, when I read in a modern history of the Middle Ages that the people of the Middle Ages were deeply concerned with religion, I wonder how we know this, and whether it is true. What we know as the facts of mediaeval history have almost all been selected for us by generations of chroniclers who were professionally occupied in the theory and practice of religion, and who therefore thought it supremely important, and recorded everything relating to it, and not much else. The picture of the Russian peasant as devoutly religious was destroyed by the revolution of 1917. The picture of mediaeval man as devoutly religious, whether true or not, is indestructible, because nearly all the known facts about him were preselected for us by people who believed it, and wanted others to believe it, and a mass of other facts, in which we might possibly have found evidence to the contrary, has been lost beyond recall. The dead hand of vanished generations of historians, scribes, and chroniclers has determined beyond the possibility of appeal the pattern of the past. "The history we read," writes Professor Barraclough, himself trained as a mediaevalist, "though based on facts, is, strictly speaking, not factual at all, but a series of accepted judgments."

But let us turn to the different, but equally grave, plight of the modern historian. The ancient or mediaeval historian may be grateful for the vast winnowing process which, over the years, has put at his disposal a manageable corpus of historical facts. As Lytton Strachey said in his mischievous way, " ignorance is the first requisite of the historian, ignorance which simplifies and clarifies, which selects and omits." When I am tempted, as I sometimes am, to envy the extreme competence of colleagues engaged in writing ancient or mediaeval history, I find consolation in the reflection that they are so competent mainly because they are so ignorant of their subject. The modern historian enjoys none of the advantages of this built-in ignorance. He must cultivate this necessary ignorance for himself—the more so the nearer he comes to his own times. He has the dual task of discovering the few significant facts and turning them into facts of history, and of discarding the many insignificant facts as unhistorical. But this is the very converse of the nineteenth-century heresy that history consists of the compilation of a maximum number of irrefutable and objective facts. Anyone who succumbs to this heresy will either have to give up history as a bad job, and take to stamp-collecting or some other form of antiquarianism, or end in a madhouse. It is this heresy, which during the past hundred years has had such devastating effects on the modern historian, producing in Germany, in Great Britain, and in the United States a vast and growing mass of dry-as-dust factual histories, of minutely specialized monographs, of would-be historians knowing more and more about less and less, sunk without trace in an ocean of facts. It was, I suspect, this heresy—rather than the alleged conflict between liberal and Catholic loyalties—which frustrated Acton as a historian. In an early essay he said of his teacher Dollinger: "He would not write with imperfect materials, and to him the materials were always imperfect." Acton was surely here pronouncing an anticipatory verdict on himself, on that

Unit 4 The Historian and His Facts (Part II)

strange phenomenon of a historian whom many would regard as the most distinguished occupant the Regius Chair of Modern History in this university has ever had—but who wrote no history. And Acton wrote his own epitaph in the introductory note to the first volume of *the Cambridge Modern History*, published just after his death, when he lamented that the requirements pressing on the historian "threaten to turn him from a man of letters into the compiler of an encyclopedia." Something had gone wrong. What had gone wrong was the belief in this untiring and unending accumulation of hard facts as the foundation of history, the belief that facts speak for themselves and that we cannot have too many facts, a belief at that time so unquestioning that few historians then thought it necessary—and some still think it unnecessary today—to ask themselves the question: What is history?

The nineteenth-century fetishism of facts was completed and justified by a fetishism of documents. The documents were the Ark of the Covenant in the temple of facts. The reverent historian approached them with bowed head and spoke of them in awed tones. If you find it in the documents, it is so. But what, when we get down to it, do these documents—the decrees, the treaties, the rent-rolls, the blue books, the official correspondence, the private letters and diaries—tell us? No document can tell us more than what the author of the document thought—what he thought had happened, what he thought ought to happen or would happen, or perhaps only what he wanted others to think he thought, or even only what he himself thought he thought. None of this means anything until the historian has got to work on it and deciphered it. The facts, whether found in documents or not, have still to be processed by the historian before he can make any use of them: the use he makes of them is, if I may put it that way, the processing process.

Let me illustrate what I am trying to say by an example which I happen to know well. When Gustav Stresemann, the Foreign Minister of the Weimar Republic, died in 1929, he left behind him an enormous mass—300 boxes full—of papers, official, semiofficial, and private, nearly all relating to the six years of his tenure of office as Foreign Minister. His friends and relatives naturally thought that a monument should be raised to the memory of so great a man. His faithful secretary Bernhardt got to work; and within three years there appeared three massive volumes, of some 600 pages each, of selected documents from the 300 boxes, with the impressive title *Stresemanns Vermachtnis*. In the ordinary way the documents themselves would have moldered away in some cellar or attic and disappeared for ever; or perhaps in a hundred years or so some curious scholar would have come upon them and set out to compare them with Bernhardt's text. What happened was far more dramatic. In 1945 the documents fell into the hands of the British and American governments, who photographed the lot and put the photostats at the disposal of scholars in the Public Record Office in London and in the National Archives in Washington, so that, if we have sufficient patience and curiosity, we can discover exactly what Bernhardt did. What he did was neither very unusual nor very shocking. When Stresemann died, his Western policy seemed to have been crowned with a series of brilliant successes—Locarno, the admission of Germany to the League of Nations, the Dawes and Young plans and the American loans, the withdrawal of allied occupation armies from the Rhineland. This seemed the important and rewarding part of Stresemann's foreign policy; and it was not unnatural that it should have been over-represented in Bernhardt's selection of documents. Stresemann's Eastern policy, on the other hand, his relations with the Soviet Union, seemed to have led nowhere in particular; and, since masses of documents about negotiations which yielded only trivial results were not very interesting and added nothing to Stresemann's reputation, the process of selection could be more rigorous. Stresemann in fact devoted a far more constant and anxious attention to relations with the Soviet Union, and they played a far larger part in his foreign policy as a whole, than the reader of the Bernhardt selection would surmise. But the Bernhardt volumes compare favorably, I suspect, with many published collections of documents on which the ordinary historian implicitly relies.

This is not the end of my story. Shortly after the publication of Bernhardt's volumes, Hitler came into power. Stresemann's name was consigned to oblivion in Germany, and the volumes disappeared from circulation: many perhaps most, of the copies must have been destroyed. Today *Stresemanns Vermachtnis* is a rather rare book. But in the West Stresemann's reputation stood high. In 1935 an English publisher brought out an abbreviated translation of Bernhardt's work—a selection from Bernhardt's selection; perhaps one third of the original was omitted. Sutton, a well-known translator from the German, did his job competently and well. The English version, he explained in the preface, was "slightly condensed, but only by the omission of a certain amount of what, it was felt, was more ephemeral matter....of little interest to English readers or students." This again is natural enough. But the result is that Stresemann's Eastern policy, already under-represented in Bernhardt, recedes still further from view, and the Soviet Union appears in Sutton's volumes merely as an occasional and rather unwelcome intruder in Stresemann's predominantly Western foreign policy. Yet it is safe to say that, for all except a few specialists, Sutton and not Bernhardt—and still less the documents themselves—represents for the Western world the authentic voice of Stresemann. Had the documents perished in 1945 in the bombing, and had the remaining Bernhardt volumes disappeared, the authenticity and authority of Sutton would never have been questioned. Many printed collections of documents gratefully accepted by historians in default of the originals rest on no securer basis than this.

But I want to carry the story one step further. Let us forget about Bernhardt and Sutton, and be thankful that we can, if we choose, consult the authentic papers of a leading participant

Unit 4 The Historian and His Facts (Part II)

in some important events in recent European history. What do the papers tell us? Among other things they contain records of some hundreds of Stresemann's conversations with the Soviet ambassador in Berlin and of a score or so with Chicherin. These records have one feature in common. They reveal his arguments as invariably well put and cogent, while those of his partner are for the most part scanty, confused, and unconvincing. This is a familiar characteristic of all records of diplomatic conversations. The documents do not tell us what happened, but only what Stresemann thought had happened. It was not Sutton or Bernhardt, but Stresemann himself, who started the process of selection. And if we had, say Chicherin's records of these same conversations, we should still learn from them only what Chicherin thought, and what really happened would still have to be reconstructed in the mind of the historian. Of course, facts and documents are essential to the historian. But do not make a fetish of them. They do not by themselves constitute history, they provide in themselves no ready-made answer to this tiresome question: What is history?

At this point I should like to say a few words on the question of why nineteenth-century historians were generally indifferent to the philosophy of history. The term was invented by Voltaire, and has since been used in different senses; but I shall take it to mean, if I use it at all, our answer to the question: What is history? The nineteenth century was, for the intellectuals of Western Europe, a comfortable period exuding confidence and optimism. The facts were on the whole satisfactory; and the inclination to ask and answer awkward questions about them was correspondingly weak. Ranke piously believed that divine providence would take care of the meaning of history if he took care of the facts; and Burckhardt with a more modern touch of cynicism observed that "we are not initiated into the purposes of the eternal wisdom." Professor Butterfield as late as 1931 noted with apparent satisfaction that "historians have reflected little upon the nature of things and even the nature of their own subject." But my predecessor in these lectures, Dr. A. L. Rowse, more justly critical, wrote of Sir Winston Churchill's *The World Crisis*—his book about the First World War—that, while it matched Trotsky's *History of the Russian Revolution* in personality, vividness, and vitality, it was inferior in one respect: it had "no philosophy of history behind it." British historians refused to be drawn, not because they believed that history had no meaning, but because they believed that its meaning was implicit and self-evident. The liberal nineteenth-century view of history had a close affinity with the economic doctrine of laissez-faire—also the product of a serene and self-confident outlook on the world. Let everyone get on with his particular job, and the hidden hand would take care of the universal harmony. The facts of history were themselves a demonstration of the supreme fact of a beneficent and apparently infinite progress towards higher things. This was the age of innocence, and historians walked in the Garden of Eden, without a scrap of philosophy to cover them, naked and unashamed before the god of history. Since then, we have known Sin and experienced a Fall; and those historians who today pretend to dispense with a philosophy of history are merely trying, vainly and self-consciously, like members of a nudist colony, to recreate the Garden of Eden in their garden suburb. Today the awkward question can no longer be evaded.

➔ Notes

1. **Spartan:** a resident of Sparta, a powerful city in ancient Greece.
2. **Corinthian:** a resident of Corinth, a port city in ancient Greece.
3. **Theban:** a Greek inhabitant of ancient Thebes.
4. **Professor Barraclough:** Geoffrey Barraclough (1908—1984) was an English historian, known as a medievalist and historian of Germany.
5. **Lytton Strachey:** Giles Lytton Strachey (1880—1932) was an English writer and critic.
6. **The Ark of Covenant:** also known as the Ark of the Testimony. In Judaism and Christianity, the ornate, gold-plated wooden chest that in biblical times housed the two tablets of the Law given to Moses by God.
7. **Weimar Republic:** an unofficial, historical designation for the German state during the years 1919 to 1933.
8. **The Rhineland:** the name used for a loosely defined area of Western Germany along the Rhine, chiefly its middle section.
9. **Chicherin:** Georgy Vasilyevich Chicherin (1872—1936) was a Marxist revolutionary and a Soviet politician. He served as People's Commissar for Foreign Affairs in the Soviet government from March 1918 to 1930.
10. **Burchhardt:** Carl Jacob Christoph Burckhardt (1818—1897) was a Swiss historian of art and culture and an influential figure in the historiography of both fields. Burckhardt's best known work is *The Civilization of the Renaissance in Italy* (1860).
11. **Professor Butterfield:** Sir Herbert Butterfield (1900—1979) was Regius Professor of History and Vice-Chancellor of the University of Cambridge.
12. **A. L. Rowse:** Alfred Leslie Rowse (1903—1997) was a British author and historian from Cornwall.
13. **Sir Winston Churchill (1874—1965):** a British politician, army officer, and writer, who was Prime Minister of the United Kingdom from 1940 to 1945 and again from 1951 to 1955.
14. **Trotsky:** Leon Trotsky (1879—1940) was a Russian revolutionary, Marxist theorist, and Soviet politician whose particular strain of Marxist thought is known as Trotskyism.

Unit 4　The Historian and His Facts (Part II)

15. **The Garden of Eden:** also called Paradise, is the biblical "garden of God" described in the Bible.

Vocabulary

1. reminiscence ['rɛmə'nɪsns]: *n.* the act of remembering things that happened in the past 回忆；追忆

2. attrition [ə'trɪʃ(ə)n]: *n.* attrition is a process in which you steadily reduce the strength of an enemy by continually attacking them 磨损；消耗

3. minute [maɪ'nut]: *adj.* paying careful attention to the smallest details 详细的

4. nagging ['nægɪŋ]: *adj.* continuing for a long time and difficult to cure or remove 纠缠不休的；难以摆脱的

5. lacuna [lə'kjuːnə]: *n.* a place where something is missing in a piece of writing 空隙

6. jig-saw ['dʒɪgsɔ]: *n.* a picture cut up into many small pieces to be fitted together 拼图玩具

7. imbue [ɪm'bju]: *vt.* to fill somebody/something with strong feelings, opinions or values 使充满；灌输

8. devout [dɪ'vaʊt]: *adj.* believing strongly in a particular religion and obeying its laws and practices 虔诚的

9. scribe [skraɪb]: *n.* someone in the past whose job was to make written copies of official documents 抄写员

10. winnow ['wɪnəʊ]: *v.* to make a list, group, or quantity smaller by getting rid of the things that you do not need or want 精选

11. heresy ['hɛrəsi]: *n.* a belief or an opinion that disagrees strongly with what most people believe 反面论点；悖论

12. antiquarianism [ˌæntɪ'kwɛrɪənɪzəm]: *n.* the study, collection or sale of valuable old objects, especially books 古文物研究（或收藏、经营）

13. monograph ['mɒnəgrɑːf]: *n.* an article or short book that discusses a subject in detail 专题著作，专题论文

14. epitaph ['ɛpɪtæf]: *n.* words that are written or said about a dead person, especially words on a gravestone 墓志铭

15. fetish ['fetɪʃ]: *n.* something to which one pays an unreasonable amount of attention or which one admires to a foolish degree 迷信；被盲目崇拜之物

16. rent-roll ['rentrəʊl]: *n.* a register of rents; includes the names of tenants and the amount of rent they pay 租金账簿

17. photostat ['fotə,stæt]: *n.* a photocopy made on a Photostat machine　福图斯泰直接影印本
18. rigorous ['rɪgərəs]: *adj.* demanding that particular rules, processes etc. are strictly followed　严格的
19. consign [kən'saɪn]: *v.* to put somebody/something in unpleasant situation　打发；发落
20. oblivion [ə'blɪvɪən]: *n.* the state in which somebody/something has been forgotten and is no longer famous or important　被遗忘；湮没
21. ephemeral [ə'fɛmərəl]: *adj.* (formal) lasting or used for only a short period of time　短暂的
22. recede [rɪ'sid]: *vi.* to move gradually away from somebody or away from a previous position　逐渐远离
23. cogent ['kəʊdʒ(ə)nt]: *adj.* if a statement is cogent, it seems reasonable and correct　使人信服的
24. scanty ['skænti]: *adj.* too little in size or amount for what is needed　偏少的；不足的
25. exude [ɪg'zud]: *vt.* to (cause to) flow out slowly and spread in all directions　流露（感觉或品质）
26. cynicism ['sɪnɪsɪz(ə)m]: *n.* the belief that people always act selfishly　愤世嫉俗
27. affinity [ə'fɪnəti]: *n.* a close relationship between two people or things that have similar qualities, structures or features　密切的关系；类同
28. serene [sə'ri:n]: *adj.* calm and peaceful　平静的；宁静的

Expressions

1. I suspect that even today one of the fascinations of ancient and mediaeval history is that it gives us the illusion of having all the facts <u>at our disposal</u> within a manageable compass…
   at one's disposal: available for use as one prefers　任某人处理；由某人自行支配
2. Our picture of Greece in the fifth century B.C. is… <u>by and large</u>, the picture formed by a tiny group of people in the city of Athens.
   by and large: on the whole; in general　大体上；总的说来
3. Our picture has been preselected and predetermined for us, not so much by accident as by people who were consciously or unconsciously <u>imbued with</u> a particular view and thought the facts which supported that view worth preserving.
   imbue somebody/something with something: to make someone or something have a quality, idea, or emotion very strongly　灌输（某人）强烈的情感或意见
4. Anyone who <u>succumbs to</u> this heresy will either have to give up history as a bad job…

Unit 4 The Historian and His Facts (Part II)

succumb to something: fail to resist the attack, an illness, a temptation, etc.   屈服；屈从

5. Stresemann's name <u>was consigned to</u> oblivion in Germany…

   consign somebody/something to something: to put somebody/something in an unpleasant situation   把……置于（令人不快的境地）

6. Many printed collections of documents gratefully accepted by historians <u>in default of</u> the originals rest on no securer basis than this.

   in default of something: because of the lack or absence of something   由于缺乏……；因为没有……

7. …and those historians who today pretend to <u>dispense with</u> a philosophy of history are merely trying, vainly and self-consciously, like members of a nudist colony, to recreate the Garden of Eden in their garden suburb.

   dispense with something: to not use or do something that people usually use or do, because it is not necessary   摒弃；不用

Comprehension

I. Discuss the Main Point and the Meanings.

1. Why does the author tend to envy the competence of colleagues engaged in writing ancient and medieval history?

2. Professor Barraclough says that "The history we read, though based on facts, is strictly speaking, not factual at all, but a series of accepted judgments." How should we understand this statement? (History is written by people imbued with a particular view.)

3. What does the story of Gustav Stresemann tell us about history?

II. Fill in the blanks with the appropriate words or expressions in the box.

facts	facts of history	factual	hard facts
history	ignorance	judgment	predetermined
preselected	reconstructed	self-confident	serene

1. Our picture of fifth-century Greece has been _____ and _____ by people who were consciously or unconsciously imbued with a particular view.

2. Professor Barraclough writes: "The history we read, though based on _____, is, strictly speaking, not _____ at all, but a series of accepted _____."

3. Lytton Strachey said in his mischievous way, "_____ is the first requisite of the historian, _____ which simplifies and clarifies, which selects and omits."

67

4. The modern historian has the dual task of discovering the few significant facts and turning them into _____, and of discarding the many insignificant facts as unhistorical.

5. What had gone wrong was the belief in this untiring and unending accumulation of _____ as the foundation of history, the belief that _____ speak for themselves and that we cannot have too many facts.

6. What really happened in the past would have to be _____ in the mind of the historian.

7. Facts and documents are essential to the historian. But they do not by themselves constitute _____.

8. The liberal nineteenth-century view of history had a close affinity with the economic doctrine of laissez-faire—also the product of a _____ and _____ outlook on the world.

→ Structure

I. Find out how the words and expression in bold are used in the following sentences.

1. Our picture of Greece in the fifth century B.C. is, **by and large**, the picture formed by a tiny group of people in the city of Athens.

2. When I am tempted, as I sometimes am, to envy the extreme competence of colleagues **engaged in** writing ancient or mediaeval history.

3. Anyone who succumbs to this heresy will either have to **give up** history as a bad job, and **take to** stamp-collecting.

4. But what, when we **get down to** it, do these documents tell us?

5. None of this means anything until the historian has got to **work on** it and deciphered it.

6. The facts have still to be processed by the historian before he can **make any use of** them.

7. Perhaps in a hundred years or so some curious scholar would have **come upon** them and **set out** to compare them with Bernhardt's text.

8. They played a far larger part in his foreign policy **as a whole**.

9. In 1935 an English publisher **brought out** an abbreviated translation of Bernhardt's work…

10. Many printed collections of documents gratefully accepted by historians in default of the originals **rest on** no securer basis than this.

11. …it was **inferior** in one respect: it had "no philosophy of history behind it."

12. Let everyone **get on with** his particular job, and the hidden hand would take care of the universal harmony.

Unit 4 The Historian and His Facts (Part II)

II. Complete the following sentences with some of the above words or expressions in bold.

1. She doesn't like being around her colleagues because she often feels _____.

2. The band _____ just _____ their second album.

3. He had to _____ his studies through lack of money.

4. _____, I enjoyed my time in the United States.

5. With the election out of the way, the government can _____ business.

6. I _____ an irresistible item at the yard sale.

7. The whole argument _____ a false assumption.

8. The government is trying to _____ the job of running the country in spite of impossible difficulties.

9. Even in prison, he continued to _____ criminal activities.

10. All this gloomy news is enough to make you _____ drink.

America in WWII

The progressive movement's zest and drive waned with the coming of World War I. When World War I burst upon Europe in August 1914, the United States hoped to stay out of the war. However, it did not take long for the worst to happen. A German submarine sank an unarmed American ship, the Algonquin. Then three more American ships were sunk. Many lives were lost. President Wilson no longer had a choice between war and peace. On April 6, 1917, Congress approved a declaration of war against Germany.

President Wilson and Congress worked together to organize the United States for war. Congress gave Wilson new wartime powers. He soon formed a council to build ships, improve industrial production, and control national transportation. He formed an agricultural agency to increase food production and food exports. And he formed an information committee to build public support for the war.

On November 11, 1918, a truce was signed ending the hostilities of World War I. The Central Powers — led by Germany — had lost. The Allies — led by Britain, France and the United States — had won.

Compared to European nations, the United States was touched relatively lightly by World War I. For all its horrendous toll, World War I brought glowing prosperity to the American economy and it propelled the United States to the center of world politics. After World War I the United States had become a world power.

The Roaring 20s

A Decade of Prosperity

After the war, Americans just wanted to live their own lives and make their own country a better place. They became more concerned with material things. Wages for most workers in the United States were higher than ever at the beginning of the 1920s. Men and women had enough money to enjoy life more than they had in the past. Technology made it possible for millions of people to improve their lives. Two of the most important new technologies were automobiles and radio. The 1920s were a time of economic progress for most Americans. It was a decade of prosperity.

A Decade of Creativity

This was also a decade of bubbling creativity. Writers, painters, and other artists produced some of the greatest works in the nation's history. In *The Wasteland* (1922), poet T. S. Eliot evoked images of a shattered culture. Ernest Hemingway wrote about love, war, sports, and other subjects. F. Scott Fitzgerald wrote especially about rich Americans searching for happiness and new values. His book *The Great Gatsby* is considered today to be one of the greatest works in the history of American writing.

The Jazz Age

Above all, American music in the 1920s meant jazz. Jazz advanced greatly as a true American kind of music in the nineteen twenties. Musicians Louis Armstrong, Duke Ellington and Eubie Blake played in gathering places and small theaters. White musicians and music experts from universities came to listen. Soon the music became popular among Americans of all kinds and around the world.

A Turbulent Era

In this decade, many young people began to challenge the traditions of their parents and grandparents. They experimented with new ideas and ways of living. People of all kinds became interested in the new popular culture. Radio and films brought them exciting news of court trials, sports heroes and wild parties. some young women began to experiment with new kinds of clothes. Many young women began to smoke cigarettes, too. Many women also began to drink alcohol with men in public for the first time. It was a revolution in social values, at least among some Americans. People openly discussed subjects that their parents and grandparents had kept private.

Mass Production, Mass Culture

The technologies of mass communication promoted cultural standardization and uniformity of thought and to a degree stifled local and regional diversity. But radio, the movies, and the mass magazines also helped forge a national culture and introduced millions of Americans to fresh viewpoints and new ways of behaving. The spread of mass culture in the 1920s opened a larger world for ordinary Americans.

Prohibition

In most ways, the 1920s were a conservative time in American life. Voters elected three conservative Republican presidents. A second sign of the conservative feelings in the 1920s was the nation's effort to ban the sale of alcoholic drinks, or liquor. On January 16, 1919, the 18th Amendment to the Constitution was ratified. It prohibited — or banned — alcoholic drinks. This policy was known as Prohibition. The term can also apply to the period during which the prohibition of alcohol was enforced.

Not surprisingly, thousands of Americans soon saw a chance to make profits from the new laws. Prohibition created a nation of criminals. The illegal liquor trade was worth ten's billions in today's money. And the gangsters were in charge. Prohibition has massively increased the stranglehold of organized crime. By the end of the decade prohibition was discredited, and in 1933 it came to an end. The 18the Amendment became the only amendment to be repealed in American history.

Great Depression

In the 1920s, America was becoming the world's leading economic nation. Increased advertising on the radio and magazines strengthened people's desire for new devices. They started installment buying or buying on credit. Investors also started buying stocks in the same way. More and more people were turning to the stock market as method of making a fast income. Many of these inexperienced investors also engaged in speculation. Speculating on stocks combined with buying those stocks on margin could mean financial doom for investors if the stock market took a turn for the worse. That is what exactly happened in the fall of 1929. In the last week of October, the stock market began to fail.

The stock market crash of October 29, 1929 (known as Black Tuesday) brought the so-called Roaring Twenties to an end. The nation soon found itself locked in a full-scale depression that did not bottom out until 1933 and whose effects lingered through the decade. The Great Depression was the longest, most widespread, and deepest depression of the 20th century.

Between 1930 and early 1933, more than 5,500 banks closed their doors. The unemployment rate rose from 3 percent in 1929 to 25 percent in 1933. Thousands of farm families lost their homes. Three hundred thousand children were out of school. The suicide rate climbed nearly 30% between 1928 and 1932.

President Herbert Hoover did take several actions to try to improve the economy. But he resisted proposals for the federal government to provide aid in a major way. And he refused to let the government spend more money than it earned. People blamed President Hoover because they thought he was not doing enough to help them.

New Deal

In the election of 1932, Americans turned away from Republican rule. They elected the Democratic presidential candidate, Franklin Delano Roosevelt. In this way, the conservative Republican policies of the 1920s changed to the more progressive policies of Roosevelt in the 1930s. Roosevelt's inauguration speech of 1933 was one of the most powerful and important speeches in American history. He gave American people hope.

Enjoying overwhelming majorities in Congress, Roosevelt proposed a series of emergency measures in his early months in office. These measures involved three components: *industrial recovery* through business-government cooperation and pump-priming federal spending; *agricultural recovery* through subsidized crop reduction; and *short-term emergency relief for the jobless*—funneled through state and local agencies when possible, but provided directly by the federal government if necessary. These measures were collectively called the First New Deal.

After the worst crisis was past, some groups of Americans began to attack Roosevelt and his programs. Conservatives were accusing him of socialism. Leftist opponents said he was doing too little to end the depression. He saw that he had to change his path. The many changes he made during this period became known as the Second New Deal. A set of laws had been enacted promoting the interests of the jobless, the elderly, the rural poor, and the blue-collar workers; regulating major business enterprises more strictly; and somewhat increasing the taxes paid by the wealthy. They included some of the most important pieces of legislation in the history of the country, such as the National Labor Relations Act and the Social Security Law.

Today, the New Deal still constitutes a watershed in American history. The Roosevelt administration began by assuming a government responsibility to promote economic prosperity and the well-being of all citizens. Such measures as Social Security, the Wagner Act, and the Fair Labor Standards Act defined the basic contours of the modern activist welfare state.

The New Deal vastly increased the power and prestige of the presidency. This development decisively altered the balance of power between the White House and Congress.

Unit 4 The Historian and His Facts (Part II)

America in WWII

On September 1, 1939, the Fuhrer's troops poured into Poland. Two days later, Britain and France, honoring their commitments to Poland, declared war on Germans.

The Roosevelt administration initially hoped that neutrality would keep America at peace and secure. But on December 7, 1941, Japan attacked Pearl Harbor, Hawaii, which brought the United States into the conflict.

Wartime spending and the military draft vanquished the unemployment of the Great Depression and stimulated an industrial boom that produced unprecedented prosperity for most Americans.

The American home front, moreover, suffered none of the devastation that swept Europe and Asia: it was neither bombed nor invaded; it endured few serious material deprivations. To the contrary, the war made the United States once again a land of opportunity and hope. After the war, the United States found itself the strongest military, economic and political power in the world.

Nifty Fifties

After WWII, the United States entered one of its longest, steadiest periods of growth and prosperity. Between 1945 and 1970, the American economy grew at an average annual rate of 3.5 percent. In terms of both income level and lifestyles, more Americans were better off than ever before in the postwar years.

In the distorting mirror of memory, the decade of the 1950s came to seem a peaceful decade of prosperity and easy living, of cheap gasoline and big cars, of comfortable suburban homes and family togetherness. The mass media portrayed the 1950s as a sunny time when almost everybody liked Ike and loved Lucy.

Yet for a full picture of the 1950s, we must look beyond the stereotypes. The decade also saw the birth of the space age, of a private nuclear-power industry, and of hydrogen bombs and intercontinental ballistic missiles. It was an era, too, of intense political passions, kindled by such influential voices as Senator Joseph McCarthy, the Warren Court, and civil-rights leader Martin Luther King, Jr. The advent of an automated and computerized postindustrial society, television's growing power, and the baby boom transformed society, as did mass suburbanization and a remarkable internal migration due to the interstate highway system.

Interstate Highway System

America's sheer size made it difficult for people to move around. The land mass is 9 million square miles, and the road system wasn't working. How could its people and goods be moved across its great lengths? Each generation has come up with its own solution. The rivers were America's first highways. Now it's time to get America's roads working like the canals and rivers before them to get the country to move again. The interstate highway system became the biggest engineering project in American history. It changed America. It connected the cities in a way that no one had seen before, on a level that no one had seen before. America's landscape has been shaped by transportation. With good roads and more cars, it became the age of the automobile.

Suburbanization

"Auto-mania" spurred white flight to suburbs throughout the country. So did government policies. As federal spending on highways skyrocketed from $79 million in 1946 to $2.9 billion in 1960, and as state and local expenditures for roads kept pace, areas once considered too remote by urban workers became desirable places to live.

Eighty-five percent of the phenomenal 13 million new homes built in the 1950s were in the suburbs. A variety of attractions lured Americans to suburbia. Some moved in search of affordable single family dwellings. Others became suburbanites to escape the crime and grime of the central cities and to distance themselves from the millions of newly urbanized minorities. And many newly married Americans headed for suburbia in quest of communities oriented toward children and education.

The suburban population of 60 million in 1960 equaled that of the central cities. And by 1970 the suburbs would contain two-thirds of the metropolitan-area population and the cities only one-third—exactly the reverse of 1950.

Babyboom

The combination of economic prosperity and Cold War saber rattling led Americans in the 1950s to wed at an earlier age than their parents, to have babies sooner, and to have more of them. In 1957, an American baby was born every seven seconds. The increase in births after the war produced what became known as the baby boom generation. An estimated seventy-eight million Americans were born between 1946 and 1964. They became the most influential and powerful group of Americans ever born.

The Silent Generation

Disaffected intellectuals denounced the young in middle-class suburbia in the 1950s as a "silent generation" because they gave in to social pressure rather than adhering to personal values. They became "organization men" bent on getting ahead by going along, "status seekers" pursuing external rewards to compensate for inner insecurities. The United States, the dissenters charged, had become a "packaged society" and its people "all items in a national supermarket—categorized, processed, labeled, priced, and readied for merchandising."

The Beat Generation

There were exceptions. One group of writers noisily repudiated the materialistic and self-congratulatory world of the middle class and the suburbs in the 1950s. These writers together with the cultural phenomenon they both inspired and documented were called the Beat Generation. The Beat writers rejected both social niceties and literary conventions, and they flaunted their freewheeling sexuality and consumption of drugs. The Beats produced some memorable prose and poetry, including Allen Ginsberg's angry incantational poem *Howl* (1956) and Jack Kerouac's novel *On the Road* (1957). Although the Beats were largely ignored during the 1950s, millions of young Americans discovered their writings and imitated their lifestyle in the 1960s. Elements of the expanding Beat movement were incorporated into the hippie and larger counterculture movements.

The Turbulent Era 1961—1974

The Hippie Movement

During the 1960s, aspects of the Beat movement metamorphosed into the counterculture of the 1960s, accompanied by a shift in terminology from "beatnik" to "hippie." Many of the original Beats remained active participants, notably Allen Ginsberg, who became a fixture of the anti-war movement.

The word "hippie" came from *hipster*, and was initially used to describe beatniks who had moved into New York City's Greenwich Village and San Francisco's Haight-Ashbury district. The early hippies inherited the language and countercultural values of the Beat Generation. Hippies created their own communities, listened to psychedelic music, embraced the sexual revolution, and used drugs such as cannabis, LSD, and psilocybin mushrooms to explore altered states of consciousness. Hippies rejected established institutions, criticized middle class values, opposed nuclear weapons and the Vietnam War, embraced aspects of Eastern philosophy.

In January 1967, the Human Be-In in Golden Gate Park in San Francisco popularized hippie culture, leading to the Summer of Love on the West Coast of the United States, and the 1969 Woodstock Festival on the East Coast.

The Human Be-In

The Human Be-In was an event in San Francisco's Golden Gate Park on January 14, 1967. The Human Be-In was announced on the cover of the fifth issue of the *San Francisco Oracle* as

"A Gathering of the Tribes for a Human Be-In." The occasion was a new California law banning the use of the psychedelic drug LSD that had come into effect on October 6, 1966. The speakers at the rally were all invited by Michael Bowen, the main organizer. They included poets like Allen Ginsberg and Timothy Leary in his first San Francisco appearance, who set the tone that afternoon with his famous phrase "Turn on, tune in, drop out". Music was provided by a host of local rock bands including Jefferson Airplane and The Grateful Dead. "Underground chemist" Owsley Stanley provided massive amounts of his "White Lightning" LSD, specially produced for the event.

The Human Be-In focused the key ideas of the 1960s counterculture: personal empowerment, cultural and political decentralization, communal living, ecological awareness, higher consciousness (with the aid of psychedelic drugs), acceptance of illicit drug use, and radical liberal political consciousness.

The national media were stunned. Reports were unable to agree whether 20,000 or 30,000 people showed up at the Be-In. Soon every gathering was an "-In" of some kind.

Publicity about this event leading to the mass movement of young people from all over America to descend on the Haight-Ashbury area. It was a prelude to San Francisco's Summer of Love, which made the Haight-Ashbury district a symbol of American counterculture and introduced the word "psychedelic" to suburbia.

The Human Be-In took its name from a chance remark by the artist Michael Bowen made at the Love Pageant Rally. The playful name combined humanist values with the scores of sit-ins that had been reforming college and university practices and eroding the vestiges of entrenched segregation, starting with the lunch counter sit-ins of 1960 in Greensboro, North Carolina, and Nashville, Tennessee.

The Summer of Love

The Summer of Love was a social phenomenon that occurred during the summer of 1967, when as many as 100,000 people converged in the Haight-Ashbury neighborhood of San Francisco. Although hippies also gathered in major cities across the U.S., Canada and Europe, San Francisco remained the epicenter of the social earthquake that would come to be known as the Hippie Revolution. Like its sister enclave of Greenwich Village, the city became even more of a melting pot of politics, music, drugs, creativity, and the total lack of sexual and social inhibition than it already was. As the hippie counterculture movement came farther and farther forward into public awareness, the activities centered therein became a defining moment of the 1960s, causing numerous "ordinary citizens" to begin questioning everything and anything about them and their environment as a result.

Unit 4 The Historian and His Facts (Part II)

Woodstock

Like sex and drugs, the music of the 1960s represented a quest to redefine reality and create a more just and joyful society.

In 1969, 500,000 young Americans gathered at a farm in New York state at the Woodstock music festival. They listened to musicians such as Jimi Hendrix and Joan Baez, and to groups like The Who and Jefferson Airplane. They reveled for three days and nights in the music of dozen of rock stars, swam nude in the lake, and openly shared drugs, sexual partners, and their contempt for the Establishment.

Woodstock became a symbol of the young peoples' rebellion against traditional values. After that a number of the young people began to dream of a peaceful "Woodstock nation" based on love, drugs, and rock music.

Toward a New Left

Along with the hippie movement and the American Civil Rights Movement, the New Left was one of three dissenting groups of the 1960s counterculture.

In 1965, 41 percent of all Americans were under the age of 20. American youths deluged colleges and spawned a student movement that provided the initial impetus for the campus political awakening of the 1960s, the so-called New Left. Their assault on traditional policies and values would bring immense changes; it would sweep away the well-kept world of the fifties; and it would provoke a preoccupation with self and a conservative backlash that would dominate U.S. culture for the next generation.

The New Left was used in contrast to earlier leftist or Marxist movements that had taken a more vanguardist approach to social justice and focused mostly on labor unionization and questions of social class.

Civil Rights Movements

The end of American Civil War meant the end of slavery, but African-Americans went in for long struggle before they were finally awarded equal rights. After Reconstruction, southern states passed a series of black codes, making blacks second-class citizens, starting the Jim Crow Era—the long era of racial segregation and discrimination.

In 1909, a group of black and white campaigners created the National Association for the Advancement of Colored People. The goal of NAACP was to increase racial equality and challenge issues like the Jim Crow laws.

The Civil Rights Movement gathered momentum in 1955 when Rosa Parks, a black woman, was arrested for refusing to give her seat to a white man on a public bus in Montgomery,

Alabama. The incident galvanized the black community and lead to a successful year long boycott of the Montgomery Bus System. It also raised public awareness of the plight of African-Americans.

In 1957, President Eisenhower ordered in the army to ensure that black students would be safe when they enrolled in a previously segregated high school in Little Rock Arkansas. Protest by blacks in combination with increasing white support followed.

An eminent leader with a great vision emerged in Martin Luther King. Jr. King's policy of non-violent resistance gained sympathy for the civil rights movement and his impassioned speeches influenced millions of Americans. In 1963, over 200,000 people participated in a march on Washington to hear Dr. King and demonstrate their support for the civil rights bill. In 1964, President Lyndon Johnson signed into law the strongest civil rights bill in the history of the country.

Law and Order

The United States Constitution guarantees freedoms such as freedom of speech, freedom of the press and freedom of religion. The Bill of Rights in the Constitution protects these and other individual rights. But the government has not always honored all of the rights in the Constitution.

In the 1700s, for example, President John Adams supported laws to stop Thomas Jefferson and the Democratic Party from criticizing the government. During the Civil War, President Abraham Lincoln took strong actions to prevent newspapers from printing military news.

McCarthyism

And, during the 1950s, Senator Joseph McCarthy accused innocent people of being communists and traitors. He led the search for communists in America.

Actually, anticommunism had been a prominent strand in the American political fabric since World War I and the Red Scare of 1919 and 1920. In 1919 and 1920, some of the most serious government attacks on personal rights took place. A number of government officials took sometimes unlawful actions against labor leaders, foreigners and others.

But the Cold War heightened anti-Communist fears, and McCarthy manipulated the fears to his advantage. He became the most successful and frightening redbaiter the country had ever seen. He accused hundreds of people of being communists or communist supporters. His targets included the State Department, the Army and the entertainment industry. He often had little evidence to support his accusations.

McCarthyism destroyed the careers of many innocent people. It demoralized and frightened federal workers and spread fear and a mood of caution among government employees. It also discouraged people from freely expressing themselves and hence from debating critical issues.

Later, McCarthyism became a synonym for public charges of disloyalty without sufficient regard for evidence.

Nixon Administration in the 1970s

In the 1970s, to combat the militants he despised, Richard Nixon drew upon the full force of the federal government. The Internal Revenue Service audited the tax returns of antiwar and civil-rights activists, and the Small Business Administration denied them loans. The Federal Bureau of Investigation illegally wiretapped leftist individuals and organizations, and the National Security Agency intercepted their telecommunications. The FBI also infiltrated the ranks of the SDS and black radical groups with informers and agents who provoked violence within these movements to discredit them. The Justice Department and the FBI worked closely with local police forces in 1969—1970 to arrest Black Panthers on dubious charges and to disrupt their operations by disinformation programs. Contrary to the specific prohibitions written into the National Security Act of 1947, moreover, the CIA investigated, and compiled dossiers on, thousands of American dissidents. To focus the nation's fear on the radical threat, Nixon authorized the Department of Justice to prosecute antiwar activists and militant blacks in highly publicized trials.

Watergate Scandal

To seek reelection, Nixon left no stone unturned, remembering his narrow loss to John F. Kennedy in 1960 and his too-slender victory over Hubert Humphrey in 1968. He created the Committee to Re-Elect the President (CREEP) to do everything necessary to ensure his reelection, and appointed his attorney general, John Mitchell, as its head. The many millions in contributions collected by CREEP finances a series of "dirty tricks" that spread dissension within Democratic ranks and paid for a special internal espionage unit to spy on the opposition. Led by Liddy and Hunt of the White House plumbers, the Republican undercover team gained Mitchell's approval for a plan to wiretap telephones at the Democratic National Committee headquarters in the Watergate apartment/office complex in Washington. Early in the morning of June 17, 1972, a security guard foiled the break-in to install the bugs. Arrested were James McCord, the security coordinator of CREEP, and several other burglars associated with Liddy and Hunt.

The congressional investigation showed that Nixon had repeatedly misused government agencies in an effort to hide wrongdoing and punish his critics. The hearings also showed that he had tried to block the investigation. Nixon was forced to resign. He is the only President ever to resign from office in American history.

Nixon's actions violated the basic trust between the American public and their elected officials. Watergate intensified the American people's loss of confidence in their government and its future.

Vocabulary of History/American History

1. The nagging distinction between **the facts of history** and **other facts about the past** vanishes.

2. The facts of mediaeval history have almost all been **selected** for us by generations of chroniclers who **recorded** everything relating to it.

3. The history we read, though based on facts, is, strictly speaking, not factual at all, but a series of accepted **judgments**.

4. History consists of the compilation of a maximum number of **irrefutable and objective facts**.

5. What had gone wrong was the belief in this untiring and unending **accumulation of hard facts** as the foundation of history.

6. The nineteenth-century fetishism of facts was completed and justified by a fetishism of **documents**.

7. I should like to say a few words on the question of why nineteenth-century historians were generally indifferent to **the philosophy of history**.

8. World War I was **touched off** when a Serbian terrorist assassinated the heir to the Austria-Hungarian throne in 1914.

9. When war **burst upon** Europe in August 1914, most Americans wished only to remain aloof.

10. On November 11, 1918, a **truce** was signed ending the hostilities of World War I.

11. In this decade, many young people began to **challenge** the traditions of their parents and grandparents.

12. They **experimented** with new ideas and ways of living.

13. In most ways, the 1920s were a **conservative** time in American life.

14. The 18th Amendment became the only amendment to be **repealed** in American history.

15. **Prohibition** has massively increased the stranglehold of **organized crime**.

16. The stock market **crashed** two months before the end of the decade.

17. The Great Depression was the longest, most widespread, and **deepest depression** of the twentieth century.

18. A set of laws had been **enacted** promoting the interests of the jobless, the elderly, the rural poor, and the blue-collar workers.

19. Many **leftists** and socialists agreed with conservatives that it was impossible to mix capitalism and socialism.

Unit 4　The Historian and His Facts (Part II)

20. Today, the New Deal still constitutes a **watershed** in American history.

21. And WWII ended American **isolationism**.

22. A variety of attractions lured Americans to **suburbia**.

23. The most obvious expression of postwar optimism was the **baby boom**.

24. Disaffected intellectuals denounced the young in middle-class suburbia as a "**silent generation**."

25. They became "**organization men**" bent on getting ahead by going along.

26. The incident galvanized the black community and lead to a successful year long **boycott** of the Montgomery Bus System.

27. Students held **sit-ins** to halt compulsory ROTC programs.

28. In the 1970s, to combat the militants he despised, Richard Nixon **drew upon** the full force of the federal government.

29. The congressional investigation showed that Nixon had repeatedly **misused** government agencies in an effort to hide wrongdoing and punish his critics.

30. Two Washington Post reporters, following clues furnished by "**Deep Throat**," wrote a succession of front-page stories about **Watergate Scandal**.

31. Richard Nixon fired his special counsel, John Dean, after Dean refused to be a **scapegoat**.

32. Even as Nixon named a new special prosecutor, the Judiciary Committee began **impeachment** proceedings.

33. In March 1974 special prosecutor Jaworski and the House Judiciary Committee **subpoenaed** the president for the tape recordings.

34. But the Senate still lacked concrete evidence of the president's criminality, the so-called **smoking gun** that would prove Nixon's guilt.

Unit 5: The Historian and His Facts (Part III)

Edward Hallett Carr

During the past fifty years a good deal of serious work has been done on the question: What is history? It was from Germany, the country which was to do so much to upset the comfortable reign of nineteenth-century liberalism, that the first challenge came in the 1880's and 1890's to the doctrine of the primacy and autonomy of facts in history. The philosophers who made the challenge are now little more than names: Dilthey is the only one of them who has recently received some belated recognition in Great Britain. Before the turn of the century, prosperity and confidence were still too great in this country for any attention to be paid to heretics who attacked the cult of facts. But early in the new century, the torch passed to Italy, where Croce began to propound a philosophy of history which obviously owed much to German masters. All history is "contemporary history," declared Croce, meaning that history consists essentially in seeing the past through the eyes of the present and in the light of its problems, and that the main work of the historian is not to record, but to evaluate; for, if he does not evaluate, how can he know what is worth recording? In 1910 the American philosopher, Carl Becker, argued in deliberately provocative language that "the facts of history do not exist for any historian till he creates them." These challenges were for the moment little noticed. It was only after 1920 that Croce began to have a considerable vogue in France and Great Britain. This was not perhaps because Croce was a subtler thinker or a better stylist than his German predecessors, but because, after the First World War, the facts seemed to smile on us less propitiously than in the years before 1914, and we were therefore more accessible to a philosophy which sought to diminish their prestige. Croce was an important influence on the Oxford philosopher and historian Collingwood, the only British thinker in the present century who has made a serious contribution to the philosophy of history. He did not live to write the systematic treatise he had planned but his published and unpublished papers on the subject were collected after his death in a volume entitled *The Idea of History*, which appeared in 1945.

The views of Collingwood can be summarized as follows. The philosophy of history is concerned neither with "the past by itself" nor with "the historian's thought about it by itself," but with "the two things in their mutual relations." (This dictum reflects the two current meanings of the word "history"—the enquiry conducted by the historian and the series of past events into which he enquires.) "The past which a historian studies is not a dead past, but a past which in some sense is still living in the present." But a past act is dead, *i.e.* meaningless to the historian, unless he can understand the thought that lay behind it. Hence "all history is the history of thought," and "history is the re-enactment in the historian's mind of the thought whose history he is studying." The reconstitution of the past in the historian's mind is dependent on empirical evidence. But it is not in itself an empirical process, and cannot consist in a mere recital of facts. On the contrary, the process of reconstitution governs the selection and interpretation of the facts: this, indeed, is what makes them historical facts. "History," says Professor Oakeshott, who on this point stands near to Collingwood, "is the historian's experience. It is 'made' by nobody save the historian: to write history is the only way of making it."

This searching critique, though it may call for some serious reservations, brings to light certain neglected truths.

In the first place, the facts of history never come to us "pure," since they do not and cannot exist in a pure form: they are always refracted through the mind of the recorder. It follows that when we take up a work of history, our first concern should be not with the facts which it contains but with the historian who wrote it. Let me take as an example the great historian in whose honor and in whose name these lectures were founded. Trevelyan, as he tells us in his autobiography, was "brought up at home on a somewhat exuberantly Whig tradition"; and he would not, I hope, disclaim the title if I described him as the last and not the least of the great English liberal historians of the Whig tradition. It is not for noting that he traces back his family tree, through the great Whig historian George Otto Trevelyan, to Macaulay, incomparably the greatest of the Whig historians. Dr. Trevelyan's finest and maturest work *England under Queen Anne* was written against that background, and will yield its full meaning and significance to the reader only when read against that background. The author, indeed, leaves the reader with no excuse for failing to do so. For if, following the technique of connoisseurs of detective novels, you read the end first, you will find on the last few pages of the third volume the best summary known to me of what is nowadays called the Whig interpretation of history; and you will see that what Trevelyan is trying to do is to investigate the origin and development of the Whig tradition, and to root it fairly and squarely in the years after the death of its founder, William III. Though this is not, perhaps, the only conceivable interpretation of the events of Queen Anne's reign, it is a valid and, in Trevelyan's hands, a fruitful interpretation. But, in order to appreciate it at its full value, you have to understand what the historian is doing. For if, as Collingwood says, the historian must re-enact in thought what has gone on in the mind of his *dramatis personae*, so the reader in his turn must re-enact what goes on in the mind of the historian. Study the historian before you begin to study the facts. This is, after all, not very abstruse. It is what is already done by the intelligent undergraduate who, when recommended to read a work by that great scholar Jones of St. Jude's, goes round to a friend at St. Jude's to ask what sort of chap Jones is, and what bees he has in his bonnet. When you read a work of history, always listen out for the buzzing. If you can detect none, either you are tone deaf or your historian is a dull dog. The facts are really not at all like fish on the fishmonger's slab. They are like fish swimming about in a vast and sometimes inaccessible ocean; and what the historian catches will depend partly on chance, but mainly on what part of the ocean he chooses to fish in and what tackle he chooses to use—these two factors being, of course, determined by the kind of fish he wants to catch. By and large, the historian will get the kind of facts he wants. History means interpretation. Indeed, if, standing Sir George Clark on his head, I were to call history "a hard core of interpretation surrounded by a pulp of disputable facts," my statement would, no doubt, be one-sided and misleading, but no more so, I venture to think, than the original dictum.

The second point is the more familiar one of the historian's need of imaginative understanding for the minds of the people with whom he is dealing, for the thought behind their acts: I say "imaginative understanding," not "sympathy," lest sympathy should be supposed to imply agreement. The nineteenth century was weak in mediaeval history, because it was too much repelled by the superstitious beliefs of the Middle Ages and by the barbarities which they inspired, to have any imaginative understanding of mediaeval people. Or take Burckhardt's censorious remark about the Thirty Years' War: "It is scandalous for a creed, no matter whether it is Catholic or Protestant, to place its salvation above the integrity of the nation." It was extremely difficult for a nineteenth-century liberal historian, brought up to believe that it is right and praiseworthy to kill in defense of one's country, but wicked and wrongheaded to kill in defense of one's religion, to enter into the state of mind of those who fought the Thirty Year's War. This difficulty is particularly acute in the field in which I am now working. Much of what has been written in English-speaking countries in the last ten years about the Soviet Union, and in the Soviet Union about the English-speaking countries, has been vitiated by this inability to achieve even the most elementary measure of imaginative understanding of what goes on in the mind of the other party, so that the words and actions of the other are always made to appear malign, senseless, or hypocritical. History cannot be written unless the historian can achieve some kind of contact with the mind of those about whom he is writing.

The third point is that we can view the past, and achieve our understanding of the past, only through the eyes of the present. The historian is of his own age, and is bound to it by the conditions of human existence. The very words which he uses—words like democracy, empire, war, revolution—have current connotations from which he cannot divorce them. Ancient historians have taken to using words like *polis* and *plebs* in the original, just in order to show that they have not fallen into this trap. This does not help them. They, too, live in the present, and cannot cheat themselves into the past by using unfamiliar or obsolete words, any more than they would become better Greek or Roman historians if they delivered their lectures in a *chlamys* or a *toga*. The names by which successive French historians have described the Parisian crowds which played so prominent a role in the French revolution—*les sansculottes, le peuple, la canaille, les bras-nus*—are all, for those who know the rules of the game, manifestos of a political affiliation and of a particular interpretation. Yet the historian is obliged to choose; the use of language forbids him to be neutral. Nor is it a matter of words alone. Over the past hundred years the changed balance of power in Europe has reversed the attitude of British historians to Frederick the Great. The changed balance of power within the Christian churches between Catholicism and Protestantism has profoundly altered their attitude to such figures as Loyola, Luther, and Cromwell. It requires only a superficial knowledge of the work of French historians of the last forty years on the French revolution to recognize how deeply it has been affected by the Russian revolution of 1917. The historian belongs not to the past but to the present. Professor Trevor-Roper tells us that the historian "ought to love the past." This is a dubious injunction. To love the past may easily be an expression of the nostalgic romanticism of old men and old societies, a symptom of loss of faith and interest in the presence or future. *Cliché for cliché*, I should prefer the one about freeing oneself from "the dead hand of the past." The function of the historian is neither to love the past nor to emancipate himself from the past, but to master and understand it as the key to the understanding of the present.

If, however, these are some of the sights of what I may call the Collingwood view of history, it is time to consider some of the dangers. The emphasis on the role of the historian in the making of history tends, if pressed to its logical conclusion, to rule out any objective history at all: history is what the historian makes. Collingwood seems indeed, at one moment, in an unpublished note quoted by his editor, to have reached this conclusion:

> St. Augustine looked at history from the point of view of the early Christian; Tillemont, from that of a seventeenth-century Frenchman; Gibbon, from that of an eighteenth-century

Englishman; Mommsen, from that of a nineteenth-century German. There is no point in asking which was the right point of view. Each was the only one possible for the man who adopted it.

This amounts to total scepticism, like Froude's remark that history is "a child's box of letter with which we can spell any word we please." Collingwood, in his reaction against "scissors-and-paste history," against the view of history as a mere compilation of facts, comes perilously near to treating history as something spun out of the human brain, and leads back to the conclusion referred to by Sir George Clark in the passage which I quoted earlier, that "there is no 'objective' historical truths." In place of the theory that history has no meaning, we are offered here the theory of an infinity of meanings, none any more right than any other—which comes to much the same thing. The second theory is surely as untenable as the first. It does not follow that, because a mountain appears to take on different shapes from different angles of vision, it has objectively either no shape at all or an infinity of shapes. It does not follow that, because interpretation plays a necessary part in establishing the facts of history, and because no existing interpretation is wholly objective, one interpretation is as good as another, and the facts of history are in principle not amenable to objective interpretation. I shall have to consider at a later stage what exactly is meant by objectivity in history.

But a still greater danger lurks in the Collingwood hypothesis. If the historian necessarily looks at his period of history through the eyes of his own time, and studies the problems of the past as a key to those of the present, will he not fall into a purely pragmatic view of the facts, and maintain that the criterion of a right interpretation is its suitability to some present purpose? On this hypothesis, the facts of history are nothing, interpretation is everything. Nietzsche had already enunciated the principle: "The falseness of an opinion is not for us any objection to it.... The question is how far it is life-furthering, life-preserving, species-preserving, perhaps species-creating." The American pragmatists moved, less explicitly and less wholeheartedly, along the same line. Knowledge is knowledge for some purpose. The validity of the knowledge depends on the validity of the purpose. But, even where no such theory has been professed, the practice has often been no less disquieting. In my own field of study, I have seen too many examples of extravagant interpretation riding roughshod over facts, not to be impressed with the reality of this danger. It is not surprising that perusal of some of the more extreme products of Soviet and anti-Soviet schools of historiography should sometimes breed a certain nostalgia for that illusory nineteenth-century heaven of purely factual history.

How then, in the middle of the twentieth century, are we to define the obligation of the historian to his facts? I trust that I have spent a sufficient number of hours in recent years chasing and perusing documents, and stuffing my historical narrative with properly footnoted facts, to escape the imputation of treating facts and documents too cavalierly. The duty of the historian to respect his facts is not exhausted by the obligation to see that his facts are accurate. He must seek to bring into the picture all known or knowable facts relevant, in one sense or another, to the theme on which he is engaged and to the interpretation proposed. If he seeks to depict the Victorian Englishman as a moral and rational being, he must not forget what happened at Stalybridge Wakes in 1850. But this, in turn, does not mean that he can eliminate interpretation, which is the life-blood of history. Laymen—that is to say, non-academic friends or friends from other academic disciplines—sometimes ask me how the historian goes to work when he writes history. The commonest assumption appears to be that the historian divides his work into two sharply distinguishable phases or periods. First, he spends a long preliminary period reading his source and filling his notebook with facts: then, when this is over, he puts away his source, takes out his notebooks, and writes his book from beginning to end. This is to me an unconvincing and unplausible picture. For myself, as soon as I have got going on a few of what I take to be the capital sources, the itch becomes too strong and I begin to write—not necessarily at the beginning, but somewhere, anywhere. Thereafter, reading and writing go on simultaneously. The writing is added to, subtracted from, re-shaped, cancelled, as I go on reading. The reading is guided and directed and made fruitful by the writing; the more I write, the more I know what I am looking for, the better I understand the significance and relevance of what I find. Some historians probably do all this preliminary writing in their head without using pen, paper, or typewriter, just as some people play chess in their heads without recourse to board and chess-men: this is a talent which I envy, but cannot emulate. But I am convinced that, for any historian worth the name, the two processes of what economists call "input" and "output" go on simultaneously and are, in practice, parts of a single process. If you try to separate them, or to give one priority over the other, you fall into one of two heresies. Either you write scissors-and-paste history without meaning or significance; or you write propaganda or historical fiction, and merely use facts of the past to embroider a kind of writing which has nothing to do with history.

Our examination of the relation of the historian to the facts of history finds us, therefore, in an apparently precarious situation, navigating delicately between the Scylla of an untenable theory of history as an objective compilation of facts, of the unqualified primacy of fact over interpretation, and the Charybdis of an equally untenable theory of history as the subjective product of the mind of the historian who establishes the facts of history and masters them through the process of interpretation, between a view of history having the center of gravity in the past and the view having the center of gravity in the present. But our situation is less precarious than it seems. We shall encounter the same dichotomy of fact and interpretation again in these lectures in other guises—the particular and the general, the empirical and the theoretical, the objective and the subjective. The predicament of the historian is a reflection of the nature of man. Man, except perhaps in earliest infancy and in extreme old age, is not totally involved in his environment and unconditionally subject to it. On the other hand, he is never totally independent of it and its unconditional master. The relation of man to his environment is the relation of the historian to his theme. The historian is neither the humble slave, nor the tyrannical master, of his facts. The relation between the historian and his facts is one of equality, of give-and-take. As any working historian knows, if he stops to reflect on what he is doing as he thinks and writes, the historian is engaged in a continuous process of molding his facts to his interpretation and his interpretation to his facts. It is impossible to assign primacy to one over the other.

The historian starts with the provisional selection of facts and a provisional interpretation in the light of which that selection has been made—by others as well as by himself. As he works, both the interpretation and the selection and ordering of facts undergo subtle and perhaps partly unconscious changes through the reciprocal action of one or the other. And this reciprocal action also involves reciprocity between present and past, since the historian is part of the present and the facts belong to the past. The historian and the facts of history are necessary to one another. The historian without his facts is rootless and futile; the facts without their historian are dead and meaningless. My first answer therefore to the question, What is history? Is that it is a continuous process of interaction between the historian and his facts, an unending dialogue between the present and the past.

Notes

1. **Dilthey:** Wilhelm Dilthey (1833—1911) was a German historian, psychologist, sociologist, and hermeneutic philosopher, who held G. W. F. Hegel's Chair in Philosophy at the University of Berlin. As a polymathic philosopher, working in a modern research university, Dilthey's research interests revolved around questions of scientific methodology, historical evidence and history's status as a science.
2. **Croce:** Benedetto Croce (1866—1952) was an Italian idealist philosopher, historian and politician, who wrote on numerous topics, including philosophy, history, historiography and aesthetics.
3. **Professor Oakeshott:** Michael Joseph Oakeshott (1901—1990) was an English philosopher and political theorist who wrote about philosophy of history, philosophy of religion, aesthetics, philosophy of education, and philosophy of law.

4. **Trevelyan:** George Macaulay Trevelyan (1876—1962), was a British historian and academic. The noted historian E. H. Carr considered Trevelyan to be one of the last historians of the Whig tradition.

5. **Whig:** the approach to historiography which presents the past as an inevitable progression towards ever greater liberty and enlightenment, culminating in modern forms of liberal democracy and constitutional monarchy. In general, Whig historians emphasize the rise of constitutional government, personal freedoms, and scientific progress. The term is often applied generally (and pejoratively) to histories that present the past as the inexorable march of progress towards enlightenment. The term is also used extensively in the history of science for historiography which focuses on the successful chain of theories and experiments that led to present-day science, while ignoring failed theories and dead ends. It is claimed that Whig history has many similarities with the Marxist–Leninist theory of history, which presupposes that humanity is moving through historical stages to the classless, egalitarian society to which communism aspires. Whig history is a form of liberalism, putting its faith in the power of human reason to reshape society for the better, regardless of past history and tradition. It proposes the inevitable progress of mankind. Its opposite is conservative history or "Toryism." The English historian A. J. P. Taylor commented, "Toryism rests on doubt in human nature; it distrusts improvement, clings to traditional institutions, prefers the past to the future."

6. **Thirty Years' War:** The Thirty Years' War was a war fought primarily in Central Europe between 1618 and 1648. One of the most destructive conflicts in human history. The war was preceded by the election of the new Holy Roman Emperor, Ferdinand II, who tried to impose religious uniformity on his domains, forcing Roman Catholicism on its peoples. The northern Protestant states, angered by the violation of their rights to choose, which had been granted in the Peace of Augsburg, banded together to form the Protestant Union. Initially a war between various Protestant and Catholic states in the fragmented Holy Roman Empire, it gradually developed into a more general conflict involving most of the European great powers. These states employed relatively large mercenary armies, and the war became less about religion and more of a continuation of the France–Habsburg rivalry for European political pre-eminence.

7. **Chlamys:** a cloak worn by soldiers in the Ancient Greek.

8. **Toga:** a distinctive garment of Ancient Rome, was a roughly semicircular cloth, between 12 and 20 feet (3.7 and 6.1 m) in length, draped over the shoulders and around the body.

9. **Frederick the Great** (1712—1786): King of Prussia from 1740 until 1786.

10. **Loyola:** Saint Ignatius of Loyola (1491—1556) was the principal founder and first Superior General of the Society of Jesus, a religious order of the Catholic Church professing direct service to the Pope in terms of mission. Members of the order are called Jesuits.

11. **Luther:** Martin Luther (1483[2] —1546) was a German professor of theology, composer, priest, monk, and a seminal figure in the Protestant Reformation.

12. **Cromwell:** Oliver Cromwell (1599—1658) was an English military and political leader. He was an intensely religious man. He became an Independent Puritan after undergoing a religious conversion in the 1630s, taking a generally tolerant view towards the many Protestant sects of his period.

13. **Professor Trevor-Roper:** Hugh Redwald Trevor-Roper (1914—2003), was a British historian of early modern Britain and Nazi Germany. He was Regius Professor of Modern History at the University of Oxford.

14. **Froude:** James Anthony Froude (1818—1894) was an English historian, novelist, biographer, and editor of Fraser's Magazine.

15. **Nietzsche:** Friedrich Wilhelm Nietzsche (1844—1900) was a German philosopher, cultural critic, composer, poet, philologist, and a Latinand Greek scholar whose work has exerted a profound influence on Western philosophy and modern intellectual history.

16. **Scylla:** In Greek mythology, Scylla was a monster that lived on one side of a narrow channel of water, opposite her counterpart Charybdis. The two sides of the strait were within an arrow's range of each other—so close that sailors attempting to avoid Charybdis would pass dangerously close to Scylla and vice versa.

Vocabulary

1. heretic ['herətɪk]: *n.* a person who is guilty of heresy   持异端者
2. cult [kʌlt]: *n.* a system of worship, esp. one that is different from the usual and established forms of religion in a particular society   狂热的崇拜，迷信
3. propound [prə'paʊnd]: *vt.* to put forward as a question or matter for consideration   提出（问题）供考虑
4. propitious [prə'pɪʃəs]: *adj.* good and likely to bring good results   吉祥的
5. treatise ['trɪtɪs]: *n.* a serious book or article that examines a particular subject   专著；专题论文
6. refract [rɪ'frækt]: *v.* (of water, glass, etc.) to cause (light) to change direction when passing through at an angle   使折射

Unit 5 The Historian and His Facts (Part III)

7. exuberantly [ɪɡˈz(j)uːb(ə)r(ə)ntli; eɡ-]: *adj.* (of people and their behavior) overflowing with life and cheerful excitement （人或行为）充满活力的

8. connoisseur [ˌkɒnəˈsɜː]: *n.* someone who knows a lot about something such as art, food, or music   内行

9. abstruse [əbˈstruːs; æb-]: *adj.* difficult to understand   深奥的；难懂的

10. vitiate [ˈvɪʃɪeɪt]: *v.* to make something less effective or spoil it   损害

11. malign [məˈlaɪn]: *adj.* harmful; causing evil   有害的；邪恶的

12. dubious [ˈdubɪəs]: *adj.* causing doubt; of uncertain value or meaning   引起怀疑的；（意义或价值）不确定的

13. injunction [ɪnˈdʒʌŋkʃən]: *n.* a command or official order to do or not to do something   命令；指令

14. perilous [ˈpɛrələs]: *adj.* very dangerous; risky   危险的；冒险的

15. untenable [ʌnˈtenəb(ə)l]: *adj.* impossible to defend   （论据等）站不住脚的

16. amenable [əˈmiːnəbl]: *adj.* ready to be guided or influenced by   易接受指导（影响）的，顺从的

17. enunciate [ɪˈnʌnsɪeɪt]: *vt.* to make a clear and reasoned statement about   清楚地表明

18. profess [prəˈfɛs]: *vt.* to declare openly or freely   公开表示；声称

19. perusal [pəˈruːz(ə)l]: *n.* the act of reading through carefully   细读

20. historiography [hɪˌstɔːrɪˈɒɡrəfɪ; -ˌstɒrɪ-]: *n.* the writing of history based on the analysis and selection of sources   历史编纂学

21. impute [ɪmˈpjuːt]: *vt.* to say, often unfairly, that someone is responsible for something bad or has bad intentions   非难

22. cavalierly [ˌkævəˈlɪrli]: *adv.* in a thoughtless and disrespectful way   唐突的；轻漫的

23. recourse [ˈriːkɔːrs]: *n.* the use of somebody or something as a means of help   求助；依靠

24. emulate [ˈɛmjuleɪt]: *vt.* to try to do as well as or better than (another person)   努力赶上（或超过）

25. precarious [prɪˈkɛrɪəs]: *adj.* not safe; not firm or steady   不稳定的；不安全的

26. provisional [prəˈvɪʒ(ə)n(ə)l]: *adj.* likely or able to be changed in the future   临时的

27. reciprocal [rɪˈsɪprək(ə)l]: *adj.* a reciprocal arrangement or relationship is one in which two people or groups do or give the same things to each other   相互的

Expressions

1. It is what is already done by the intelligent undergraduate who... goes round to a friend at St. Jude's to ask what sort of chap Jones is, and <u>what bees he has in his bonnet</u>.

bee in one's bonnet: a fixed idea about something 对（某事物的）固执想法

2. When you read a work of history, you <u>listen out</u> for the buzzing.

listen out: to listen carefully, esp. for an expected sound 留心听

3. Indeed, if, <u>standing Sir George Clark on his head</u>, I were to call history "a hard core of interpretation surrounded by a pulp of disputable facts,"...

stand somebody on his head: to show he is completely wrong 推翻他的理论

4. In my own field of study, I have seen too many examples of extravagant interpretation <u>riding roughshod over</u> facts, not to be impressed with the reality of this danger.

ride roughshod over something: to ignore someone else's feelings or ideas because you have the power or authority to do this 粗暴地对待

5. The writing is added to, <u>subtracted from</u>, re-shaped, cancelled, as I go on reading.

subtract from: to take (a number, an amount) from something larger 减去

Comprehension

I. Discuss the Main Point and the Meanings.

1. In Croce's view, all history is contemporary history. How do you understand this view of history?

2. How can Collingwood's belief that "all history is the history of thought" make sense to you?

3. Why can't we have pure facts in history?

4. Different historians look at history from different points of view, then how can we have objective history?

5. What is history according to Edward Carr?

II. Fill in the blanks with the appropriate words or expressions in the box.

dialogue	equality	evaluate	facts of the past
interaction	meaning	mutual relations	significance
the mind of the recorder	the present	the thought	the understanding of the present

1. Croce declared that all history is "contemporary history," meaning that history consists essentially in seeing the past through the eyes of _____ and in the light of its problems, and that the main work of the historian is not to record, but to _____.

2. The philosophy of history is concerned neither with "the past by itself" nor with "the historian's thought about it by itself," but with "the two things in their _____."

Unit 5 The Historian and His Facts (Part III)

3. "All history is the history of thought," and "history is the re-enactment in the historian's mind of _____ whose history he is studying."

4. The facts of history never come to us "pure," since they are always refracted through _____.

5. Historians need to have _____ for the minds of the people with whom he is dealing, for the thought behind their act.

6. We can view the past, and achieve our understanding of the past, only through the eyes of _____.

7. The function of the historian is to master and understand the past as the key to _____.

8. Either you write scissors-and-paste history without _____ or _____; or you write propaganda or historical fiction, and merely use _____ to embroider a kind of writing which has nothing to do with history.

9. The relation between the historian and his facts is one of _____, of give-and-take.

10. History is a continuous process of _____ between the historian and his facts, an unending _____ between the present and the past.

Structure

I. Find out how words and expression in bold are used in the following sentences.

1. Croce began to propound a philosophy of history which obviously **owed** much **to** German masters.

2. History consists essentially in seeing the past through the eyes of the present and **in the light of** its problems.

3. The views of Collingwood can be summarized **as follows**.

4. The reconstitution of the past is not **in itself** an empirical process.

5. **It follows that** when we take up a work of history, our first concern should be with the historian who wrote it.

6. Trevelyan was "**brought up** at home on a somewhat exuberantly Whig tradition."

7. The emphasis on the role of the historian in the making of history tends to **rule out** any objective history at all.

8. This **amounts to** total scepticism.

9. It does not follow that, because a mountain appears to **take on** different shapes from different angles of vision, it has objectively either no shape at all or an infinity of shapes.

10. Man is not totally involved in his environment and unconditionally **subject to** it.

11. The historian starts with the **provisional** selection of facts and a provisional interpretation in the light of which that selection has been made.

12. As he works, both the interpretation and the selection and ordering of facts undergo subtle and perhaps partly unconscious changes through the **reciprocal** action of one or the other.

II. Complete the following sentences with some of the above words or expressions in bold.

1. Let's form a _____ government until we can hold an election.

2. She hasn't actually refused, but it _____ the same thing.

3. She _____ to respect the laws.

4. I wanted to go to the movie with you, but _____ the changed circumstances, I'd better go to the hospital.

5. The winners are _____: Johnson, Miller and Smith.

6. The book _____ is not about racism, but the title is misleading.

7. _____ doesn't necessarily _____ you're going to do well academically even if you are highly intelligent.

8. All citizens _____ the laws of this country.

9. The couple next door have a _____ loathing for each other.

10. We can't _____ the possibility that she lost her passport.

→ *America in Cold War*

American historian Arthur Schlesinger Jr. writes in the "Cycles of American History" that American foreign policy has been swinging between isolationism and internationalism (interventionism). This can be used to describe American foreign policy up to the Second World War.

By the end of the war, the United States became the strongest country in the world. As the sole possessor of atomic bombs, with over 70% of the gold reserve of the world in its coffers and over 50% of industrial production of the world in its hand, the planners of the United States were visualizing a Pax Americana. They wanted a world order dominated by the United States, a world market which was free and open to American goods and services and more and more countries modeling on American institutions and values.

In February 1946, George F. Kennan, a leading student of Soviet politics who had been stationed in the U.S.S.R. since the 1930s, warned that the Soviet Union was a political force committed to the belief that there could be no permanent peace with the United States. The only answer was a "long-term, patient but firm and vigilant containment of Russian expansive tendencies." The idea that only strong, sustained U.S. resistance could "contain" Soviet expansionism suited the mood of Truman.

A week later, Truman accompanied Winston Churchill to Westminster College in Missouri, where the former British prime minister delivered a speech. Stalin, Churchill intoned, had drawn an iron curtain across the eastern half of Europe. He called for an alliance of the English-speaking people against the Soviet Union. Truman in the spring of 1946 shifted his foreign policy in the direction prescribed by Kennan and Churchill.

Truman Doctrine

The first major application of the containment policy came in 1947, when both Greece and Turkey became destabilized. On March 12, in an address to a joint session of Congress, the president requested military assistance to Greece and Turkey. Especially momentous in the dramatic speech were the words that would guide U. S. policymakers for almost a half century: "I believe that it must be the policy of the United States to support free peoples who are resisting attempted subjugation by armed minorities or by outside pressures." The Truman Doctrine was meant to be as comprehensive as the Monroe Doctrine's "Keep out" sign posted on the Western Hemisphere. The president's declaration committed the United States in theory to the role of global policeman.

The counterpart to the Truman Doctrine in the economic sphere was the European Recovery Program, commonly known as the Marshall Plan. By the time of its termination on December 31, 1951, a total of $12.5 billion had been spent in support of Marshall Plan operations. The Marshall Plan marked the final step toward the cold war. In January 1949, Moscow established the Council for Mutual Economic Assistance (Molotov Plan) as the Eastern counterpart to the Marshall Plan.

Thus the line was drawn between the Communist and Western worlds. The cold war now was in full sway, and the next half-decade one crisis followed closely on another. The moves and countermoves culminated in the establishment of the two confrontational military alliances: the North Atlantic Treaty Organization, or NATO (April 4, 1949), which included the United States, Canada, and western European states, and the Warsaw Pact (May, 1965), comprising the Soviet Union and its eastern European allies. Thus, Europe, as well as Germany, was cut in two by the cold war.

The contest between the United States and the Soviet Union soon acquired the name Cold War. The Cold War got its name because both sides were afraid of fighting each other directly. In a "hot war," nuclear weapons might destroy everything. So, instead, both sides fought each other indirectly.

They expressed the conflict through military coalitions, strategic conventional force deployments, extensive aid to states deemed vulnerable, proxy wars, espionage, propaganda, conventional and nuclear arms races, appeals to neutral nations, rivalry at sports events, and technological competitions such as the Space Race.

Cold War tensions increased, then eased, then increased again over the years. The changes came as both sides attempted to influence political and economic developments around the world.

The most tense conflicts involved the Berlin Blockade (1948—1949), the Korean War (1950—1953), the Berlin Crisis of 1961, the Vietnam War (1955—1975), the Cuban Missile Crisis (1962), the Soviet war in Afghanistan (1979—1989), and the Able Archer 83 NATO exercises in November 1983.

The Berlin Blockade

The 1945 Potsdam Agreement had divided Germany into four separate zones (administered by France, Great Britain, the Soviet Union, and the United States) and had created a joint four-power administration for Germany's capital, Berlin. As the Cold War unfolded, however, the West began to view a revived Germany as a buffer against the Soviet-controlled East. The Western powers gradually united their zones, and Stalin responded in April 1948 by impeding the flow of supplies and people from the west of Germany into Berlin. Truman ordered a massive airlift to provide Berliners with the thousands of tons of food and fuel necessary for their survival. In May 1949 the Soviets ended the blockade. The Berlin Blockade marked a very high point of American cold war history.

The Korean War

On June 24, 1950, North Korean troops had conflicts with South Korean troops. North Korea's move seemed to Truman more a case of Soviet-directed aggression than an internal Korean matter. The president decided to intervene. Without consulting Congress or asking for a formal declaration of war, Truman quickly secured the United Nations' sanction for a common "police action" against North Korea.

On June 27 Truman ordered American air and sea forces to the aid of the South Koreans and appointed seventy-year old General Douglas MacArthur to command the U.N. effort in Korea.

On October 1, South Korean troops entered North Korea. They captured the capital, Pyongyang. Then they moved toward the Yalu River, the border between North Korea and China. China warned against moving closer to the border. General MacArthur ordered the troops to continue their attacks. He repeatedly said he did not believe that China would enter the war in force.

MacArthur was wrong. Several hundred thousand Chinese soldiers crossed into North Korea in October and November. They pushed the American forces into retreat and advanced steadily south. Then a stalemate developed as battle lines stabilized near the 38th parallel. The war dragged on for another two years and finally ended on on July 26, 1953 after a lot of negotiations for peace. The Korean War is often dismissed as America's forgotten war. Unlike WWII, it did not capture the nation's attention.

The Berlin Crisis of 1961

To stabilize the East German economy, on August 13, 1961 Soviet and East German troops sealed the border between East and West Berlin. In response, President John F. Kennedy judged that so long as Western rights in West Berlin were not being directly challenged the United States could not interfere. This decision led to widespread criticism of American inaction. The Berlin Wall came to symbolize the Cold War division of Germany and the world between the communist and noncommunist blocs.

Vietnam War

Vietnam had gained its independence from France in 1954. The country was divided into North and South. The North had a communist government led by Ho Chi Minh. The CIA mission in Vietnam helped install Ngo Dinh Diem in the South.

CIA agents worked with Diem to train his armed forces and secret police, to eliminate political opposition, and to block the election to reunify Vietnam that the Geneva agreements had specified.

In 1957, communist rebels — the Viet Cong — launched a violent campaign in the South. They were supported by the government of North Vietnam and later by North Vietnamese troops. Their goal was to overthrow the government in the South.

President Johnson believed that the United States had to support South Vietnam. In early 1965 Johnson ordered the sustained bombing of North Vietnam. Unable to turn the tide by bombing, Johnson made a fateful decision to escalate the U.S. commitment by sending combat troops to Vietnam.

As casualty figures surpassed those of the Korean War, and total costs approached $100 billion, the war's unpopularity, even among the ambivalent majority, deepened. Hundreds of thousands of Americans participated in antiwar marches and demonstrations in 1967. In 1973, the Paris Peace Accords withdrew the American troops from southeast Asia. And in 1975, south Vietnam was defeated, ending a deeply divisive era in two parts of the globe.

Vietnam became the site of American's longest war (1955—1975). The war did not involve vital U.S. interests, whose costs far outweighted potential benefits, and worsened domestic problems and social divisions. Although not considered the military defeat, the Vietnam War was a humiliating political defeat for the United States.

CIA Intervention

Vietnam War is the most extensive CIA operations in the 1950s. Established by the National Security Act of 1947 mainly to conduct espionage and to analyze information on foreign nations, the Central Intelligence Agency fought a covert war against those thought to be imperiling American interests. They became involved in various undercover operations to topple regimes believed hostile to the United States.

In 1953 the agency plotted with Iranian army officers to overthrow the popularly elected government that had taken possession of the rich oil resources long exploited by Britain. Fearing a precedent that might jeopardize Western oil interests in the Middle East, the CIA secretly returned the deposed Shah of Iran to power and restored the oil wells to British firms. In 1954 it equipped and trained a force of Guatemalans to stage a military coup against the incumbent regime, which had seized 225, 000 acres from the American-owned United Fruit Company. After destroying the leftist government, the CIA's Guatemalan agents instituted a military opposition.

After the election of the Marxist Salvado Allende to the presidency of Chile in 1970, Nixon secretly funneled $10 million to the CIA to fund opponents of the leftist Chilean government.

Under director William Casey, the CIA in 1982 organized and financed a ten-thousand-man anti-Sandinista guerrilla army, called contras, based in neighboring Honduras and Costa Rica. The contras, many with links to the deposed Somoza regime, conducted raids, planted mines, and carried out sabotage inside Nicaragua.

Bay of Pigs Invasion

At a secret base in the Guatemala Jungle, American CIA agents had been training Cuban exiles to invade Cuba. The plan was presented to the new President—John F. Kennedy. Kennedy agreed to the invasion, but demanded crucial changes to hide America's involvement.

On April 17, armed Cuban exiles tried to invade Cuba, less than 150 kilometers from the American state of Florida. The exiles came ashore at Cuba's Bay of Pigs. American planes were to protect the invasion force to stay and hit the beach. But Kennedy, now faced with international condemnation for the initial bombing, canceled the air support. Without American air support or resupply, the invasion force was outnumbered and outgunned. Within 72 hours, most of the exiles were killed or captured. Kennedy was devastated by the fiasco of the Bay of Pigs. It was a failure in his political life.

Cuban Missile Crisis

The United States had all along been regarding Latin America as its backyard and would not allow other powers to put their fingers on this region. The Soviet Union, taking advantage of the Bays of Pigs of Invasion to expand its influence in the region, introduced medium range and intermediated range missiles into Cuba without being detected by the United States. The United States was not aware of the existence of missiles in Cuba until the U-2 spy plane brought back photos in October, 1962, showing that the launching pads were near completion. After much discussion and deliberation, President Kennedy decided to place a blockade around Cuba to prevent further shipment of weapons into Cuba and demand the total removal of missiles in place in Cuba. There were tense negotiations with the Soviets. Khrushchev demanded a promise that the United States would not invade Cuba. Kennedy agreed, and did so publicly. Secretly he also agreed to another demand. He promised that the United States would remove its Jupiter missiles based in Turkey, after the crisis was over. In the end, the Soviet Union withdrew the missiles from Cuba. The Cuban missile crisis lasted thirteen days. It raised fears of a nuclear war.

Vocabulary of History/American History

1. The **reconstitution of the past** in the historian's mind is dependent on empirical evidence.
2. But it is not in itself an empirical process, and cannot consist in a mere **recital of facts**.
3. The reader must **re-enact** in thought what has gone on in the mind of the historian.
4. We shall encounter the same dichotomy of fact and interpretation again in these lectures in other guises—the particular and the general, the empirical and the theoretical, the **objective** and the **subjective**.
5. The historian starts with the provisional selection of facts and a **provisional** interpretation in the light of which that selection has been made—by others as well as by himself.
6. As he works, both the **interpretation** and the **selection** and ordering of facts undergo subtle and perhaps partly unconscious changes through the **reciprocal** action of one or the other.
7. My first answer therefore to the question, What is history? Is that it is a continuous process of **interaction** between the historian and his facts, an unending **dialogue** between the present and the past.
8. The only answer was a "long-term, patient but firm and vigilant **containment** of Russian expansive tendencies."

9. Stalin, Churchill intoned, had drawn an **iron curtain** across the eastern half of Europe.

10. As the Cold War **unfolded**, however, the West began to view a revived Germany as a **buffer** against the Soviet-controlled East.

11. Cold War tensions increased, then **eased**, then increased again over the years.

12. American historian Arthur Schlesinger Jr. writes in the "Cycles of American History" that American foreign policy has been swinging between **isolationism** and **internationalism** (**interventionism**).

13. Established by the National Security Act of 1947 mainly to conduct **espionage** and to analyze information on foreign nations, the Central Intelligence Agency fought a **covert** war against those thought to be imperiling American interests.

14. The contras, many with links to the deposed Somoza regime, conducted raids, planted mines, and carried out **sabotage** inside Nicaragua.

15. But Kennedy, now faced with international **condemnation** for the initial bombing, canceled the air support.

Unit 6

A Nation of Welfare Families

Stephanie Coontz

The current political debate over family values, personal responsibility, and welfare takes for granted the entrenched American belief that dependence on government assistance is a recent and destructive phenomenon. Conservatives tend to blame this dependence on personal irresponsibility aggravated by a swollen welfare apparatus that saps individual initiative. Liberals are more likely to blame it on personal misfortune magnified by the harsh lot that falls to losers in our competitive market economy. But both sides believe that "winners" in America make it on their own, that dependence reflects some kind of individual or family failure, and that the ideal family is the self-reliant unit of traditional lore — a family that takes care of its own, carves out a future for its children, and never asks for handouts. Politicians at both ends of the ideological spectrum have wrapped themselves in the mantle of these "family values," arguing over *why* the poor have not been able to make do without assistance, or whether aid has exacerbated their situation, but never questioning the assumption that American families traditionally achieve success by establishing their independence from the government.

The myth of family self-reliance is so compelling that our actual national and personal histories often buckle under its emotional weight. "We always stood on our own two feet," my grandfather used to say about his pioneer heritage, whenever he walked me to the top of the hill to survey the property in Washington State that his family had bought for next to nothing after it had been logged off in the early 1900s. Perhaps he didn't know that the land came so cheap because much of it was part of a federal subsidy originally allotted to the railroad companies, which had received 183 million acres of the public domain in the nineteenth century. These federal giveaways were the original source of most major Western logging companies' land, and when some of these logging companies moved on to virgin stands of timber, federal lands trickled down to a few early settlers who were able to purchase them inexpensively.

Like my grandparents, few families in American history — whatever their "values" — have been able to rely solely on their own resources. Instead, they have depended on the legislative, judicial, and social-support structures set up by governing authorities, whether those authorities were the clan elders of Native American societies, the church courts and city officials of colonial America, or the judicial and legislative bodies established by the Constitution.

At America's inception, this was considered not a dirty little secret but the norm, one that confirmed our social and personal interdependence. The idea that the family should have the sole or even primary responsibility for education and socializing its members, finding them suitable work, or keeping them from poverty and crime was not only ludicrous to colonial and revolutionary thinkers but dangerously parochial.

Historically, one way that government has played a role in the well-being of its citizens is by regulating the way that employers and civic bodies interact with families. In the early twentieth century, for example, as a response to rapid changes ushered in by a mass-production economy, the government promoted a "family wage system." This system was designed to strengthen the ability of the male breadwinner to support a family without having his wife or children work. This family wage system was not a natural outgrowth of the market. It was a *political* response to conditions that the market had produced: child labor, rampant employment insecurity, recurring economic downturns, an earnings structure in which 45 percent of industrial workers fell below the poverty level and another 40 percent hovered barely above it, and a system in which thousands of children had been placed in orphanages or other institutions simply because their parents could not afford their keep. The state policies involved in the establishment of the family wage system included abolition of child labor, government pressure on industrialists to negotiate with unions, federal arbitration, expansion of compulsory schooling — and legislation discriminating against women workers.

But even such extensive regulation of economic and social institutions has never been enough: government has always supported families with direct material aid as well. The two best examples of the government's history of material aid can be found in what many people consider the ideal models of self-reliant families: the Western pioneer family and the 1950s suburban family. In both cases, the ability of these families to establish and sustain themselves required massive underwriting by the government.

Pioneer families, such as my grandparents, could never have moved west without government-funded military mobilizations against the original Indian and Mexican inhabitants or state-sponsored economic investment in transportation systems. In addition, the Homestead Act of 1862 allowed settlers to buy 160 acres for $10 — far below the government's cost of acquiring the land — if the homesteader lived on and improved the land for five years. In the twentieth century, a new form of public assistance became crucial to Western families: construction of dams and other federally subsidized irrigation projects. During the 1930s, for example, government electrification projects brought pumps, refrigeration, and household technology to millions of families.

The suburban family of the 1950s is another oft-cited example of familial self-reliance. According to legend, after World War II a new, family-oriented generation settled down, saved their pennies, worked hard, and found well-paying jobs that allowed them to purchase homes in the suburbs. In fact, however, the 1950s suburban family was far more dependent on government assistance than any so-called underclass family of today. Federal GI benefit payments, available to 40 percent of the male population between the ages of twenty and twenty-four, permitted a whole generation of men to expand their education and improve their job prospects without forgoing marriage and children. The National Defense Education Act retooled science education in America, subsidizing both American industry and the education of individual scientists. Government-funded research developed the aluminum clapboards, prefabricated walls and ceilings, and plywood paneling that comprised the technological basis of the post-war housing revolution. Government spending was also largely responsible for the new highways, sewer systems, utility services, and traffic-control programs that opened up suburbia.

In addition, suburban home ownership depended on an unprecedented expansion of federal regulation and financing. Before the war, banks often required a 50 percent down payment on homes and normally issued mortgages for five to ten years. In the postwar period, however, the Federal Housing Authority, supplemented by the GI Bill, put the federal government in the business of insuring and regulating private loans for single-home construction. FHA policy required down payments of only 5 to 10 percent of the purchase price and guaranteed mortgages of up to thirty years at interest rates of just 2 to 3 percent. The Veterans Administration required a mere dollar down from veterans. Almost half the housing in suburbia in the 1950s depended on such federal programs.

The drawback of these aid programs was that although they worked well for recipients, nonrecipients — disproportionately poor and urban — were left far behind. While the general public financed the roads that suburbanites used to commute, the streetcars and trolleys that served urban and poor families received almost no tax revenues, and our previously thriving rail system was allowed to decay. In addition, federal loan policies, which were a boon to upwardly mobile white families, tended to systematize the pervasive but informal racism that had previously characterized the housing market. FHA red-lining practices, for example, took entire urban areas and declared them ineligible for loans, while the government's two new mortgage institutions, the Federal National Mortgage Association and the Government National Mortgage Association (Fannie Mae and Ginny Mae) made it possible for urban banks to transfer savings out of the cities and into new suburban developments in the South and West.

Despite the devastating effects on families and regions that did not receive such assistance, government aid to suburban residents during the 1950s and 1960s produced in its beneficiaries none of the demoralization usually presumed to afflict recipients of government handouts. Instead, federal subsidies to suburbia encouraged family formation, residential stability, upward occupational mobility, and rising educational aspirations among youth who could look forward to receiving such aid. Seen in this light, the idea that government subsidies intrinsically induce dependence, undermine self-esteem, or break down family ties is exposed as no more than a myth.

I am not suggesting that the way to solve the problems of poverty and urban decay in America is to quadruple our spending on welfare. Certainly there are major reforms needed in our current aid policies to the poor. But the debate over such reform should put welfare in the context of *all* federal assistance programs. As long as we pretend that only poor or single-parent families need outside assistance, while normal families "stand on their own two feet," we will shortchange poor families, overcompensate rich ones, and fail to come up with effective policies for helping out families in the middle. Current government housing policies are a case in point. The richest 20 percent of American households receives three times as much federal housing aid — mostly in tax subsidies — as the poorest 20 percent receives in expenditures for low-income housing.

Historically, the debate over government policies toward families has never been over *whether* to intervene but *how*: to rescue or to warehouse, to prevent or to punish, to moralize about values or mobilize resources for education and job creation. Today's debate, lacking such a historical perspective, caricatures the real issues. Our attempt to sustain the myth of family self-reliance in the face of all the historical evidence to the contrary has led policymakers into theoretical contortions and practical miscalculations that are reminiscent of efforts by medieval philosophers to maintain that the earth and not the sun was the center of the planetary system. In the sixteenth century, leading European thinkers insisted that the planets and the sun all revolved around the earth — much as American politicians today insist that our society revolved around family self-reliance. When evidence to the contrary mounted, defenders of the Ptolemaic universe postulated all sorts of elaborate planetary orbits in order to reconcile observed reality with their cherished theory. Similarly, rather that admit that all families need some kind of public support, we have constructed ideological orbits that explain away each instance of middle-class dependence as an "exception," an "abnormality," or even an illusion. We have distributed public aid to families through convoluted bureaucracies that have become impossible to track; in some cases the system has become so cumbersome that it threatens to collapse around our ears. It is time to break through the old paradigm of self-reliance and substitute a new one that recognizes that assisting families is, simply, what government does.

Notes

1. **The Homestead Act of 1862:** The Homestead Acts were several laws in the United States by which an applicant could acquire ownership of government land or the public domain, typically called a "homestead." In all, more than 270 million acres of public land, or nearly 10 percent of the total area of the U.S., was given away free to 1.6 million homesteaders; most of the homesteads were west of the Mississippi River. The first of the acts, the Homestead Act of 1862, opened up millions of acres. Any adult who had never taken up arms against the U.S. government could apply. Women and immigrants who had applied for citizenship were eligible.

2. **GI Bill:** The Servicemen's Readjustment Act of 1944, also known as the G.I. Bill, was a law that provided a range of benefits for returning World War II veterans (commonly referred to as G.I.s). The goal was to provide immediate rewards for practically all World War II veterans.

3. **Ptolemaic universe:** the theory named after Claudius Ptolemy, a Greco-Roman mathematician, astronomer, geographer, astrologer, and poet of a single epigram in the Greek Anthology. According to this theory, on the spherical form of the heavens, the spherical Earth lies motionless as the center, with the fixed stars and the various planets revolving around the Earth.

Vocabulary

1. entrench [ɪn'trɛntʃ]: *vt.* to establish something very firmly so that it is very difficult to change   牢固确立

2. aggravate ['ægrəvet]: *vt.* to make an illness or a bad or unpleasant situation worse   使严重；使恶化

3. sap [sæp]: *vt.* to make something/somebody weaker; to destroy something gradually   削弱；逐渐破坏

4. initative [ɪ'nɪʃətɪv]: *n.* the ability to decide and act on your own without waiting for somebody to tell you what to do   主动性；积极性；自发性

5. **lore** [lɔːr]: *n.* the stories and traditions of a particular group of people （某一群体的）传说，传统

6. **exacerbate** [ɪɡ'zæsərbeɪt]: *vt.* to make something worse, especially a disease or problem 使加剧；使恶化；激怒

7. **buckle** ['bʌk(ə)l]: *vi.* to become crushed or bent under a weight or force （被）压垮；压弯

8. **trickle** ['trɪkl]: *vi.* to flow, or to make something flow, slowly in a thin stream （使）滴，淌

9. **inception** [ɪn'sɛpʃən]: *n.* the start of an institution, an organization, etc. （机构、组织等的）开端，创始

10. **ludicrous** ['ludɪkrəs]: *adj.* ridiculous and unreasonable 荒唐的；不合理的

11. **parochial** [pə'rokɪəl]: *adj.* (disapproving) only concerned with small issues that happen in your local area and not interested in more important things 地方观念的；狭隘的

12. **rampant** ['ræmpənt]: *adj.* (of something bad) existing or spreading everywhere in a way that cannot be controlled 泛滥的；猖獗的

13. **hover** ['hʌvər]: *vi.* to stay close to something, or to stay in an uncertain state 靠近（某事物）

14. **underwrite** [ˌʌndər'raɪt]: *vt.* to accept financial responsibility for an activity so that you will pay for special costs or for losses it may make 承担经济责任（包括支付特别费用或损失）

15. **subsidize** ['sʌbsə'daɪz]: *vt.* to give money to somebody or an organization to help pay for something 资助

16. **forgo** [fɔr'go]: *vt.* to decide not to have or do something that you would like to have or do 放弃

17. **retool** [ˌri'tul]: *vt.* to organize something in a new or different way 重新安排

18. **sewer** ['suər]: *n.* an underground pipe that is used to carry sewage away from houses, factories, etc. 下水道

19. **utility** [ju'tɪləti]: *n.* a service provided for the public, for example an electricity, water, or gas supply 公用事业

20. **mortgage** ['mɔːrɡɪdʒ]: *n.* a legal agreement by which a bank or similar organization lends you money to buy a house, etc, and you pay the money back over a particular number of years 按揭贷款

21. **boon** [bʊn]: *n.* something that is very helpful and makes life easier for you 非常有用的东西；益处

22. **eligible** ['ɛlɪdʒəbl]: *adj.* qualified for or worthy of being chosen 合格的

23. intrinsic [ɪn'trɪnsɪk]: *adj.* belonging to or part of the real nature of something/somebody 内在的

24. warehouse ['wɛrhaʊs]: *vi.* to store in a warehouse 储入仓库

25. caricature ['kærɪkətʃər]: *vt.* to describe or present somebody as a type of person you would laugh at or not respect 滑稽地描述

26. contortion [kən'tɔːʃən]: *n.* the act of twisting or deforming the shape of something 扭曲

27. postulate ['pɑstʃəlet]: *vt.* to suggest or accept that something is true so that it can be used as the basis for a theory, etc. 假定；假设

28. convoluted ['kɑnvəluːtɪd]: *adj.* extremely complicated and difficult to follow 错综复杂的

29. cumbersome ['kʌmbərsəm]: *adj.* large and heavy; slow and complicated 笨重的；繁琐的

30. paradigm ['pærə'daɪm]: *n.* a typical example or pattern of something 典范；样式

Expressions

1. Politicians at both ends of the ideological spectrum have wrapped themselves in <u>the mantle of</u> these "family values,"…

   the mantle of somebody/something: the role and responsibility of an important person or job, especially when they are passed on from one person to another （可继承的）责任，职责，衣钵

2. Politicians at both ends of the ideological spectrum have wrapped themselves in the mantle of these "family values," arguing over *why* the poor have not been able to <u>make do</u> without assistance…

   make do (with/without something): *infml* to use (something) even though it may not be exactly what is wanted or needed 凑合着对付过去

3. …his family had bought for next to nothing after it had been <u>logged off</u> in the early 1900s.

   log off: to cut down trees in a forest for their wood 伐木

4. …because much of it was part of a federal subsidy originally <u>allotted to</u> the railroad companies…

   allot something (to somebody/something)/allot (somebody/something) something: to give time, money, tasks, etc. to somebody/something as a share of what is available 分配，配给（时间、钱财等）

5. …this was considered not a dirty little secret but <u>the norm</u>…

   the norm: a situation or a pattern of behavior that is usual or expected 常态

6. Before the war, banks often required a 50 percent <u>down payment</u> on homes and normally issued mortgages for five to ten years.

   down payment: the amount of money that you pay to start with, and then you pay the rest later 预付款；先付款

Comprehension

I. Discuss the Main Point and the Meanings.

1. Why does the author say that families rely solely on their own resources to take care of their members is a traditional lore in America?

2. How can the government play a role in the well-being of its people?

3. How has government aid to suburban residents during the 1950s and 1960s affected the beneficiaries?

4. What does the author suggest to solve the problems of poverty and urban decay in America?

II. Fill in the blanks with the appropriate words or expressions in the box.

all federal assistance programs	assisting families	direct material aid
individual initiative	on their own	overcompensate
personal irresponsibility	personal misfortune	regulating
shortchange	their own resources	encouraged

1. Conservatives tend to blame dependence on government assistance on _____ aggravated by a swollen welfare apparatus that saps _____.

2. Liberals are more likely to blame the dependence on government assistance on _____ magnified by the harsh lot that falls to losers in our competitive market economy.

3. Both conservatives and liberals believe that "winners" in America make it _____.

4. Few families in American history have been able to rely solely on _____.

5. Historically, one way that government has played a role in the well-being of its citizens is by _____ the way that employers and civic bodies interact with families.

6. Government has always supported families with _____ as well.

7. Federal subsidies to suburbia _____ family formation, residential stability, upward occupational mobility, and rising educational aspirations among youth.

8. As long as we pretend that only poor or single-parent families need outside assistance, while normal families "stand on their own two feet," we will _____ poor families, _____ rich ones, and fail to come up with effective policies for helping out families in the middle.

9. The reforms in America's aid policies to the poor should put welfare in the context of _____.

10. _____ is, simply, what government does.

Structure

I. Find out how the words and expression in bold are used in the following sentences.

1. The current political debate **takes for granted** the entrenched American belief…

2. Conservatives tend to **blame** this dependence **on** personal irresponsibility.

3. But both sides believe that "winners" in America **make it on their own**.

4. The ideal family **carves out** a future for its children.

5. They have depended on the legislative, judicial, and social-support structures **set up** by governing authorities.

6. Government regulates the way that employers and civic bodies **interact** with families.

7. …as a response to rapid changes **ushered in** by a mass-production economy, the government promoted a "family wage system."

8. …after World War II a new, family-oriented generation **settled down**…

9. Government-funded research developed the aluminum clapboards, prefabricated walls and ceilings, and plywood paneling that **comprised** the technological basis of the post-war housing revolution.

10. Government spending was also largely responsible for the new highways, sewer systems, utility services, and traffic-control programs that **opened up** suburbia.

11. In addition, suburban home ownership depended on an **unprecedented** expansion of federal regulation and financing.

12. …nonrecipients — disproportionately poor and urban — were **left far behind**.

13. …federal loan policies …tended to systematize the pervasive but informal racism that had **previously** characterized the housing market.

14. …government subsidies intrinsically induce dependence, undermine self-esteem, or **break down** family ties…

15. Current government housing policies are **a case in point**.

16. Our attempt to sustain the myth of family self-reliance **in the face of** all the historical evidence to the contrary…**are reminiscent of** efforts by medieval philosophers to maintain that the earth and not the sun was the center of the planetary system.

17. …the sun all **revolved around** the earth…

18. Ptolemaic universe postulated all sorts of elaborate planetary orbits in order to **reconcile** observed reality **with** their cherished theory.

19. It is time to **break through** the old paradigm of self-reliance.

II. Complete the following sentences with some of the above words or expressions in bold.

1. It is hard to _____ her career ambitions _____ the needs of her children.

2. Some of the things happening now may seem _____ the old cold war.

3. The national government became involved in areas that _____ had been the responsibility of the states.

4. The railway _____ the west of the country.

5. The stripes symbolize the 13 colonies that originally _____ the United States.

6. The change of management _____ fresh ideas and policies.

7. Police _____ the accident _____ drunken driving.

8. When are you going to _____ and have a family.

9. Britain _____ in the race for new markets.

10. The council _____ a committee to look into unemployment.

11. It's hard to _____ to the top in show business.

12. The 13 stripes in the American Flag represent the 13 colonies that originally _____ the United States.

13. This agreement will _____ the barriers to free trade.

14. _____ great hardship, she managed to keep her sense of humor.

15. I can't carry out the plan _____. It's too time-consuming.

→ American Government

I. The Constitution

The Constitution of the United States is the basis for the machinery and institutions of the U.S. government. The Constitution is the world's oldest charter of national government in continuous use. In 1788, after nine states ratified it, the Constitution became the law of the land.

Unit 6 A Nation of Welfare Families

The Constitution consists of a preamble, seven original articles, twenty-seven amendments, and a paragraph certifying its enactment by the constitutional convention. The Founders established three branches of government—the executive, the legislative, and the judicial. The functions of these branches are described in the first three articles of the Constitution.

Article IV sets up cooperative arrangements between the states and the federal government regarding fugitives and criminals, and requires that states respect one other and one other's citizens. It also establishes the process by which territories become states, an important function during the 19th and early 20th centuries. Finally, Article IV guarantees a republican—or representative—form of government for all states. Article V establishes procedures for amending the Constitution. Article VI is a catchall article; its most important section establishes the Constitution and the laws of the United States as "the Supreme Law of the Land." Article VII of the Constitution establishes procedures that were used in 1788 and 1789 for the approval and subsequent adoption of the document by the states.

In 1790 Congress and the states ratified ten amendments known as the Bill of Rights. These amendments guarantee personal liberties and prevent the federal government from infringing on the rights of states and citizens. The First Amendment is the basic statement of American freedoms. It protects freedom of religion, freedom of speech and freedom of the press. The Second Amendment guarantees the peoples' right to keep weapons as part of an organized militia.

Some other most important amendments are the 15th, 19th, and 26th amendments, which, respectively, gave blacks, women, and 18-year-olds the right to vote. Also important are the 17th Amendment, which gave the people the right to elect United States senators, and the 22nd Amendment, which restricted the number of terms a president can serve to two. These amendments extended the principles of democracy to more Americans, and in the case of the president, limited the power of a chief executive by restricting the length of his or her tenure. Besides these amendments, the 14th Amendment is an important safeguard for minority rights because under its "due process" clause, it extends the protections of the Bill of Rights to individual residents of states. In the same way that the Bill of Rights limits federal power, the 14th Amendment limits the power of the states over their citizens.

II. Fundamental Principles of the Constitution

Checks and Balances

American political system is built on the Constitution. The Constitution establishes a system of checks and balance on government power. The three branches of government—the legislative, the executive, and the judicial—restrain and stabilize one another through their separated functions.

The president can veto acts of Congress; Congress could override the president by a two-thirds majority in each house. The president could conduct diplomacy, but only the Senate could ratify treaties. The president named his cabinet, but only with Senate approval. The president and all his appointees could be removed from office by a joint vote of Congress, but only for "high crimes," not for political disagreements.

Separation of Powers

The legislative branch (Congress) has the power to make certain kinds of laws. The executive branch headed by the president has the power to enforce or carry out laws. The judicial branch headed by the Supreme Court is to interpret and apply the law in federal court cases.

Republicanism

In a republican form of government, people elect representatives to govern. In the United States, the people vote for members of the House and Senate and elect the members of the Electorate College to elect the president.

Federalism

The American government is a federal one, which means that authority and jurisdiction are divided among national, state, and local governments. The relationship between the national government and the state and local governments has continued to change. Since the U.S. Civil War, the powers of the Federal Government have generally expanded greatly, although there have been periods when states' rights proponents have succeeded in limiting federal power through legislative action, executive prerogative or by constitutional interpretation of the courts. In the twentieth century the courts have tended to favor policies that give more power to the national government at the expense of the states.

III. Legislative Branch—Congress

Congress is the legislative branch of the government of the United States. The Constitution divides Congress into two structures—a House of Representatives and a Senate. These structures are jointly assigned "all legislative powers" in the national government. Each chamber could block hasty measures demanded by the other.

The House of Representatives is made up of 435 representatives—the number per state varies by population—elected every two years. The internal organization of the House is based on a system of committees and subcommittees. All Representatives serve on several committees, and these committees consider all legislation before it is presented to the House as a whole. The committees work to transform ideas into detailed, complex bills. Because the committee process is very important, committee chairmen and chairwomen are some of the most powerful people in the House. The most powerful individual in the House is the Speaker of the House, who presides over the chamber, refers bills to committees, appoints Representatives to special committees, and grants Representatives the right to speak during chamber debates. The Speaker of the House is elected by the entire body and is always a member of the party with a majority of seats in the House.

The Senate is composed of 100 senators—two each from the 50 states—who serve six-year terms. The procedures and workings of the Senate are similar to those of the House, though because of its smaller membership there are fewer committees and subcommittees. The vice president of the United States serves as the president of the Senate. One of the few designated duties of the vice president is to break tie votes in the Senate. However, because the vice president has such a limited role in the Senate, he or she rarely attends its sessions. The Senate selects a *president pro tempore* (temporary president), who is usually the senior senator of the majority party. He or she supervises the Senate most of the time.

IV. Judiciary Branch—the Federal Courts

Today the federal judiciary is based on a three-tiered hierarchy of courts. On the bottom are the 94 U.S. District Courts in the 50 states and the U.S. dependent territories. These courts have jurisdiction to hear only those cases allowed under the Constitution and by federal law. These include cases where crimes have been committed that violate federal laws, and disputes between citizens of different states. The next tier above the district courts contains the 13 Circuit Courts of Appeal. These courts can hear only cases where the ruling of a district court has been appealed (contested) by one of the parties involved. The circuit courts, like other appeals courts, cannot question the facts of a case, they can consider only questions of law and legal interpretation. The top of the pyramid is the United States Supreme Court, which is the highest court in the country. Rulings of the circuit courts may be appealed to the Supreme Court, but in practice the court hears only cases of important constitutional significance. Congress is responsible for creating and maintaining the federal courts.

Despite their high visibility, the federal courts deal with only one percent of the nation's judicial business. The state and local courts—the latter usually at the county, municipal, and township level—hear most of the judicial cases. Like those at the federal level, state court systems are arranged into a three-tiered system of trial, appellate, and supreme courts. Decisions by the state supreme courts can be appealed to the U.S. Supreme Court, which can overturn state laws.

V. Executive Branch

The President presides over the executive branch of the Federal Government, a vast organization numbering about 4 million people. The heads of the 15 departments, form a council of advisors generally known as the President's "Cabinet." In addition to departments, there is a number of staff organizations grouped into the Executive Office of the President. These include the White House staff, the National Security Council, the Office of Management and Budget, the Council of Economic Advisers, the Office of the U. S. Trade Representative, the Office of National Drug Control Policy and the Office of Science and Technology Policy.

There are also independent agencies such as the National Aeronautics and Space Administration, the Central Intelligence Agency, and the Environmental Protection Agency. In addition, there are government-owned corporations such as the Federal Deposit Insurance Corporation, the National Railroad Passenger Corporation and the United States Postal Service.

It has always been necessary for presidents to work with Congress, but in the second half of the twentieth century, relations between the two have often been strained and divided by political-party affiliation. Until after World War II (1939—1945) most presidents worked with a government in which their political party also controlled the House and Senate, making relations smoother. But since 1952 presidents have often confronted a Congress where the opposition party has a majority in at least one House. Such circumstances have limited the effectiveness of presidential leadership.

VI. The Presidential Election

The US presidential elections take place every 4 years on the first Tuesday after the first Monday in November.

Who can run

Article Two of the United States Constitution stipulates any individual who is a natural-born citizen of the United States, at least 35 years old, and a resident of the United States for a period of no less than 14 years can run for American president. But most people have little chance of being president. Most candidates for president are, in fact, senators or governors.

Primaries & Caucuses

Primaries and caucuses are where the presidential candidates for the two main political parties are chosen. They occur between January and June of election year. Some states use only primaries. Others use only caucuses, and some use both. These systems are quite different.

Primaries are government-run and are decided by secret ballot. There are two kinds of primaries. In a closed primary, you can only vote for a candidate in your political party. In an open primary, you can vote for the candidate in any party.

Caucuses are organized by the parties themselves. Party members meet and break into groups based on which candidate they support and try to sway undecided votes to support their candidate. At the end, whoever has the most supporters of the caucuses wins.

National Convention

The National Convention is the event in which each party's nominees for president and vice-president are officially announced and their platforms are discussed. The chosen candidates then campaign by travelling the country to meet the public and give speeches. They also participate in televised debates leading to the election day.

Electoral College

The United States Electoral College is a body of electors established by the United States Constitution, constituted every four years for the sole purpose of electing the president and vice president of the United States. The Electoral College consists of 538 electors, and an absolute majority of 270 electoral votes is required to win an election. Each state's number of electors is equal to the combined total of the state's membership in the Senate and House of Representatives; currently there are 100 senators and 435 representatives. Additionally, the Twenty-third Amendment provides that the District of Columbia (D.C.) is entitled to a number of electors no greater than that of the least populous state. Candidates for the Electoral College are nominated by the political parties and are voted by the public on the election day. This is called an indirect vote.

General Election Day

In most states on the general election day, voters in each state actually cast a single ballot for the members of the Electoral College pledged to support the candidates for president and vice-president nominated by their party at the national convention. In other words, voters indirectly vote for presidential and vice presidential candidates; it is these members of Electoral College, rather than the presidential and vice presidential nominees, for whom the people vote in the election. This set of electors is called the electoral college. The slate of elector-candidates that wins the most popular votes in a state (not necessarily a majority) becomes the electors for that state and gets all of that state's electoral votes (winner-take-all system).

The Electoral College members chosen by the public on the election day meet on the first Monday after the second Wednesday in December in their states' capital to cast ballots for president and vice president. On January 6, the following year, the winner of that vote is announced. Once the candidate is officially announced, he or she is inaugurated president on January 20 and serves the next four years in the White House.

VII. Political Parties—the Democratic party vs. Republican party

By the end of Washington's second term, politically conscious Americans had split into two hostile parties, Federalists and Republicans.

Federalists led by Treasury Secretary Alexander Hamilton, wanted a strong national government with a powerful president and courts. They supported policies that helped bankers and wealthy businessmen. They urged close economic and diplomatic ties with Britain. They did not like democracy, which they described as mob rule.

Republicans led by Secretary of State Thomas Jefferson supported the Constitution as a plan of government. But they did not think the Constitution gave the national government unlimited powers. They supported policies that helped the nation's farmers and small businessmen. They urged closer ties with the French people, who were rebelling against their king. And they demanded more rights, more democracy, for the people of the United States.

The War of 1812 eliminated the Federalists as a national political force.

By 1824 the Republican party of Thomas Jefferson was coming apart at the seams under pressures generated by industrialization in New England, the spread of cotton cultivation in the South, and westward expansion. These forces sparked issues that would become the basis for the new political division between Democrats and Whigs. In general, those Republicans (augmented by a few former Federalists) who retained Jefferson's suspicion of a strong federal government and preference for states' rights became Democrats; those Republicans (along with many former Federalists) who believed that the national government should actively encourage economic development became Whigs. In 1828, the second American party system was taking place. Andrew Jackson and Martin Van Buren led the Democratic party in the 1830s, and John Quincy Adams and Henry Clay, helped to guide the rival National Republican (or Whig) party in the 1830s.

For two decades the Whigs and the Democrats had battled, often on even terms. Then, within the four years of Pierce's administration, the Whig party disintegrated. In its place the Republican party, arose.

Unit 6　A Nation of Welfare Families

Unlike the Whig party, the Republican party was a purely sectional, northern party. Born in the chaotic aftermath of the Kansas-Nebraska Act, the Republican party sprang up in several northern states in 1854 and 1855. The Republicans would become the main opposition to the Democratic party, and they would win each presidential election from 1860 through 1880.

From the 1860s to the 1950s the Republican Party was considered to be the more classically liberal of the two major parties and the Democratic Party the more classically conservative/populist of the two.

During the second half of the twentieth century the overall political philosophy of both the Republican Party and the Democratic Party underwent a dramatic shift from their earlier philosophies.

Now generally Republican officeholders and candidates tend to be more conservative. The Republican party comprises an uneasy coalition of traditional economic conservatives, who favor a reduced role for the government, and the "social issues" right, which draws its strength especially from religious groups like the Christian Coalition.

The Democratic party is similarly divided between traditional liberals and a centrist wind led by the Democratic Leadership Council. The first group favors a continuation and extension of New Deal and 1960s policies on economic issues, civil rights, education, welfare and the environment. The second group favors a more pragmatic blend of policy reforms and new initiatives designed to cope with these and other issues such as health care, industrial competitiveness, crime, and immigration.

The Republican party of the 1990s has built on its strong base in the west and south. The Democratic party's strength, conversely, now lies on the two coasts and in the industrial states of the upper Midwest.

The Democratic party's core of support remains grounded in the groups that made up the enormously successful New Deal coalition: African Americans, union members, the poor, Jews, Catholics, and liberals. Republican support is strongest among conservatives, the affluent, and white Protestants. Southern whites, once steadfast Democrats, have become increasingly Republican. Beginning in the 1960s, the Republican party has managed to chip away at Democratic support among all of these groups except African Americans. By contrast, the Democrats have picked up support only among southern blacks, whose right to vote was ensured only after the passage of the Voting Right Act of 1965.

Given this alignment of voters, Democrats can count on winning in urban areas and Republicans are sure to rack up big numbers in the countryside. By contrast, the suburbs are an electoral battleground.

VIII. Interest Groups

A political interest group is any organized group of individuals who share one or more common policy goals and seek to influence government's policy-making in its favor. Interest groups may also be referred to as special interests, pressure groups, organized interests or lobbies. Thousands of interest groups exist in Washington D. C. They spend time, money, resources and lobby in congressional committees, in congressional staff offices, at the White House, at executive agencies, at Washington cocktail parties with the hope of influencing decisions in their favor.

A 1990 Hudson Institute study found that 7 of 10 Americans belong to at least one association, the vast majority of which engage in lobbying. America has become a nation of lobbyists.

Vocabulary of American Government

1. Dependence on **government assistance** is a recent and destructive phenomenon.
2. **Conservatives** tend to blame this dependence on personal irresponsibility.
3. **Liberals** are more likely to blame it on personal misfortune.
4. But even such extensive **regulation** of economic and social **institutions** has never been enough.
5. But the debate over such reform should put **welfare** in the context of all federal assistance programs.
6. Historically, the debate over government **policies** toward families has never been over whether to **intervene** but how.
7. American **politicians** today insist that our society revolved around family self-reliance.
8. In 1788, after nine states **ratified** it, the Constitution became the law of the land.
9. The **Constitution** consists of a **preamble**, seven original articles, twenty-seven **amendments**, and a paragraph certifying its enactment by the constitutional convention.
10. The Founders established three branches of government—the **executive**, the **legislative**, and the **judicial**.
11. The president can **veto** acts of Congress; Congress could **override** the president by a two-thirds majority in each house.
12. **The House of Representatives** is made up of 435 **representatives**…
13. **The Senate** is composed of 100 **senators**…
14. Rulings of the circuit courts may be appealed to **the Supreme Court**…

15. But since 1953 presidents have often confronted Congress where the **opposition party** has a **majority** in at least one House.

16. The presidential elections occur **quadrennially** on the first Tuesday after the first Monday in November.

17. The slate of elector—candidates that wins the most popular votes in a state (not necessarily a majority) becomes the electors for that state and gets all of that state's electoral votes (**winner-take-all** system).

18. They spend time, money, resources and **lobby** in congressional committees, in congressional staff offices, at the White House, at executive agencies, at Washington cocktail parties with the hope of influencing decisions in their favor.

Unit 7　Toward a Hidden God

John T. Elson

Is God dead? It is a question that tantalizes both believers, who perhaps secretly fear that he is, and atheists, who possibly suspect that the answer is no.

Is God dead? The three words represent a summons to reflect on the meaning of existence. No longer is the question the taunting jest of skeptics for whom unbelief is the test of wisdom and for whom Nietzsche is the prophet who gave the right answer a century ago. Even within Christianity, now confidently renewing itself in spirit as well as form, a small band of radical theologians has seriously argued that the churches must accept the fact of God's death, and get along without him. How does the issue differ from the age-old assertion that God does not and never did exist? Nietzsche's thesis was that striving, self-centered man had killed God, and that settled that. The current death-of-God group believes that God is indeed absolutely dead, but proposes to carry on and write a theology without theos, without God. Less radical Christian thinkers hold that at the very least God in the image of man, God sitting in heaven, is dead, and—in the central task of religion today—they seek to imagine and define a God who can touch men's emotions and engage men's minds.

If nothing else, the Christian atheists are waking the churches to the brutal reality that the basic premise of faith—the existence of a personal God, who created the world and sustains it with his love—is now subject to profound attack. "What is in question is God himself," warns German Theologian Heinz Zahrnt, "and the churches are fighting a hard defensive battle, fighting for every inch." "The basic theological problem today," says one thinker who has helped define it, Langdon Gilkey of the University of Chicago Divinity School, "is the reality of God."

A Time of No Religion

Some Christians, of course, have long held that Nietzsche was not just a voice crying in the wilderness. Even before Nietzsche, Soren Kierkegaard warned that "the day when Christianity and the world become friends, Christianity is done away with." During World War II, the anti-Nazi Lutheran martyr Dietrich Bonhoeffer wrote prophetically to a friend from his Berlin prison cell: "We are proceeding toward a time of no religion at all."

For many, that time has arrived. Nearly one of every two men on earth lives in thralldom to a brand of totalitarianism that condemns religion as the opiate of the masses—which has stirred some to heroic defense of their faith but has also driven millions from any sense of God's existence. Millions more, in Africa, Asia and South America, seem destined to be born without any expectation of being summoned to the knowledge of the one God.

Princeton theologian Paul Ramsey observes that "ours is the first attempt in recorded history to build a culture upon the premise that God is dead." In the traditional citadels of Christendom, grey Gothic cathedrals stand empty, mute witnesses to a rejected faith. From the scrofulous hobos of Samuel Beckett to Antonioni's tired-blooded aristocrats, the anti-heroes of modern art endlessly suggest that waiting for God is futile, since life is without meaning.

For some, this thought is a source of existential anguish: the Jew who lost his faith in a providential God at Auschwitz, the Simone de Beauvoir who writes:

"It was easier for me to think of a world without a creator than of a creator loaded with all the contradictions of the world." But for others, the God issue — including whether or not he is dead—has been put aside as irrelevant. "Personally, I've never been confronted with the question of God," says one such politely indifferent atheist, Dr. Claude Lévi-Strauss, professor of social anthropology at the Collège de France, "I find it's perfectly possible to spend my life knowing that we will never explain the universe." Jesuit Theologian John Courtney Murray points to another variety of unbelief: the atheism of distraction, people who are just "too damn busy" to worry about God at all.

Johannine Spirit

Yet, along with the new atheism has come a new reformation — The open-window spirit of Pope John XXIII and Vatican II have revitalized the Roman Catholic Church.

Less spectacularly but not less decisively, Protestantism has been stirred by a flurry of experimentation in liturgy, church structure, ministry. In this new Christianity, the watchword is witness: Protestant faith now means not intellectual acceptance of an ancient confession, but open commitment — perhaps best symbolized in the U.S. by the civil rights movement — to eradicating the evil and inequality that beset the world.

The institutional strength of the churches is nowhere more apparent than in the U.S., a country where public faith in God seems to be as secure as it was in medieval France. According to a survey by Pollster Lou Harris last year, 97% of the American people say they believe in God. Although clergymen agree that the postwar religious revival is over, a big majority of believers continue to display their faith by joining churches. In 1964, reports the National Council of Churches, denominational allegiance rose about 2%, compared with a population gain of less than 1.5%. More than 120 million Americans now claim a religious affiliation; and a recent Gallup survey indicated that 44% of them report that they attend church services weekly.

For uncounted millions, faith remains as rock-solid as Gibraltar. Evangelist Billy Graham is one of them. "I know that God exists because of my personal experience," he says. "I know that I know him. I've talked with him and walked with him. He cares about me and acts in my everyday life." Still another is Roman Catholic Playwright William Alfred, whose off-Broadway hit, *Hogan's Goat*, melodramatically plots a turn-of-the-century Irish immigrant's struggle to achieve the American dream. "People who tell me there is no God," he says, "are like a six-year-old boy saying that there is no such thing as passionate love—they just haven't experienced it."

Practical Atheists

Plenty of clergymen, nonetheless, have qualms about the quality and character of contemporary belief. Lutheran Church Historian Martin Marty argues that all too many pews are filled on Sunday with practical atheists—disguised nonbelievers who behave during the rest of the week as if God did not exist. Jesuit Murray qualifies his conviction that the U.S. is basically a God-fearing nation by adding: "The great American proposition is 'religion is good for the kids, though I'm not religious myself.'" Pollster Harris bears him out: of the 97% who said they believed in God, only 27% declared themselves deeply religious.

Christianity and Judaism have always had more than their share of men of little faith or none. "The fool says in his heart, 'there is no God,'" wrote the Psalmist, implying that there were plenty of such fools to be found in ancient Judea. But it is not faintness of spirit that the churches worry about now: it is doubt and bewilderment assailing committed believers.

Particularly among the young, there is an acute feeling that the churches on Sunday are preaching the existence of a God who is nowhere visible in their daily lives. "I love God," cries one anguished teenager, "but I hate the church." Theologian Gilkey says that "belief is the area in the modern Protestant church where one finds blankness, silence, people not knowing what to say or merely repeating what their preachers say." Part of the Christian mood today, suggests Christian Atheist William Hamilton, is that faith has become not a possession but a hope.

Anonymous Christianity. In search of meaning, some believers have desperately turned to psychiatry, Zen or drugs. Thousands of others have quietly abandoned all but token allegiance to the churches, surrendering themselves to a life of "anonymous Christianity" dedicated to civil rights or the Peace Corps. Speaking for a generation of young Roman Catholics for whom the dogmas of the church have lost much of their power, Philosopher Michael Novak of Stanford writes: "I do not understand God, nor the way in which he works. If, occasionally, I raise my heart in prayer, it is to no God I can see, or hear, or feel. It is to a God in as cold and obscure a polar night as any non-believer has known."

Even clergymen seem to be uncertain. "I'm confused as to what God is," says no less a person than Francis B. Sayre, the Episcopal dean of Washington's National Cathedral, "but so is the rest of America." Says Marty's colleague at the Chicago Divinity School, the Rev. Nathan Scott, who is also rector of St. Paul's Episcopal Church in Hyde Park: "I look out at the faces of my people, and I'm not sure what meaning these words, gestures and rituals have for them."

...

Secularization, science, urbanization—all have made it comparatively easy for the modern man to ask where God is, and hard for the man of faith to give a convincing answer, even to himself. It is precisely to this problem—how do men talk of God in the context of a culture that rejects the transcendent, the beyond?—that theologians today are turning.

...

Four Options

What unites the various contemporary approaches to the problem of God is the conviction that the primary question has become not what God is, but how men are justified in using the word. There is no unanimity about how to solve this problem, although theologians seem to have four main options: stop talking about God for a while, stick to what the Bible says, formulate a new image and concept of God using contemporary thought categories, or simply point the way to areas of human experience that indicate the presence of something beyond man in life.

It is not only the Christian Atheists who think it pointless to talk about God. Some contemporary ministers and theologians, who have no doubts that he is alive, suggest that the church should stop using the word for a while, since it is freighted with unfortunate meanings. They take their clue from Bonhoeffer, whose prison-cell attempt to work out a "nonreligious interpretation of Biblical concepts" focused on Jesus as "the man for others." By talking almost exclusively about Christ, the argument goes, the church would be preaching a spiritual hero whom even non-believers can admire. Yale's Protestant Chaplain William Sloane Coffin reports that "a girl said to me the other day, 'I don't know whether I'll ever believe in God, but Jesus is my kind of guy.'"

In a sense, no Christian doctrine of God is possible without Jesus, since the suffering redeemer of Calvary is the only certain glimpse of the divine that churches have. But a Christ-centered theology that skirts the question of God raises more questions than it answers. Does it not run the risk of slipping into a variety of ethical humanism? And if Jesus is not clearly related in some way to God, why is he a better focus of faith than Buddha, Socrates or even Albert Camus? Rather than accept this alternative, a majority of Christians would presumably prefer to stay with the traditional language of revelation at any cost. And it is not merely conservative evangelists who believe that the words and ideas of Scripture have lost neither relevance nor meaning.

The century's greatest Protestant theologian, Karl Barth of Switzerland, has consistently warned his fellow churchmen that God is a "wholly other" being, whom man can only know by God's self-revelation in the person of Christ, as witnessed by Scripture. Any search for God that starts with human experience, Barth warns, is a vain quest that will discover only an idol, not the true God at all.

Holy Being

The word of God, naked and unadorned, may be fine for the true believer, but some theologians argue that Biblical terminology has ceased to be part of the world's vocabulary, and is in danger of becoming a special jargon as incomprehensible to some as the equations of physicists. To bridge this communications gap, they have tried to reinterpret the concept of God into contemporary philosophical terms. Union Seminary's John Macquarrie, for example, proposes a description of God based on Martin Heidegger's existential philosophy, which is primarily concerned with explaining the nature of "being" as such. To Heidegger, "being" is an incomparable, transcendental mystery, something that confers existence on individual, particular beings. Macquarrie calls Heidegger's mystery "Holy Being," since it represents what Christians have traditionally considered God.

Other philosophical theologians, such as Schubert Ogden of Southern Methodist University and John Cobb of the Southern California School of Theology, have been working out a theism based on the process thinking of Alfred North Whitehead. In their view, God is changing with the universe. Instead of thinking of God as the immutable Prime Mover of the universe, argues Ogden, it makes more sense to describe him as "the ultimate effect" and as "the eminently relative One, whose openness to change contingently on the actions of others is literally boundless." In brief, the world is creating God as much as he is creating it.

Perhaps the most enthusiastic propagandists for a new image of God are the Tweedledum and Tweedledee of Anglican theology, Bishop Robinson of Woolwich, England, and Bishop James A. Pike of California. Both endorse the late Paul Tillich's concept of God as "the ground of being." Pike, who thinks that the church should have fewer but better dogmas, also suggests that the church should abandon the Trinity, on the ground that it really seems to be preaching three Gods instead of one. Christianity, in his view, should stop attributing specific actions to persons of the Trinity—creation to the Father, redemption to the Son, inspiration to the Holy Spirit—and just say that they were all the work of God.

Discernment Situations

The contemporary world appears so biased against metaphysics that any attempt to find philosophical equivalents for God may well be doomed to failure. "God," says Jerry Handspicker of the World Council of Churches, "has suffered from too many attempts to define the indefinable." Leaving unanswered the question of what to say God is, some theologians are instead concentrating on an exploration of the ultimate and unconditional in modern life. Their basic point is that while modern men have rejected God as a solution to life, they cannot evade a questioning anxiety about its meaning. The apparent eclipse of God is merely a sign that the world is experiencing what Jesuit Theologian Karl Rahner calls "the anonymous presence" of God, whose word comes to man not on tablets of stone but in the inner murmurings of the heart.

Following Tillich, Langdon Gilkey argues that the area of life dealing with the ultimate and with mystery points the way toward God. "When we ask, 'Why am I?', 'What should I become and be?', 'What is the meaning of my life?'— then we are exploring or encountering that region of experience where language about the ultimate becomes useful and intelligible." That is not to say that God is necessarily found in the depths of anxiety. "Rather we are in the region of our experience where God may be known, and so where the meaningful usage of this word can be found." To Oxford theologian Ian Ramsey, this area of ultimate concern offers what he calls "discernment situations"—events that can be the occasion for insight, for awareness of something beyond man. It is during these insight situations, Ramsey says, that the universe "comes alive, declares some transcendence, and to which we respond by ourselves coming alive and finding another dimension."

A discernment situation could be falling in love, suffering cancer, reading a book. But it need not be a private experience. The Rev. Stephen Rose, editor of Chicago's Renewal magazine, argues that "whenever the prophetic word breaks in, either as judgment or as premise, that's when the historical God acts." One such situation, he suggests, was Watts—an outburst of violence that served to chide men for lack of brotherhood. Harvey Cox of the Harvard Divinity School sees God's hand in history, but in a different way. The one area where empirical man is open to transcendence, he argues, is the future: man can be defined as the creature who hopes, who has taken responsibility for the world. Cox proposes a new theology based on the premise that God is the source and ground of this hope—a God "ahead" of man in history rather than "out there" in space.

German Theologian Gerhard Ebeling of Tubingen University finds an arrow pointing the way to God in the problem in language. A word, he suggests, is not merely a means of conveying information; it is also a symbol of man's power over nature and of his basic impotence: one man cannot speak except to another, and language itself possesses a power that eludes his mastery of it. God, he proposes, is the source of the mystery hidden in language, or, as he obscurely puts it, "the basic situation of man as word-situation."

"The Kingdom Within You." For those with a faith that can move mountains, all this tentative groping for God in human experience may seem unnecessary. The man-centered approach to God runs against Barth's warning that a "God" found in human depths may be an imagined idol—or a neurosis that could be dissolved on the psychiatrist's couch. Rudolf Bultmann answers that these human situations of anxiety and discernment represent "transformations of God," and are the only way that secular man is likely to experience any sense of the eternal and unconditional.

This theological approach is not without scriptural roots. A God who writes straight with crooked lines in human history is highly Biblical in outlook. The quest for God in the depths of experience echoes Jesus' words to his Apostles, "The kingdom of God is within you." And the idea of God's anonymous presence suggests Matthew's account of the Last Judgment, when Jesus will separate the nations, telling those on his right: "I was hungry and you gave me food, I was thirsty and you gave me drink." But when? they ask. "And the King will answer them, Truly, I say to you, as you did it to one of the least of these my brethren, you did it to me.'"

The theological conviction that God is acting anonymously in human history is not likely to turn many atheists toward him. Secular man may be anxious, but he is also convinced that anxiety can be explained away. As always, faith is something of an irrational leap in the dark, a gift of God. And unlike in earlier centuries, there is no way today for churches to threaten or compel men to face that leap; after Dachau's mass sadism and Hiroshima's instant death, there are all too many real possibilities of hell on earth.

The new approaches to the problem of God, then, will have their greatest impact within the church community. They may help shore up the faith of many believers and, possibly, weaken that of others. They may also lead to a more realistic, and somewhat more abstract, conception of God. "God will be seen as the order in which life takes on meaning, as being, as the source of creativity," suggests Langdon Gilkey. "The old-fashioned personal God who merely judges, gives grace and speaks to us in prayer, is, after all, a pretty feeble God." Gilkey does not deny the omnipotence of God, nor undervalue personal language about God as a means of prayer and worship. But he argues that Christianity must go on escaping from its too-strictly anthropomorphic past, and still needs to learn that talk of God is largely symbolic.

No More Infallibilities

The new quest for God, which respects no church boundaries, should also contribute to ecumenism. "These changes make many of the old disputes seem pointless, or at least secondary," says Jesuit Theologian Avery Dulles. The churches, moreover, will also have to accept the empiricism of the modern outlook and become more secular themselves, recognizing that God is not the property of the church, and is acting in history as he wills, in encounters for which man is forever unprepared.

To some, this suggests that the church might well need to take a position of reverent agnosticism regarding some doctrines that it had previously proclaimed with excessive conviction.

Many of the theologians attempting to work out a new doctrine of God admit that they are uncertain as to the impact of their ultimate findings on other Christian truths; but they agree that such God-related issues as personal salvation in the afterlife and immortality will need considerable re-study. But Christian history allows the possibility of development in doctrine, and even an admission of ignorance in the face of the divine mystery is part of tradition. St. Thomas Aquinas declared that "we cannot know what God is, but rather what he is not."

Gabriel Vahanian suggests that there may well be no true faith without a measure of doubt, and thus contemporary Christian worry about God could be a necessary and healthy antidote to centuries in which faith was too confident and sure. Perhaps today, the Christian can do no better than echo the prayer of the worried father who pleaded with Christ to heal his spirit-possessed son: "I believe; help my unbelief."

→ Notes

1. This article is an excerpt from the April 8, 1966, cover story for the news magazine, *Time*.
2. **Nietzsche:** Friedrich Wilhelm Nietzsche (1844—1900) was a German philosopher, cultural critic, composer, poet, philologist, and a Latin and Greek scholar whose work has exerted a profound influence on Western philosophy and modern intellectual history.

3. **Soren Kierkegaard:** Soren Aabye Kierkegaard (1813—1855) was a Danish philosopher, theologian, poet, social critic and religious author who is widely considered to be the first existentialist philosopher. He wrote critical texts on organized religion, Christendom, morality, ethics, psychology, and the philosophy of religion, displaying a fondness for metaphor, irony and parables.

4. **Gothic:** Gothic architecture is a style that flourished in Europe during the High and Late Middle Ages. It evolved from Romanesque architecture and was succeeded by Renaissance architecture. Originating in 12th-century France, it was widely used, especially for cathedrals and churches, until the 16th century.

5. **Samuel Beckett** (1906—1989): Irish-born poet, novelist, and playwright, who won international fame with his play *En attendant Godot* (*Waiting for Godot*), which premiered in 1953.

6. **Antonioni:** Michelangelo Antonioni (1912—2007) was an Italian film director, screenwriter, editor, and short story author.

7. **Auschwitz:** The Auschwitz concentration camp was a complex of over 40 concentration and extermination camps built and operated by Nazi Germany in occupied Poland during World War II and the Holocaust.

8. **Jesuit:** Society of Jesus, religious order of men in the Roman Catholic church, founded by Saint Ignatius of Loyola in 1534 and confirmed by Pope Paul III in 1540. The motto of the order is *Ad majorem Dei gloriam* (Latin for "to the greater glory of God"), and its object is the spread of the church by preaching and teaching or the fulfillment of whatever else is judged the most urgent need of the church at the time. Education has been its chief activity almost from the outset, and it has made notable contributions to scholarship in both theology and the secular disciplines.

9. **Johannine Spirit**: John the Apostle (c. AD 6—c.100) was one of the Twelve Apostles of Jesus according to the New Testament. Generally listed as the youngest apostle. The traditions of most Christian denominations have held that John the Apostle is the author of several books of the New Testament.

10. **Lou Harris** (1921—2016): an American opinion polling entrepreneur, journalist, and author. He ran one of the best-known polling organizations of his time, Louis Harris and Associates, which conducted The Harris Poll.

11. **Gallup Survey:** Gallup, Inc. is an American analytics and advisory company based in Washington, D.C. Founded by George Gallup in 1935, the company became known for its public opinion polls conducted worldwide.

12. **Gibraltar:** a British Overseas Territory located at the southern tip of the Iberian Peninsula.

13. **Evangelist:** In Christianity, Evangelism is the commitment to or act of publicly preaching of the Gospel with the intention of spreading the message and teachings of Jesus Christ. Christian groups who encourage evangelism are sometimes known as evangelistic or evangelist.

14. **Billy Graham:** William Franklin Graham Jr. (1918—2018) was an American evangelist, a prominent evangelical Christian figure, and an ordained Southern Baptist minister who became well known internationally in the late 1940s.

15. **Lutheran:** Lutheranism is a major branch of Protestant Christianity which identifies with the theology of Martin Luther (1483—1546), a German friar, ecclesiastical reformer and theologian.

16. **Psalmist:** the writer of Psalms in the Bible.

17. **Judea:** the ancient Hebrew and Israelite biblical, the exonymic Roman/English, and the modern-day name of the mountainous southern part of the region of Palestine.

18. **Peach Corps:** The Peace Corps is a volunteer program run by the United States government. Its official mission is to provide social and economic development abroad through technical assistance, while promoting mutual understanding between Americans and populations served. Peace Corps Volunteers are American citizens, typically with a college degree, who work abroad for a period of two years after three months of training. Volunteers work with governments, schools, non-profit organizations, non-government organizationss, and entrepreneurs in education, business, information technology, agriculture, and the environment. After 24 months of service, volunteers can request an extension of service.

19. **Episcopal Church:** The Episcopal Church (TEC) in the United States is a member church of the worldwide Anglican Communion. It is a mainline Christian denomination divided into nine provinces. The Episcopal Church was active in the Social Gospel movement of the late 19th and early 20th centuries. Since the 1960s and 1970s, the church has pursued a decidedly more liberal course. It has opposed the death penalty and supported the civil rights movement and affirmative action. Some of its leaders and priests are known for marching with influential civil rights' demonstrators such as Martin Luther King Jr. The Church calls for the full legal equality of LGBT people. In 2015, the Church's 78th triennial General Convention passed resolutions allowing the blessing of same-sex marriages and approved two official liturgies to bless such unions.

20. **Washington National Cathedral:** an American cathedral of the Episcopal Church. The cathedral is located in Washington, D.C., the capital of the United States. It is both the second-largest church building in the United States, and the fourth-tallest structure in

Washington, D.C. The cathedral is the seat of both the Presiding Bishop of the Episcopal Church, Michael Bruce Curry, and the bishop of the Diocese of Washington, Mariann Edgar Budde. Over 270,000 people visit the structure annually.

21. **Hyde Park:** a Grade I-listed major park in Central London.
22. **Socrates** (c. 470—399 B.C.): was a classical Greek (Athenian) philosopher credited as one of the founders of Western philosophy, and as being the first moral philosopher, of the Western ethical tradition of thought.
23. **Albert Camus** (1913—1960): French-Algerian novelist, essayist, dramatist, and journalist, a Nobel laureate whose concepts of the absurd and of human revolt address and suggest solutions to the problem of meaninglessness in modern human life.
24. **Scripture:** the Bible.
25. **Martin Heidegger** (1889—1976): a German philosopher and a seminal thinker in the Continental tradition and philosophical hermeneutics, and is "widely acknowledged to be one of the most original and important philosophers of the 20th century." Heidegger is best known for his contributions to phenomenology and existentialism.
26. **Alfred North Whitehead** (1861—1947): an English mathematician and philosopher. He is best known as the defining figure of the philosophical school known as process philosophy, which today has found application to a wide variety of disciplines, including ecology, theology, education, physics, biology, economics, and psychology, among other areas.
27. **Tweedledum and Tweedledee:** fictional characters in an English nursery rhyme and in Lewis Carroll's *Through the Looking-Glass, and What Alice Found There*. Their names may have originally come from an epigram written by poet John Byrom. The names have since become synonymous in western popular culture slang for any two people who look and act in identical ways, generally in a derogatory context.
28. **Paul Tillich** (1886—1965): a German-American Christian existentialist philosopher and Lutheran Protestant theologian who is widely regarded as one of the most influential theologians of the twentieth century.
29. **Watts:** a district of Los Angeles, California. It was the scene of severe racial tensions and violence in 1965.
30. **Rudolf Bultmann** (1884—1976): a German Lutheran theologian and professor of New Testament at the University of Marburg. He was one of the major figures of early-20th-century biblical studies and a prominent voice in liberal Christianity.
31. **Matthew:** one of the twelve apostles of Jesus and, according to Christian tradition, one of the four Evangelists.

32. **Last Judgment:** Some Christian denominations consider the Second Coming of Christ to be the final and eternal judgment by God of the people in every nation resulting in the glorification of some and the punishment of others.

33. **Dachau:** Bavarian town, 16 km (10 mi) northwest of Munich, Germany. Chartered in 1391, Dachau has a 16th-century castle and a 17th-century town hall and church. During World War II (1939—1945), the town was the site of the Dachau concentration camp. The concentration camp was organized in 1933 and, before the end of the war, over 160,000 slave laborers had been confined there under appalling conditions. On April 29, 1945, United States troops liberated the infamous camp. Thousands of starving men were found in the camp during the liberation, and there were facilities for the mass murder and cremation of the camp's inmates. The concentration camp in Dachau was also a medical research center for the German Schutzstaffel (Defense Corps), or SS, where experiments were carried out on over 3500 prisoners. In November and December of 1945, war crimes trials of 40 SS men were held, and 36 of them were sentenced to death. Population (2001 estimate) 38,400.

34. **Hiroshima:** city on southwestern Honshu Island, Japan, capital of Hiroshima Prefecture, at the head of Hiroshima Bay. On August 6, 1945, during World War II (1939—1945), the first atomic bomb to be used against an enemy position was dropped on the city by the United States Army Air Forces. According to U.S. estimates 60,000 to 70,000 people were killed or missing as a result of the bomb and many more were made homeless. (In 1940 the population of Hiroshima had been 343,698.) The blast also destroyed more than 10 sq km (4 sq mi) of the city, completely destroying 68 percent of Hiroshima's buildings; another 24 percent were damaged. Every August 6 since 1947, thousands participate in interfaith services in the Peace Memorial Park built on the site where the bomb exploded. In 1949 the Japanese dedicated Hiroshima as an international shrine of peace.

35. **St. Thomas Aquinas** (1225—1274): an Italian Dominican friar, Catholic priest, and Doctor of the Church. He was an immensely influential philosopher, theologian, and jurist in the tradition of scholasticism.

36. **Gabriel Vahanian** (1927—2012): a French Protestant Christian theologian who was most remembered for his pioneering work in the theology of the "death of God" movement within academic circles in the 1960s, and who taught for 26 years in the U.S. before finishing a prestigious career in Strasbourg, France.

Readings on American Culture and Society

Vocabulary

1. tantalize ['tæntəlaɪz]: *vt.* to excite (another) by exposing something desirable while keeping it out of reach 挑逗
2. taunt [tɔːnt]: *vt.* to reproach in a mocking, insulting, or contemptuous manner 奚落
3. strive [straɪv]: *vi.* to try very hard to achieve something or to defeat something 努力；奋斗
4. totalitarianism [toˌtælə'tɛrɪən]: *n.* a country or system of government in which there is only one political party that has complete power and control over people 极权主义
5. citadel ['sɪtəd(ə)l; -del]: *n.* a fortress in a commanding position in or near a city 堡垒
6. cathedral [kə'θidrəl]: *n.* the main church of a district, under the care of a Bishop 教区总教堂
7. scrofulous ['skrɒfjələs]: *adj.* morally degenerate; corrupt 堕落的；道德败坏的
8. hobo ['həʊbəʊ]: *n.* a homeless person, especially an impoverished vagrant 流浪汉
9. Johannine [dʒəu'hænaɪn]: *adj.* of John （宗教）使徒约翰的；《约翰福音》的
10. providential [ˌprɒvɪ'dɛnʃl]: *adj.* happening just when needed; lucky 幸运的；及时的
11. liturgy ['lɪtədʒɪ]: *n.* a prescribed form or set of forms for public Christian ceremonies; ritual 礼拜仪式
12. eradicate [ɪ'rædɪket]: *vt.* to destroy or get rid of something completely, especially something bad 根除；杜绝
13. denomination [dɪˌnɑmɪ'neʃən]: *n.* a branch of the Christian Church （基督教）教派
14. allegiance [ə'lidʒəns]: *n.* a person's continued support for a party, religion, ruler, etc. （对政党、宗教、统治者的）忠诚
15. qualm [kwɑːm; kwɔːm]: *n.* an uneasy feeling about the propriety or rightness of a course of action 疑虑
16. pew [pju]: *n.* a long wooden seat in a Church 教堂长椅
17. Zen [zɛn]: *n.* Zen Buddhism 禅宗
18. rector ['rɛktə]: *n.* a cleric in charge of a parish in the Protestant Episcopal Church. A cleric in charge of a parish in the Protestant Episcopal Church 教区牧师
19. unanimity [ˌjunə'nɪmətɪ]: *n.* complete agreement about something among a group of people 一致同意
20. freight [freɪt]: *vt.* (usually passive) (literary) to fill something with a particular mood or tone 使充满（某种心情或口气）
21. Calvary ['kælvəri]: *n.* a model which represents the death of Christ (CRUCIFIXION) 耶

耶稣基督（被钉在十字架上的）受难像

22. skirt [skɜːt]: *vt.* to avoid talking about a subject, especially because it is difficult or embarrassing 绕开，回避（话题）

23. seminary ['sɛmənɛri]: *n.* a college where priests, ministers or rabbis are trained 神学院

24. immutable [ɪ'mjutəbl]: *adj.* cannot be changed 永恒不变的

25. eminently ['ɛmɪnəntlɪ]: *adv.* (formal) (used to emphasize a positive quality) very; extremely 非常；极其

26. contingently [kən'tɪndʒ(ə)ntlɪ]: *adv.* dependent on or resulting from a future and as yet unknown event or circumstance 偶发地，临时地

27. metaphysics [ˌmɛtə'fɪzɪks]: *n.* the branch of philosophy that deals with the nature of existence, truth and knowledge 形而上学

28. neurosis [nʊ'rosɪs]: *n.* a mental illness in which a person suffers strong feelings of fear and worry 神经病

29. apostle [ə'pɑsl]: *n.* any one of the twelve men that Christ chose to tell people about him and his teachings 耶稣十二门徒之一

30. anthropomorphic [ˌænθrəpə'mɔrfɪk]: *adj.* relating to the idea that an animal, a god, or an object has feelings or characteristics like those of a human being 神、人同形同性论的

31. ecumenism [ɪ'kjumənɪzəm]: *n.* A movement promoting unity among Christian churches or denominations 促进基督教会或各派别大联合的运动

32. agnostic [æg'nɑstɪk]: *n.* a person who is not sure whether or not God exists or who believes that we cannot know whether God exists or not 不可知论者

➡ *Expressions*

1. The current death-of-God group believes that God is indeed absolutely dead, but proposes to <u>carry on</u> and write a theology without theos, without God.
   carry on: to continue, esp. in spite of an interruption or difficulties （尤指不顾干扰或困难）坚持

2. Nearly one of every two men on earth <u>lives in thralldom to</u> a brand of totalitarianism…
   in thrall (thralldom) to somebody/something: controlled or strongly influenced by somebody/something 受……控制；深受……影响

3. Still another is Roman Catholic Playwright William Alfred, whose <u>off-Broadway</u> hit, *Hogan's Goat*, melodramatically plots a turn-of-the-century Irish immigrant's struggle to achieve the American dream.

off-Broadway: an off-Broadway play is one that is performed outside the Broadway entertainment area in New York City and does not involve as much money as the famous plays on Broadway.

4. Pollster Harris <u>bears</u> him <u>out</u>…

bear out: If someone or something bears a person out or bears out what that person is saying, they support what that person is saying. 证实

5. They may help <u>shore up</u> the faith of many believers and, possibly, weaken that of others.

shore up: to support (something that is in danger of falling) 支撑

Comprehension

I. Discuss the Main Point and the Meanings.

1. What of Christian faith is under attack?

2. What is the difference between practical atheism and anonymous Christianity?

3. What are the new approaches to the problem of God?

4. According to the author, theologians seem to find out a viable way to talk about God in modern life. What is that?

5. What changes should churches make correspondingly in modern life?

6. What is St. Thomas Aquinas' answer for the problem of God?

II. Fill in the blanks with the appropriate words or expressions from the text.

a questioning anxiety	an irrational leap	a measure of doubt	development
discernment situations	disguised nonbelievers	empiricism	reverent agnosticism
secular	symbolic	the anonymous presence	the order
the ultimate	transformations of God	unanswered	what he is not

1. Practical atheists are _____ who behave during the rest of the week as if God did not exist.

2. Leaving _____ the question of what to say God is, some theologians are instead concentrating on an exploration of the ultimate and unconditional in modern life.

3. While modern men have rejected God as a solution to life, they cannot evade _____ about its meaning.

4. The apparent eclipse of God is merely a sign that the world is experiencing what Jesuit theologian Karl Rahner calls "_____" of God, whose word comes to man not on tablets of stone but in the inner murmurings of the heart.

5. Langdon Gilkey argues that the area of life dealing with _____ and with mystery points the way toward God.

6. To Oxford theologian Ian Ramsey, the area of ultimate concern offers what he calls "_____" —events that can be the occasion for insight, for awareness of something beyond man.

7. Rudolf Bultmann answers that these human situations of anxiety and discernment represent "_____," and are the only way that secular man is likely to experience any sense of the eternal and unconditional.

8. As always, faith is something of _____ in the dark, a gift of God.

9. God will be seen as _____ in which life takes on meaning, as being, as the source of creativity, suggests Langdon Gilkey.

10. Langdon Gilkey argues that Christianity must go on escaping from its too-strictly anthropomorphic past, and still needs to learn that talk of God is largely _____.

11. The churches, moreover, will also have to accept the _____ of the modern outlook and become more _____ themselves.

12. To some, this suggests that the church might well need to take a position of _____ regarding some doctrines that it had previously proclaimed with excessive conviction.

13. But Christian history allows the possibility of _____ in doctrine, and even an admission of ignorance in the face of the divine mystery is part of tradition.

14. St. Thomas Aquinas declared that "we cannot know what God is, but rather _____ _____."

15. Gabriel Vahanian suggests that there may well be no true faith without _____, and thus contemporary Christian worry about God could be a necessary and healthy antidote to centuries in which faith was too confident and sure.

Structure

I. Find out how the words and expression in bold are used in the following sentences.

1. The three words represent a summons to **reflect on** the meaning of existence.

2. Even within Christianity… a small band of radical theologians has seriously argued that the churches must accept the fact of God's death, and **get along** without him.

3. …the day when Christianity and the world become friends, Christianity is **done away with**.

4. But for others, the God issue—including whether or not he is dead—has been **put aside** as irrelevant.

5. They take their clue from Bonhoeffer, whose prison-cell attempt to **work out** a "nonreligious interpretation of Biblical concepts" **focused on** Jesus as "the man for others."

6. **In a sense**, no Christian doctrine of God is possible without Jesus…

7. To Heidegger, "being" is an incomparable, transcendental mystery, something that **confers** existence **on** individual, particular beings.

8. **In brief**, the world is creating God as much as he is creating it.

9. Christianity, in his view, should stop **attributing** specific actions **to** persons of the Trinity…

10. …whenever the prophetic word **breaks in**, either as judgment or as premise, that's when the historical God acts.

11. **As always**, faith is something of an irrational leap in the dark, a gift of God.

12. The new quest for God, which respects no church boundaries, should also **contribute to** ecumenism.

II. Complete the following sentences with some of the above words or expressions in bold.

1. The fall in the number of deaths from heart disease _____ generally _____ improvements in diet.
2. The President trusted him so much that he _____ him the role of "Principal Advisor".
3. What he says is right _____.
4. You must _____ your pride and call her.
5. He had time to _____ his successes and failures.
6. Don't worry, we'll _____ without you.
7. People thought that the use of robots would _____ boring low-paid factory jobs.
8. He felt he needed to _____ more _____ his career.
9. Here are today's headlines _____.
10. The truth, _____, is more complicated.

Religion in the United States

I. Overview

In his book *Democracy in America* Alexis de Tocqueville drew a startling conclusion: religion was "the foremost of the political institutions" of the United States. When polled, 70 percent of those asked will say that they believe in a personal God. In fact, religion has always played an important role in the history of the United States.

Freedom of religion is guaranteed by the first article of Bill of Rights. The fundamental American belief in individual freedom and the right of individuals to practice their own religion is at the center of religious experience in the United States. The great diversity of ethnic backgrounds has produced religious pluralism; most of the religions of the world are now practiced in the United States. According to a 2014 study by the Pew Research Center, 70.6 percent of the American population identified themselves as Christians, with 46.5 percent professing attendance at a variety of churches that could be considered Protestant, and 20.8 percent professing Roman Catholic beliefs. The same study says that other religions (including Judaism, Buddhism, Hinduism, and Islam) collectively make up about 6% of the population.

According to a 2012 survey by the Pew forum, 36 percent of Americans state that they attend services nearly every week or more. Religious participation varies immensely depending on many factors, including race, age, social class, economic condition, amount of education, and region of the country. Older people, married people with children, and middle-income people are also more regular church-goers than younger people, single people, the poor, and the rich.

According to a 2016 Gallup poll, Mississippi with 63 percent of its population described as very religious (say that religion is important to them and attend religious services almost every week) is the most religious state in the country, while New Hampshire with only 20 percent as very religious is the least religious state.

Some other states such as Oklahoma, Arkansas, Tennessee, and Alabama also report higher weekly church attendance than other areas of the country. These states are in the area of the country commonly called *the Bible Belt*.

The Bible Belt

The beginning of the twentieth century saw the development of Fundamentalism, a conservative Protestant movement that crosses many denominational lines and emphasizes a literal interpretation of the Bible. Not as extreme as the Pentecostal movement, it forged a Bible Belt across the nation where Fundamentalism is widely practiced. This Bible Belt stretched from the upper South, through the southern plains, and into parts of California.

Unchurched Belt

Unchurched Belt refers to a region in the far Western United States that has low rates of religious participation. The term derives from *Bible Belt* and the notion of the unchurched.

The term was first applied to the West Coast of the United States in 1985 by Rodney Stark and William Sims Bainbridge, who found that California, Oregon, and Washington had the

United States' lowest church membership rates in 1971, and that there was little change in this pattern between 1971 and 1980. Since 1980, however, California's church membership rate has increased; in 2000, the state had a higher percentage of church members than several states in the Northeast and Midwest. Some religious groups are under-counted in surveys of religious membership.

Now there has been debate as to whether the Western United States is still the most irreligious part of the United States due to the New England area surpassing it as the region with the highest percentage of residents unaffiliated with any religion.

The Meaning of Religion

Generalizations about what religion really means to Americans are quite difficult to make. For many Americans, churches and religious sects are expressions of group solidarity rather than of rigid adherence to doctrine. People go to church and it helps them feel that they have a place in a community. The major American religions also provide the comfort of a personal God to turn to in times of trouble. In the U.S., religion provides the customs and ceremonies that mark life's most important events—the naming of a baby, coming-of-age ceremonies, weddings, and funerals. Perhaps most important, many religions promise the believer some form of eternal life, which is a great comfort, especially to the old and the sick.

II. Christianity in the United States

1. Christianity

Christianity has always been the dominant American faith. Generally Christians see themselves belonging to one of three different schools of thought: Roman Catholic, the various national denominations of the Eastern Orthodox churches, and hundreds of different Protestant denominations and sects.

For Christians their religion really emerges from the teachings and the life example of Jesus Christ. In the Christian view he is the messiah as prophesized by the Hebrew Scripture. Christians generally approaches Jesus in two different ways. The first is the faith of Jesus which means Christians emulate Jesus's example of unconditional love, of compassion, of forgiveness and of empathy. The second approach is the faith about Jesus which recognized the resurrection as the final sacrifice that allows all of us to live a new life without sin.

The core doctrine of their faith can be summarized into the law of the prophets which is to love God with all your heart and love your neighbor as yourself. Even though Christians view the Hebrew Scripture as authoritative, the primary spiritual text or sacred text is the New Testament which contains within it the teachings of the Gospels. Most Christians do believe in the doctrine of the Trinity which also views God as a being with three component parts: the Father, the Son and the Holy Spirit.

The goal of Christian life is really to achieve salvation, eternal life with God in heaven after we die. Christian life is really oriented around a personal relationship with Jesus Christ as Savior.

2. Roman Catholicism

Roman Catholicism is by far the largest unified religious group. This is due in part to Roman Catholicism's hierarchical structure and willingness to allow a degree of debate within its ranks, even while insisting on certain core beliefs.

The members acknowledge the supreme authority of the Pope who is the Bishop of Rome and recognize that he is the lawful successor of the Apostle Peter to whom Christ gave the keys of the Kingdom. The often-heard term—infallibility of the Pope applies only to his pronouncements on faiths and morals when speaking as Head of the Universal Church. Whatever the Church regards as infallible, a Catholic must accept, including the teaching that the Catholic Church is the one true church established by Christ because it alone has the four marks of the true church. First it is one in doctrine and authority. Second, it is holy. Third, it is Catholic, administering the same sacraments the world over. And fourth, it is apostolic, tracing its ancestry by tradition to the Apostle Peter and the first apostolic college.

Catholic mass is not the same as Protestant communion. As it is believed, as the priest pronounces the word consecration—the bread by transubstantiation actually becomes the body of Christ, the wine becomes his blood—a literal realization of the word spoken in the last supper. This moving ceremony is the source of Holy Eucharist—one of the seven sacraments acknowledged by the Roman Catholic Church. The other sacraments are baptism, confirmation, penance including confession, holy orders, the sacraments of the sick and matrimony—all are considered to have been instituted by Christ in all confirmed grace.

But American Catholics do not strictly follow the Pope's decrees. The overwhelming majority of American Catholics practice birth control, half get divorced.

3. Protestantism

Protestantism has been, by far, the dominant religious tradition in America, although the denominational diversity of Protestantism has rendered its influence more diffuse.

Protestantism began as a movement to reform the Western Christian church in the sixteenth century, resulting in the Protestant Reformation, which severed the reformed churches from the Roman Catholic Church. The declared aim of the original reformers was to restore the Christian faith as it had been at its beginning, while keeping what they thought valuable from the Roman Catholic tradition that had developed during the intervening centuries.

Martin Luther never set foot in North America, but the movement he unleashed in the sixteenth century profoundly shaped society and culture in America, informing everything from social policy and architecture to literature and health care. Luther believed, as do most Protestants today, in the priesthood of all believers; everyone is accountable for himself or herself before God, thereby obviating the necessity of priests as dispensers of grace. Whereas Rome taught the twin bases for authority — scripture and tradition (as interpreted by the church)—Luther insisted on *sola scriptura*, the Bible alone was the only authority on faith and practice. In worship, Luther emphasized the centrality of the sermon as a means of proclaiming the gospel and educating the laity. By implication, he rearticulated the importance of the Eucharist or Holy Communion; Catholics believe in transubstantiation, that the bread and wine actually become the body and blood of Jesus in the saying of the mass, while Luther believed that the real presence of Christ was in the bread and wine, assuring believers of God's grace.

Luther's spirited defense of sola scriptura, the vernacular Bible, and the priesthood of believers virtually ensured that the Protestant Reformation would become diverse and unwieldy. Within Luther's own lifetime various sects arose, each claiming the infallibility of its own interpretation of the Bible, some insisting, for instance, solely on adult baptism or on nonviolence.

The combined Protestant groups form the largest religious body in the United States. The largest Protestant groups are the Southern Baptist Convention, the United Methodist Church, and the National Baptist Convention.

4. Baptism

"Baptist," to many people, means Southern Baptist and brings to mind two of its most famous adherents, the Reverend Billy Graham and, until he left the denomination in 2000, former U.S. president Jimmy Carter. But although the Southern Baptist Convention is the largest Protestant denomination in the United States, there are many more Baptist denominations, ranging from the mainline American Baptist Church to the smaller Conservative Baptists and Baptist General Conference. Then there are less well known Baptist denominations such as the Six Principle Baptists, Independent Baptists, and Charismatic Baptists.

Baptists came to America with the Puritan Roger Williams, who settled Providence, Rhode Island, in 1636. They have always been reluctant to force creeds and formulas, but, although their denominations are legion, they share certain doctrines and theological positions.

First, they practice adult baptism, almost always by full immersion in water. To be accepted into church membership, individuals must publicly confess conversion to Jesus Christ as Lord and Savior. This means they have become, in the words of John 3:3, "born again," or spiritually awakened to God. Having thus "accepted Jesus into their hearts" and received God's forgiveness for their sins, believers are baptized, usually in a public ceremony, "in the name of the Father, the Son, and the Holy Spirit."

Second, Baptists tend to be conservative in theology, ranging from fundamentalists to evangelicals. Christ is generally acknowledged as sole and absolute spiritual authority, speaking to each believer individually. The Bible is God's voice in all matters relating to faith and practice.

Third, Baptists practice congregational autonomy. Each congregation, although belonging to the denomination, is free to own its own buildings, call its own pastors, elect its own deacons, and manage its own affairs free from denominational hierarchy.

Fourth, worship is generally nonliturgical, featuring music, preaching, and teaching.

5. Methodism

Methodism, worldwide Protestant movement dating from 1729, when a group of students at the University of Oxford, England, began to assemble for worship, study, and Christian service. Their fellow students named them the Holy Club and "methodists," a derisive allusion to the methodical manner in which they performed the various practices that their sense of Christian duty and church ritual required.

Socially methodism was a transforming force. Methodism made an important contribution to the leadership of working-class movements like trade unionism and chartism by providing opportunities for self-education and training in leadership and organization in running the chapel. The general culture of methodism was toward respectability through living a temperate, thrifty, hard-working life. Indeed, historians have argued (somewhat exaggeratedly) that it was Methodism that prevented revolution in Britain during the revolutionary decades 1789—1848.

Most of the eighteenth century "people called Methodists" were of humble origin without advantages of education, wealth, or social position. However, their puritan virtues brought them worldly prosperity and, by the 1830s and 1840s, the big Wesleyan chapels in northern towns were dominated by wealthy mill-owners and businessmen. Yet underneath there was a more liberal and democratic spirit.

III. Mainline vs. Evangelical Protestants

There has been a steady decline since the denominational heyday of the 1950s, when most people identified strongly with either the Protestant, the Catholic, or the Jewish faiths. Over the past half century, the boundaries among these groups have blurred as the baby boomers have adopted a more consumerist approach to religion, and as more and more people have married members of other faiths. There is some evidence that old boundaries have been replaced by a liberal-conservative polarization, in which denominational membership is less important than whether a person is a member of a mainline or evangelical church. At the close of the twentieth century American Protestants remained profoundly divided between liberal and conservative, mainline and evangelical.

The mainline Protestant churches (also called mainstream American Protestant) are a group of Protestant denominations in the United States that contrast in history and practice with evangelical, fundamentalist, and charismatic Protestant denominations. Mainline Protestants were a majority of all Christians in the United States until the mid-20th century, but now constitute a minority among Protestants.

As a group, the mainline churches have maintained religious doctrine that stresses social justice and personal salvation. Politically and theologically, mainline Protestants are more liberal than non-mainline Protestants. Members of mainline denominations have played leadership roles in many aspects of life, including politics, business, science, the arts, and education. They founded most of the country's leading institutes of higher education. The leadership of mainline Protestant denominations supported racial desegregation, ordained women to the ministry, and endorsed the civil rights of gays and lesbians. They had also shown greater receptivity to new intellectual currents in the latter half of the nineteenth century, including Darwin's theory of evolution and an approach to the Bible called higher criticism, which cast doubts on the authorship of several books of the Bible.

Mainline denominations peaked in membership in the 1950s and have declined steadily in the last half century.

Evangelical Protestantism is a worldwide, transdenominational movement within Protestant Christianity which maintains the belief that the essence of the gospel consists of the doctrine of salvation by grace through faith in Jesus Christ's atonement. Evangelicals believe in the centrality of the conversion or the "born again" experience in receiving salvation, in the authority of the Bible as God's revelation to humanity, and in spreading the Christian message. The movement gained great momentum during the 18th and 19th centuries with the Great Awakenings in the United Kingdom and North America. Evangelicals are found across many Protestant branches, as well as in various denominations not subsumed to a specific branch. Its community forms a quarter of the population, is politically important and based mostly in the Bible Belt.

While targeting specific issues such as abortion, pornography, and public-school prayer, evangelicals also embraced a strongly conservative world view.

IV. Interesting Religious Groups

Two interesting religious groups founded in the US are the Mormons and the Christian Scientists. The Mormons (officially known as the Church of Jesus Christ of Latter-day Saints) were organized in New York in 1830. It is the largest indigenous religious group in America. Because it was customary for Mormon men to have more than one wife, at one time, Mormons were forced out of several established communities. They traveled westward and settled in the unpopulated valley of the Great Salt Lake in Utah, where they built a successful community. Today, there are 6.3 million Mormon church members in the US. Most of them live in Utah and in eastern Idaho, where they are the major religious sect. Its attempts to convert everyone to Mormonism and to establish a religious government in Utah, as well as the widespread practice of polygamy, confronted the First Amendment's ideas of religious pluralism, separation of church and state, and the common belief in sanctity of the family: one husband, one wife. The result was long years of religious persecution with Congressional and constitutional insistence that Utah be free of church control.

Its founder, Joseph Smith, refused to view himself merely as the founder of another denomination; instead, he saw himself as a prophet of the kingdom of God and was called a "Second Mohammed." Mormonism would be to Christianity what Christianity had been to Judaism: an all-encompassing, higher form of religion. Joseph Smith claimed that an angel led him to a buried book of revelation and to special stones for use in translating it. He completed his translation of this Book of Mormon in 1829. Mormonism appealed to the downtrodden and insecure rather than to the prosperous and secure. It offered the downcast an explicit alternative to dominant religious and social practices. In this respect, Mormonism mirrored the efforts of several religious communal societies whose members resolutely set themselves apart from society.

The Christian Science Church was founded by Mary Baker Eddy in 1879. Christian Scientists believe that healing of sickness results from spiritual understanding rather than standard medical treatment.

Another interesting religious group is the Amish. Originally from Switzerland, this group (about 40,000 people) is now centered in the US and Canada. Within the US, they have developed farming communities in 23 states, mostly in Pennsylvania and midwestern states of Ohio, Indiana, Iowa, and Illinois. The Amish are easy to spot. Their clothing is old-fashioned and plain. The men have beards and wear wide-brimmed hats and the women wear long dresses and bonnets. Jewelry and buttons are not allowed. The Amish travel in horse-drawn wagons because their religion forbids them to use cars. They have no telephones or electricity in their homes. Amish children are educated through eighth grade only and are trained to be farmers.

V. Separation of Church and State

The First Amendment to the Constitution forbids the establishment of an official national religion and prohibits governmental assistance to religious groups. It also prohibits state or federal interference with religious institutions or practices.

Separation of church and state has been interpreted to mean that any institution supported by the federal government or a state government must be free from the influence of religion.

But it may seem inconsistent, many official American ceremonies and documents make reference to God. Sessions of Congress and state legislatures begin with prayers. The national motto (printed on US money) is "In God We Trust."

→ *Vocabulary of Religion*

1. **Atheists** possibly suspect that the answer is no.

2. No longer is the question the taunting jest of **skeptics**.

3. Even within **Christianity** a small band of radical **theologians** has seriously argued that the churches must accept the fact of God's death.

4. In the traditional citadels of Christendom, grey Gothic cathedrals stand empty, mute witnesses to a rejected **faith**.

5. The open-window spirit of Pope John XXIII and Vatican II have revitalized **the Roman Catholic Church**.

6. Less spectacularly but not less decisively, **Protestantism** has been stirred by a flurry of experimentation in **liturgy**, church structure, **ministry**.

7. **Denominational allegiance** rose about 2 percent.

8. More than 120 million Americans now claim a religious **affiliation**.

9. 44% of them report that they **attend church services** weekly.

10. Plenty of **clergymen**, nonetheless, have qualms about the quality and character of contemporary **belief**.

11. All too many pews are filled on Sunday with practical atheists—disguised **nonbelievers** who behave during the rest of the week as if God did not exist.

12. For a generation of young Roman Catholics the **dogmas** of the church have lost much of their power.

13. I'm not sure what meaning these words, gestures and **rituals** have for them.

14. In a sense, no Christian **doctrine** of God is possible without Jesus, since the suffering **redeemer** of Calvary is the only certain glimpse of the **divine** that churches have.

Unit 7   Toward a Hidden God

15. But a Christ-centered **theology** that skirts the question of God raises more questions than it answers.

16. A majority of Christians would presumably prefer to stay with the traditional language of **revelation** at any cost.

17. And it is not merely conservative evangelists who believe that the words and ideas of **Scripture** have lost neither relevance nor meaning.

18. Other philosophical theologians have been working out a **theism** based on the process thinking of Alfred North Whitehead.

19. Christianity, in his view, should stop attributing specific actions to persons of the Trinity—**creation** to the Father, **redemption** to the Son, **inspiration** to the Holy Spirit—and just say that they were all the work of God.

20. The great diversity of ethnic backgrounds has produced **religious pluralism**; most of the religions of the world are now **practiced** in the United States.

21. **Religious participation** varies immensely depending on many factors.

22. Fundamentalism, crosses many **denominational** lines and emphasizes a **literal** interpretation of the Bible.

23. For many Americans, churches and religious sects are expressions of group solidarity rather than of **rigid adherence** to doctrine.

24. Most Christians do believe in the doctrine of the **Trinity**.

25. Catholics believe in **transubstantiation**.

26. Whatever the Church regards as **infallible**, a Catholic must accept.

27. To be accepted into church membership, individuals must publicly confess **conversion** to Jesus Christ as Lord and Savior.

28. Baptists tend to be conservative in theology, ranging from **fundamentalists** to **evangelicals**.

29. Worship is generally **nonliturgical**.

Unit 8 — The Feel-Good Trap

Richard Weissbourd

In the last twenty-five years, self-esteem has become a watchword in American education. Some schools have set up self-esteem classes and days. Others tack posters to the walls that exhort and praise: "YOU CAN DO ANYTHING." "YOU ARE BEAUTIFUL." The manifest risibility of this trend has prompted a sneering backlash; *commentary* pages and Doonesbury panels alike have lampooned the self-esteem movement as a baleful confluence of 1960s liberal indulgence and soft psychology that distracts from schools' central mission of teaching the basics. Even Bob Dole exploited the issue as a 1996 campaign plank. He attacked the demise of old-fashioned pedagogical tools such as spelling bees, ridiculing the notion that "such competitions can only deal a blow to the self-esteem of those who don't win."

Plenty of liberals as well as conservatives agree that this attention to self-esteem is not just useless but dangerous. Yet the self-esteem movement has at least tried to deal with serious problems that its critics have ignored. Indeed, the critics' back-to-basics call to teach just reading and writing will also fail large numbers of children. Instead, educators need to embark on a third path: developing a wide range of intellectual and social skills in children and creating more sustained relationships between children and adults. Such a plan is ambitious, to be sure, but, unlike the current solutions, it at least stands a chance of helping more children prosper in adult life.

The self-esteem movement arose not only out of a national infatuation, beginning in the late 1960s, with the inner life but also as a way to solve a host of problems plaguing children in schools. Poor and black students lagged behind their non-poor and white peers, it was argued, because racism and classism eroded their self-worth. The issue was not their ability to learn but their *confidence* in their ability to learn. Raising their self-esteem would boost their achievement.

The notion fast became a panacea in some quarters, and by 1990, a California state task force enshrined "the promotion of self-esteem" as a central goal of the curriculum, calling it a "social vaccine" that would inoculate children against academic failure, drug use, welfare dependence, violence and other ills. This task force has since become the whipping boy for the self-esteem critics.

For good reason. Thousands of studies on self-esteem have shown that the tenets of the movement just don't hold up. While there are different definitions of self-esteem and problems in measuring it, a multitude of studies reach the same conclusions. Programs to raise self-esteem—defined as a positive, global evaluation of the self—are not raising it. And the very premise that greater self-esteem will boost academic achievement is simply wrong. Self-esteem has little or no impact on academic achievement or on drug use, violence, or any other serious problems. Violent criminals, studies show, often have high self-esteem. And black children *already* have levels of self-esteem similar to white children; they take an equally positive view of themselves, but they're less likely to have a sense of efficacy: they see the outside world as placing obstacles in their path.

What's going on? For one thing, self-esteem doesn't lead to greater academic achievement unless a child values such achievement—high-school athletes may have self-esteem but no interest in school—and it's no secret that large numbers of children don't. Nor should we expect self-esteem to reduce violence or encourage ethical self-conduct. Self-esteem comes in part from feeling powerful, and playground bullies, violent gang leaders, and all sorts of other nonacademic achievers can feel powerful. If children grow up in cultures that condone unethical conduct, they may end up feeling good about such conduct.

Further, there's a problem with the concept of self-esteem. Though some violent children have high self-esteem, the self that is being esteemed is immature, incapable of empathy, unaware of itself. Many violent children lash out not because of low self-worth but because they are highly prone to shame (that's why so much violence is triggered by acts of disrespect). Even if schools could jack up children's self-esteem, it might not affect their academic competence, their ability to manage humiliation, or their maturity. These are largely separate problems and require largely separate solutions.

Even more troubling, the self-esteem movement has often been harmful. Children know when they have really accomplished something and when they haven't, and too much unconditional praise produces not self-confidence but cynicism about adults and doubts about themselves. Talking about children's selves all the time can also teach them to make how they feel about themselves paramount. As developmental psychologist Robert Karen puts it, too much talk about the value of a child's entire being "trains children to think globally, to make their selves the issue in whatever they do, and thus to be prone to both grandiosity and self-contempt."

All this advertises for seriously rethinking the entire self-esteem movement. Some of this rethinking has argued that self-esteem is the *result* of academic achievement, not vice versa; others say academic achievement is important for its own sake, regardless of what it does for self-esteem. Both groups argue that schools should be dedicated to academic achievement—in some cases to rudimentary skills. As John Leo writes in *U.S. News and World Report*, "[U]ntil we grapple with the real agenda of the self-esteem movement—ersatz therapeutic massage instead of learning—there will probably be no reform at all."

There's no question schools should focus on academic achievement, both for its own sake and because it builds self-esteem in some (though not all) children. While children should be aware of racism and discrimination, no amount of talking about discrimination can substitute for raising nonwhite children's achievements. And the focus on self-esteem has sometimes, as critics contend, detracted from academics; teachers dumb down curricula, inflate grades, and avoid discussing real academic problems with parents. A special education teacher who works with almost all poor students told me the last thing she wanted was "for a child to fail," so she spent her time providing "a lot of hugs and kisses." It's hard to imagine a greater threat to poor children's learning than this kind of dismal assessment of their capacities.

Nonetheless, to harp on academic achievement is irrelevant and insulting to most educators. It simply doesn't answer the question they struggle with daily. Most teachers care deeply that children learn basic skills. The problem is how to overcome the hurdles that interfere with that learning. Educators know what self-esteem critics don't: Huge numbers of children suffer from social and emotional problems that both shrink their self-esteem and choke their ability to learn. Some children can't concentrate in class, for instance, because they have been abandoned by a parent, or because their violence-wracked neighborhoods deprive them of an elementary sense of control, or because they live with caregivers who are too depressed to be involved in their lives. For all its failings, the self-esteem movement has at least tried to deal with these problems. To talk of academic achievement without addressing these devastating troubles is fantasy for these children.

Further, academic achievement often doesn't boost self-esteem. Many children, girls especially, achieve at high levels yet have little self-esteem. And anyone who believes academic achievement is a royal road to self-esteem should spend time with first-year law students at Harvard, who are disgusted with themselves because they find themselves ranked not at the top but wallowing somewhere in the middle of their classes.

Finally, harping on achievement ignores the evidence that both effectiveness in adult life and self-esteem depend on a wide range of intellectual and social competencies. Harvard education professor Howard Gardner has documented many different types of intelligence, including interpersonal skills, that are crucial to success in adult life. Cultivating capacities such as self-awareness, control of one's impulses, and persistence needn't detract from teaching academics. Good teachers build these competencies in the course of academic instruction. Teaching literature can clearly impart all sorts of social and moral lessons.

Schools need to forget about self-esteem altogether as an explicit goal. They should instead set high expectations of children, cultivate in them a wide range of competencies, coping strategies, and ethical sensibilities and show them the value of these abilities. Nonwhite children need to be given tools for understanding and responding to discrimination while still meeting high academic expectations. If schools want children to be less violent and more ethical, they should, among other things, provide them with opportunities to give to others, help them to manage their frustration and shame when they feel disrespected, and enable them to see moral issues from multiple points of view. A teacher might, for example, ask a violent child to host a talk show on gun control or create a classroom city government and ask a scapegoated kid to be mayor.

To prepare children for adult life schools also need to focus on something else, which neither self-esteem proponents nor critics talk about. Critical qualities that children need to develop for adulthood—persistence, the capacity to handle shame and disappointment, the ability to recognize the needs of others, and to balance them with one's own—cannot be simply transmitted. They are the ingredients of maturity, and this kind of maturity typically develops when children have a certain kind of relationship with adults.

The psychoanalyst Heinz Kohut argues that a child's self matures in two ways: by being mirrored by adults and by being esteemed by consistent, admired adults. By "mirroring," Kohut meant that all children need adults who listen to and understand them and regularly reflect their understanding; such reflections develop children's sense of coherence and rightness in the world. Kohut also recognized that at certain stages of development, every child needs adults whom he or she idealizes. Psychologists have long recognized that in adolescence, children get a second chance to internalize the confident expectations of esteemed adults. That chance should not be squandered.

To listen and reflect, adults need first to spend more time with children. The self-esteem movement's constant praising of children is a short cut, a desperate substitute for the inability of teachers and other adults to pay sufficient attention to any one child. But time and attention are real to a child in ways that praise is not. Parents, of course, best provide this time and attention, but when parents cannot or do not do so, other adults should. This doesn't entail "babysitting":

It means spending a few (or more) hours a week listening to, challenging, and developing the strengths of a child.

Schools need to push beyond the academic achievement versus self-esteem debates and embark on a variety of strategies that involve adults more in children's lives. Class sizes need to come down. Schools need to work harder to involve parents, including absentee fathers, in their children's education. And schools need to keep trying to bring more adults into children's lives who are worthy of esteem by making teaching and other types of work with children more attractive, including through higher status and better pay. Granted, this all amounts to a tall order. Yet these steps, taken together, would be far more meaningful than focusing simply on a nostrum like returning to basics or on a spurious metasolution like self-esteem.

Notes

1. **Doonesbury:** a comic strip by American cartoonist Garry Trudeau that chronicles the adventures and lives of an array of characters of various ages, professions, and backgrounds, from the President of the United States to the title character, Michael Doonesbury, who has progressed from a college student to a youthful senior citizen over the decades.
2. **1960s liberal indulgence:** young people in America in the 1960s demanded more participatory democracy and wanted to take part in the making of the decisions that influenced their lives. They rebelled against tradition and the establishment. They started a counter culture movement in the 1960s.
3. **whipping boy:** a person who is often blamed or punished for things other people have done.
4. **a tall order:** a formidable task or requirement.

Vocabulary

1. watchword ['wɑtʃwɜ·d]: *n.* a word or phrase that expresses somebody's beliefs or attitudes, or that explains what somebody should do in a particular situation 口号；格言
2. tack [tæk]: *vt.* If you tack something to a surface, you pin it there with tacks or drawing pins 以大头针钉住
3. exhort [ɪgˈzɔrt]: *vt.* try hard to persuade or encourage them to do it 激励；告诫
4. risibility [ˌrɪzɪˈbɪləti]: *n.* a sense of the ludicrous or amusing 可笑或滑稽的感觉
5. backlash [ˈbæklæʃ]: *n.* a sudden, strong reaction against a tendency or recent development in society or politics （政治或社会上的）对抗性反应

6. lampoon [læm'puːn]: *vt.* criticize them very strongly, using humorous means 讥讽

7. baleful ['beɪlfʊl; -f(ə)l]: *adj.* harmful, or expressing harmful intentions 有害的

8. confluence ['kɒnfluəns]: *n.* A flowing together of two or more streams 合流

9. plank [plæŋk]: *n.* a main point in the policy of an organization, especially a political party （政党等的）政策准则，政纲的核心

10. demise [dɪ'maɪz]: *n.* the end or failure of an institution, an idea, a company, etc 终止；失败

11. pedagogical [ˌpedə'gɒdʒɪkl]: *adj.* concerning teaching methods 教学法的

12. erode [ɪ'rəʊd]: *vt.* to gradually destroy something or make it weaker over a period of time 逐渐毁坏；削弱

13. panacea [ˌpænə'siːə]: *n.* something that will solve all the problems of a particular situation 万灵药

14. enshrine [ɪn'ʃraɪn]: *vt.* to cherish as sacred 把……奉为神圣

15. vaccine [væk'siːn]: *n.* a substance that is put into the blood and that protects the body from a disease 疫苗

16. inoculate [ɪ'nɒkjʊleɪt]: *vt.* to inject a weak form of a disease into their body as a way of protecting them against the disease 预防注射

17. tenet ['tɛnɪt]: *n.* one of the principles or beliefs that a theory or larger set of beliefs is based on 原则；信条

18. premise ['premɪs]: *n.* something that you suppose is true and that you use as a basis for developing an idea 前提

19. efficacy ['efɪkəsɪ]: *n.* the effectiveness and the ability to do what it is supposed to 功效

20. condone [kən'dəʊn]: *vt.* to overlook, forgive, or disregard (an offense) without protest or censure 宽恕（冒犯行为）

21. empathy ['empəθɪ]: *n.* the ability to share another person's feelings and emotions as if they were your own 认同和理解别人的处境、感情和动机

22. paramount ['pærəmaʊnt]: *adj.* more important than anything else 至为重要的

23. grandiosity [ˌgrændi'ɒsəti]: *n.* the fact that seeming very impressive but too large, complicated, expensive, etc. to be practical or possible 华而不实；不切实际

24. ersatz ['ɛrsats]: *adj.* artificial and not as good as the real thing or product 人造的；合成的

25. wallow ['wɒləʊ]: *vi.* to move with difficulty in a clumsy or rolling manner 蹒跚

26. impart [ɪm'pɑrt]: *vt.* to pass information, knowledge, etc. to other people 传授

27. squander ['skwɒndə]: *vt.* waste money, resources or opportunities 浪费

28. nostrum ['nɒstrəm]: *n.* something old-fashioned or even wrong in some way 秘方

29. spurious ['spjʊərɪəs]: *adj.* seems to be genuine, but is false 似是而非的

Expressions

1. Thousands of studies on self-esteem have shown that the tenets of the movement just don't <u>hold up</u>.

    hold up: If an argument or theory holds up, it is true or valid, even after close examination 经受考验

2. Many violent children <u>lash out</u> not because of low self-worth but because they <u>are highly prone to</u> shame (that's why so much violence is triggered by acts of disrespect).

    lash out: to criticize someone angrily 抨击

    be prone to: be likely to suffer from something, especially something bad or harmful 易于发生（不愉快的事）的

3. Even if schools could <u>jack up</u> children's self-esteem, it might not affect their academic competence, their ability to manage humiliation, or their maturity.

    jack up: to raise a heavy object off the ground using a jack 顶起，托起

4. [U]ntil we <u>grapple with</u> the real agenda of the self-esteem movement…

    grapple with: to work hard, to deal with something difficult 努力设法解决

5. …teachers <u>dumb down</u> curricula, inflate grades, and avoid discussing real academic problems with parents.

    dumb down: to make something easier for people to understand, especially when this spoils it. 使……通俗易懂

6. Nonetheless, to <u>harp on</u> academic achievement is irrelevant and insulting to most educators.

    harp on: to keep on talking about it in a way that other people find annoying. 喋喋不休

Comprehension

I. Discuss the Main Point and the Meanings.

1. What should be schools' central mission according to the author?

2. What are the problems the self-esteem movement supposed to solve? Could the movement accomplish this goal?

3. What is the problem with the special education teacher in Paragraph 9?

Unit 8 The Feel-Good Trap

4. In the author's opinion, what are the critical qualities schools should cultivate in order for the children to be effective in adult life?

5. How could adults be involved in educating the children according to the author?

II. Fill in the blanks with the appropriate words or expressions in the box.

1960s liberal indulgence	a wide range of intellectual and social skills	adults
idealizes	ingredients of maturity	set high expectations of children
talking	teaching academics	teaching the basics
unconditional praise	values such achievement	we are two nations

1. *Commentary* pages and Doonesbury panels alike have lampooned the self-esteem movement as a baleful confluence of _____ and soft psychology that distracts from schools' central mission of _____.

2. Indeed, the critics' back-to-basics call to teach just reading and writing will also _____ _____ large numbers of children.

3. Instead, educators need to embark on a third path: developing _____ in children and creating more sustained relationships between children and adults.

4. Self-esteem doesn't lead to greater academic achievement unless a child _____.

5. Too much _____ produces not self-confidence but cynicism about adults and doubts about themselves.

6. No amount of _____ about discrimination can substitute for raising nonwhite children's achievements.

7. Cultivating capacities such as self-awareness, control of one's impulses, and persistence needn't detract from _____.

8. Schools should _____, cultivate in them a wide range of competencies, coping strategies, and ethical sensibilities and show them the value of these abilities.

9. Persistence, the capacity to handle shame and disappointment, the ability to recognize the needs of others, and to balance them with one's own are the _____.

10. All children need _____ who listen to and understand them and regularly reflect their understanding. At certain stages of development, every child needs adults whom he or she _____.

→ *Structure*

I. Find out how the words and expressions in bold are used in the following sentences.

1. Instead, educators **embark on** a third path.

2. It **at least stands a chance of** helping more children prosper in adult life.

3. Poor and black students **lagged behind** their non-poor and white peers.

4. They're less **likely to** have a sense of efficacy.

5. Self-esteem doesn't **lead to** greater academic achievement unless a child values such achievement.

6. If children grow up in cultures that condone unethical conduct, they may **end up** feeling good about such conduct.

7. Many violent children lash out because they **are** highly **prone to** shame.

8. **As** developmental psychologist Robert Karen **puts it**…

9. All this **advertises for** seriously rethinking the entire self-esteem movement.

10. Others say academic achievement is important **for its own sake**, **regardless of** what it does for self-esteem.

11. No amount of talking about discrimination can **substitute for** raising nonwhite children's achievements.

12. …because their violence-wracked neighborhoods **deprive** them **of** an elementary sense of control…

13. **For all** its failings, the self-esteem movement has at least tried to deal with these problems.

14. They should, among other things, **provide** them **with** opportunities to give to others.

15. **Granted**, this all amounts to a tall order.

II. Complete the following sentences with some of the above words or expressions in bold.

1. He is a teacher _____ respect.

2. The Industrial Revolution, _____, necessarily produced general literacy.

3. The recipe says you can _____ yogurt _____ the sour cream.

4. The law requires equal treatment for all, _____ race, religion, or sex.

5. That little girl is interested in writing _____.

6. Most slimmers _____ putting weight back on.

7. His reluctance to help could, _____, be explained by his laziness.

8. When women joined the organization, it "took on a new look," _____ news reports _____.

9. _____ her efforts, she didn't succeed.

10. _____, the music is not perfect, but the flaws are outweighed by the sheer joy of the piece.

Education in the United States

1. American Education System

The United States does not have a national school system. Nor, with the exception of the military academies, are these schools run by the federal government.

The US Department of Education has very limited supervisory powers, but it does research, makes suggestions for national standards. It contributes approximately seven percent of the total costs of education to the states. The states have constitutional authority over education. State Boards of Education set minimum requirements for teacher qualifications, student attendance, and course offerings. All states have compulsory school attendance laws, they generally require school attendance from age 6 to 16.

But real control devolves to more local levels. The day-to-day management of the 90,000 public schools and 2.7 million teachers is delegated to 14,600 independent school districts. School districts are administered by school boards elected or appointed from the local communities or counties. School boards decide what will be taught in their schools and administer the funding.

Generally, half the money to operate schools comes from the state and the remaining half is raised through local property and local taxes, as decided by each community. Those communities that have high property values or a willingness to increase their taxes can provide high-quality facilities, the newest software, and the best teachers for their schools. Americans research the differences among schools when they make decisions on home purchases or job relocation, often making the final decision exclusively on the school district their children will enter.

Overall, Americans have built a system that is decentralized, comprehensive, (Americans expect their high schools to give comprehensive educations, wide-ranging and unspecialized), universal, (compulsory education for all children from age 6 to 16) and professional.

2. Elementary & Secondary Education

Elementary Education

Free public education begins with kindergarten, usually half day classes for 5-year-olds.

Formal academic work is divided into 12 levels called grades. One school year (from late August or early September to mid-June) is required to complete each grade.

The first academic institution that a student attends is called elementary school or grammar school. In some school systems, elementary school goes through eighth grade. In others, there is a second division called junior high school or middle school. It usually includes grades 6—8, 5—8 or 7—9.

The typical school day is about 6 hours long and ends about 3:00 P.M. Classes are in session between Monday through Friday. Traditional vacation periods includes a two-week winter vacation, a one-week spring vacation, and a two-month summer vacation. In addition, there are several one-day holidays.

Secondary Education

American high schools have a commitment to offer both a general college preparation program for those interested in higher education and vocational training for students who plan to enter the work force immediately after high school graduation.

Many high schools group students according to academic ability and motivation. Some subjects are offered at two, three, or even four different levels of difficulty.

Starting from the ninth grade, grades become part of a student's official transcript, including academic studies and attendance records.

Many high schools provide Advanced Placement (AP) or International Baccalaureate (IB) courses: intended for 11th or 12th graders, honor classes where the curriculum is more challenging and lessons more aggressively paced than standard courses, even to the degree equivalent of the first year of college courses. Most post-secondary institutions take AP or IB exam results into consideration in the admission process.

Public Schools

Eighty-six percent of Americans receive their elementary and high school education in public schools.

The public schools have important characteristics in common:

1) They are supported by state and local taxes, and do not charge tuition.

2) Most are neighborhood schools, open to students who live in the district.

3) They are coeducational, which means that boys and girls attend the same schools and have nearly all their classes together.

4) They are locally controlled. The individual states, not the federal government, are responsible for education. Public schools are required to follow some state guidelines regarding, for example, curriculum and teacher qualifications. But most decisions about a school district

are made by an elected board of education and the administrators that board hires. This system creates strong ties between the district's schools and its local community.

5) American public schools are free from the influence of any religion.

The largest public school system in the United States is in New York City, where more than one million students are taught in 1,200 separate public schools. Because of its immense size — there are more students in the system than residents in eight US states — the New York City public school system is nationally influential in determining standards and materials, such as textbooks.

Private Schools

In addition to these government-funded public schools, the United States has many schools that are privately financed and maintained. More than 10 percent of all elementary and secondary students in the United States attend private schools.

Private schools are divided into two categories: parochial (supported by a particular religious group) and independent (not affiliated with any religious group). Private schools charge tuition and are not under direct public control, although many states set educational standards for them. Parochial (mostly Catholic) schools make up the largest group of private schools.

Charter Schools

These schools are directly authorized by the state and receive public funding, but they operate largely outside the control of local school districts. Charter schools have special agreement with their state board of education that free them from some of the restrictions placed upon regular public schools. Parents and teachers enforce self-defined standards for these charter schools. Charter schools have more autonomy to try innovative teaching methods, serve specific students needs, and reduce class sizes—with the requirement to produce positive academic results.

Magnet Schools

Admission to individual public schools is usually based on residency. To compensate for differences in school quality based on geography, school systems serving large cities and portions of large cities often have "magnet schools" that provide enrollment to a specified number of non-resident students in addition to serving all resident students. This special enrollment is usually decided by lottery with equal numbers of males and females chosen. Some magnet schools cater to gifted students or to students with special interests, such as the sciences or performing arts. Admission to some of these schools is highly competitive and based on an application process.

3. Education Policy

School Voucher

In some states, families could get a voucher worth a few thousand dollars per child. That voucher could be used to purchase education via enrollment into public or private schools and would pay the cost for the average public school in each school district. If parents selected a private school or a more costly public school, they would pay the difference.

On April 27, 2011 Indiana passed a statewide voucher program, the largest in the US. It offers up to $4,500 to students with household income under $41,000, and lesser benefits to households with higher incomes. Of the ten state-run voucher programs in the United States at the beginning of 2011, however, four targeted low-income students, two targeted students in failing schools, and six targeted students with special needs. (Note that Louisiana ran a single program targeting all three groups.)

Tracking System

Most schools have tried a "tracking" system that places students in classes by ability, still teaching everyone but often at vastly different levels. The most exclusive private "college preparatory" schools select only students with certain IQ scores and/or proven ability, as well as those whose parents stand high in the community or who will donate sizable monetary gifts to the school.

No Child Left Behind

The role of the federal government in setting education policy increased significantly with the passage by Congress of the No Child Left Behind Act of 2001, a sweeping education reform law that revised the Elementary and Secondary Education Act of 1965. Signed by President George W. Bush in 2002, the new law seeks to identify poorly performing public schools by requiring states to test students in grades three through eight annually in reading and math. Schools that fail to make "adequate yearly progress" toward state proficiency standards must allow students to transfer to better-performing public schools. If poor performance continues, schools must offer supplemental services such as private tutoring; persistently failing schools must take corrective actions, such as replacing certain teachers or changing the curriculum, or risk being restructured or taken over by the state. The law also requires all public school teachers to be "highly qualified" in their subject areas by the end of the 2006 school year.

Every Student Succeeds

President Obama signed a new law in 2015 which replaced the controversial No Child Left Behind law. It still requires mandatory testing and emphasis on test scores to indicate groups of students who were failing. But power returns to states to decide what to do with failing and underperforming students. The president of the American Federation of Teachers call it a course correction, saying it moves toward the policy where the states have more authority in educating children. Critics are concerned that without government overseeing them, states may be less willing to fix failing schools.

4. Higher Education

"The more you learn, the more you earn." Americans often say. In the US, almost all jobs that pay well require some education or technical training beyond high school. In this high-tech society, college graduates outearn those without a college education, and people with advanced degrees are likely to earn even more.

Universities are the gatekeepers to the most lucrative occupations and much of the class division in America stems from how much or how little education an individual has obtained. Two-thirds of American high school graduates enroll in college. Almost one-quarter of Americans over age 25 are college graduates.

Higher Institutes

Two main categories of institutions of higher learning are public and private. All schools get money from tuition and from private contributors. However, public schools are also supported by the state in which they're located. Private schools do not receive state funding. As a result, tuition is generally lower at public schools, especially for permanent residents of that state. A third category is proprietary (for profit) school. These usually teach a particular workplace skill. Some of these schools are quite expensive.

There are three major tracks which students follow beyond the high school experience. The first is the technical institute whose primary purpose is to train students for particular occupations in technical, service, and professional areas usually within one or three calendar years depending on the field. Certificates and/or associate degrees awarded in these areas are generally recognized for acceptance into certain positions in government, business, or industry, but the curriculum is primarily vocational and thus most credits are not transferable to the other two post-secondary tracks.

Junior or community colleges, primarily two-year institutions which grant associate degrees or branch campuses of larger four-year colleges and universities, are the fastest growing segments in post-secondary education with over 1,300 institutions and 38.4 percent of the total student enrollment in higher education. The third major track in post-secondary education is the four-year undergraduate degree program offered at specialized, general baccalaureate, comprehensive, and doctoral institutions.

Specialized institutions are those which emphasize one academic field of study, such as business or engineering. General baccalaureate colleges are primarily concerned with providing general four-year liberal arts or undergraduate degrees. Comprehensive institutions have diverse undergraduate and post-bachelor's programs but do not engage in significant doctoral level education. Doctoral institution have varied programs, offering research activities and grant the highest academic degrees available.

Standardized Tests

High school seniors wishing to apply to competitive colleges and universities take standardized tests commonly called ACTs (American College Test) and SATs (Scholastic Achievement Test). A student may take the SAT, ACT, or both depending upon the post-secondary institutions the student plans to apply to for admission. Most competitive schools also require two or three SAT Subject Tests, (formerly known as SAT IIs), which are shorter exams that focus strictly on a particular subject matter. The tests help students demonstrate the ability to do college level work. Most colleges use these scores plus the students' high school grades to evaluate applicants. These tests are given several times a year throughout the U. S. and in other countries.

Grades in high school courses and scores on tests like the SAT are very important, but so are the students' extracurricular activities. It is by participating in these activities that students demonstrate their special talents, their level of maturity and responsibility, their leadership qualities, and their ability to get along with others. In making their decisions about which students to admit, colleges look for students who are "well-rounded."

Courses & Credits

An undergraduate degree takes a minimum of four years to complete and consists typically of 36—40 different courses. American colleges are uniform in requiring that one-third of a student's curriculum be in general classes in science, philosophy, history, literature, math, and language so that students will be broadly-informed democratic citizens. After completing these required courses, students select a major and take 9-12 specialized courses. The remaining classes needed for graduation are electives which students choose to supplement other areas of interest or to concentrate on a minor field which strengthens the major.

If a student wants to go on to graduate school, he or she first takes a standardized test, the Graduate Record Exam (GRE), which does what the SAT did at the undergraduate level. A Master's degree usually means an additional 6—18 courses plus a thesis, and a Ph.D. could add another 6—18 courses plus a dissertation, depending upon the specific program and whether or not classes are on the quarter or semester system. In most fields, a master's degree can be earned in 1 or 2 academic years of study beyond the B.S. or B.A. Earning a Ph.D. degree (doctor of philosophy) usually takes at least 3 years beyond the master's.

Professional degrees such as law, medicine, pharmacy, and dentistry, are offered as graduate study after earning at least three years of undergraduate schooling or after earning a bachelor's degree depending on the program. These professional fields do not require a specific undergraduate major, though medicine, pharmacy, and dentistry have set prerequisite courses that must be taken before enrollment.

More Information

At most colleges, the academic year is divided into either two semesters or three quarters, excluding the summer session. On many campuses, social life revolves around fraternities (social and, in some cases, residential clubs for men) and sororities (similar clubs for women). Some are national groups with chapters at many schools. Their names are Greek letters, such as Alpha, Delta, Phi.

Adult education or continuing education are offered in many high schools, colleges, and museums. Many schools also offer distance learning—"attending" class and interacting with professors and classmates via the internet.

Ivy League

Ivy League, eight long-established colleges and universities in the United States with prestigious academic and social reputations. Members of the Ivy League are Brown University in Providence, Rhode Island; Columbia University in New York City; Cornell University in Ithaca, New York; Dartmouth College in Hanover, New Hampshire; Harvard University in Cambridge, Massachusetts; University of Pennsylvania in Philadelphia; Princeton University in Princeton, New Jersey; and Yale University in New Haven, Connecticut. They are regarded to be the cradle for American presidents.

Affirmative Action

Affirmative action became a general social commitment during the last quarter of the 20th century. In education, it meant that universities and colleges gave extra advantages and opportunities to blacks, Native Americans, women, and other groups that were generally underrepresented at the highest levels of business and in other professions. Many American colleges set aside a certain number of places specifically for applicants from these groups.

Affirmative action also included financial assistance to members of minorities who could not otherwise afford to attend colleges and universities. Affirmative action has allowed many minority members to achieve new prominence and success. The issue became a matter of serious discussion and is one of the most highly charged topics in education today. Up to now, some states have eliminated affirmative action in their state university admissions policies.

Vocabulary of Education

1. Instead, **educators** need to embark on a third path.

2. A California state task force enshrined "the promotion of self-esteem" as **a central goal** of the **curriculum**.

3. **Cultivating** capacities such as self-awareness, control of one's impulses, and persistence needn't detract from teaching **academics**.

4. **School districts** are administered by **school boards**.

5. Starting from the ninth grade, grades become part of a student's official **transcript**.

6. Many high schools provide **Advanced Placement** (AP) or **International Baccalaureate** (IB) courses.

7. Grades in high school courses and scores on tests like the SAT are very important, but so are the students' **extracurricular** activities.

8. In making their decisions about which students to admit, colleges look for students who are "**well-rounded**."

9. To earn **a bachelor's degree**, students usually take general subjects during their first two years.

10. **A Master's degree** usually means an additional 6-18 courses.

11. Earning a **Ph.D. degree** (doctor of philosophy) usually takes at least 3 years beyond the master's.

12. At most colleges, the academic year is divided into either two **semesters** or three **quarters**, excluding the summer session.

13. On many campuses, social life revolves around **fraternities** (social and, in some cases, residential clubs for men) and **sororities** (similar clubs for women).

14. **Alumni** refer to the school they attended as their **alma mater** (Latin for "fostering mother").

15. **Adult education** or **continuing education** are offered in many high schools, colleges, and museums.

Unit 9

Jockpop: Popular Sports and Politics

James Combs

Sports and Learning

In the famous opening sequence of the movie *Patton*, General Patton (George C. Scott) delivered a speech to an audience of soldiers. He said in part:

Men, all this stuff you've heard about America not wanting to fight, wanting to stay out of the war, is a lot of horsedung. Americans traditionally love to fight. All real Americans love the sting of battle. When you were kids you all admired the champion marble shooter, the fastest runner, the big league ballplayers, the toughest boxers. Americans play to win all the time. I wouldn't give a hoot in hell for a man who lost and laughed. That's why Americans have never lost, and will never lose a war, because the very thought of losing is hateful to Americans.

Let us reflect a moment, as General Patton urges, on growing up. When we were kids, we all quickly learned the importance of sports. Playing was fun, and indeed gave us a chance to prove ourselves. We discovered that organized sports at school and the Little League gave us an opportunity to play. We discovered that some could play better than others, that winning was valued, that there was a huge adult interest in sports. We found that there was a big world of sports in which adult athletes played before gigantic audiences for large amounts of money and glory. We adopted heroes among athletes in high school or more remotely in the pro leagues. We attempted to bat, or dribble, or pass like them, even to act like them. If we hung around locker rooms or played, we heard the slogans: "Quitters never win, and winners never quit." Some of us experienced the "thrill of victory and agony of defeat." We heard the speeches at sports banquets. We won letters, were cheerleaders and pompom girls, went to the school games. We talked about sports, followed college and pro sports, maybe even dreamed dreams of athletic glory.

And what effect did it all have on us? Specifically here, what impact does the play-world of sports have on politics? Like the other areas of the American play-world, popular sports is not "just a game." Rather, we learn much about the world from sports. Whether consciously or not, the "lessons of sports" help to orient us to the world. It is not an idle metaphor when we speak of the "game of life." For games, and what we are told about games, give us much learning about life, and even politics. Sports is a form of play which we early on learn is important, come to value, and link to "real life."

Sports and Drama

The root of this may well be in the fact that sports are dramatic. Games are an organized play-area, in which dramatic struggle (*agon*) occurs. The game becomes a public arena for the enactment of the more interesting aspects of human life—competition, teamwork, risk-taking, aggression and defense, winning and losing. Because sports dramatize in microcosm both eternal human truths and specific cultural truths, we are drawn in the same way we are drawn to drama. The drama "represents" life, lets us look at a heightened reality which dramatizes in the story what we want to know about life. Popular drama like soap operas dramatizes exemplary situations with which we can identify. Similarly, sports interest us because they possess such dramatic qualities. We learn from the "story" of a game because we can relate it to our lives....

Sports and Politics

The dramatization of the American Dream in sports suggests that sports has important meanings for us. It is likely that we "read into" sports a variety of messages, including political ones. So we should expect that sports would have political meanings and realize that these meanings have not been lost on politicians and observers of politics. Sometimes the sports-politics connection is obvious, sometimes subtle, but it is nevertheless there. For if sports is a key part of our cultural mythology, and it is a play-setting for the dramatization of American myths, then its relevance for the world of politics and government exists. Therefore, we can explore some of the political meanings and uses of sports: sports as a setting for political *ritual*; as a metaphor for political *rhetoric*; as a dramatic microcosm of political *conflicts*; and as a political *resource*. We will consider these in turn.

Sports as a Setting for Political Ritual

Remember that we have stressed the ways that popular culture is a political teacher. We learn things about ourselves as political beings from the social messages that a popular playform communicates. An important part of our political socialization was through patriotic ritual at school — saluting the flag, saying the Pledge of Allegiance, school spirit assemblies. But this is not the only setting for such symbolic dramas. We all remember the patriotic rituals attached to sporting events — the national anthem, raising the flag, color guards, and so forth. We would feel uneasy if a high school or college football game did not include such patriotic rituals.

These generalized rituals are more or less universal. Indeed, we commonly expect sporting events to be clothed in not only political symbolism, but also religious symbolism as well. We all recall the invocations given before games, the players all praying in the huddle, and singing "God Bless America." Patriotic and religious symbols are, of course, closely linked in sports ritual. The presence of such rituals underscores that the event is not merely a game, but a play-event conducted with proper deference by participants and audience to transcendent values. The appeal is very largely to the moral community, as when the invocation prays that the players conduct the game with respect to moral values. Thus, the folk drama of sports comes to be imbued with patriotic rituals which remind us not only in what country the game is being played, but that the game occurs in the context of national values.

Now when a political crisis ensues, such patriotic ritual takes on a more intensely felt meaning. During the Iranian crisis, it was common for football game rituals to recognize the hostages through moments of silence immediately before the national anthem was played, a dramatic reminder with political significance. Immediately after the release of the hostages, the 1981 Super Bowl became a festive setting for the ritual recognition of that celebrated event — everyone there wore yellow ribbons, and even the Superdome had a massive yellow ribbon on the outside.

But when the country is divided over some political issue, political rituals at sports events can become controversial and excessive. During the height of the Vietnam War, there was a clear increase in the number of college football halftime shows that involved patriotic themes and pageantry. Indeed, in 1970 ABC refused to televise a halftime show planned by the University of Buffalo band which dramatized antiwar, antiracist, and antipollution themes through music and skits on the grounds that it would be a "political demonstration." But later that season ABC did televise a halftime show at the Army-Navy game which honored Green Berets who had just conducted an unsuccessful raid on a prisoner of war camp in North Vietnam, including statements by military officers critical of antiwar activity at home. So it depends upon whose moralistic myth is to be ritualized! Such incidents do remind us that sports involve the affirmation of cultural myths, since sports "participate" in the social order. Thus, "negative" rituals which celebrate a counter-myth conflict with the traditional patriotic function that sporting rituals have served.

In the past, political rituals which celebrated the symbols of government seemed especially appropriate for sporting events, since major sports seemed to embody so nicely aspects of the American Dream. If myths of the State come to be disbelieved or doubted, then such rituals may ring hollow for many people. One may wonder what sorts of feelings playing the national anthem before a game conjures up in our breasts. But whether we still believe or not, the fact remains that sports is a major stage for the dramatization of political symbols.

Sports as a Metaphor for Political Rhetoric

Politicians like to draw upon familiar symbols to illustrate some political point, and sports offer familiar and widely used metaphors. The language of the locker room permeates politics. Sports is a major repository of American mythology, so politicians can utilize the analogy, safely assuming wide familiarity with the "lessons" of sports. Since politics has many game-like aspects, reference to the dynamics of sporting games as similar to "the game of politics" is natural. Both coaches and political figures seem to believe in the necessity of inspiration, which is the most common political use of sports analogies, allegories, parables, and so on.

The "values" of sports can also be for a variety of political uses. In particular, sports can illustrate the "truth" of either moralistic or materialistic myths. The American sports creed includes many tenets, most of which can be used to support or illustrate different political messages. Even though there is wide popular consensus that sports makes us "better citizens," what that means is subject to interpretation. For instance, Americans repeatedly agree on the positive lessons of sports: e.g., sports are worthwhile because they teach us "self-discipline"; sports are good because they promote "fair play" and sports are positive because they teach "respect for authority and good citizenship." However, such virtues can be variously interpreted.

Let us illustrate this by reference to two often competing aspects of the sports creed: sportsmanship and winning. The ideal of sportsmanship has persisted in political rhetoric as a norm by which the game is supposed to be played, i.e., that one plays fair, enjoys the contest, and accepts victory with magnanimity and defeat with grace. Being a "good sport" was a trait admirable in all areas of life. The "truth" of sports was not whether one won or lost, but how you played the game. A "sportsman" was a gentleman committed to excellence, but within ethical bounds and without cheap tactics. Such an image smacks of the "Ivy League" pop books of an earlier age about sports heroes such as Frank Merriwell.

This venerable notion has been applied to democratic politics again and again. In a classic book about democracy, we learn that sportsmanship, on the field or in politics, consists of such attitudes as tolerating and honoring the opposition; being a gracious winner and loser; and playing "the game of politics" within the bounds of rules and fair play.

This motif is complicated by a conflicting norm: winning. Winning isn't everything, goes Lombardi's Law, it's the only thing. Nice guys, Durocher's Dictum has it, finish last. The winning motif is related to the idea of sports as war, in which winning takes precedence over gentlemanly traits, and indeed where sportsmanship is a hindrance to victory. The implicit locker room message is often that since winning is paramount, any means, including bending or breaking the rules, unfair play, and intimidation, are justified. At the extreme, this can justify the virtue of sheer winning in politics. Indeed, the Nixon Administration's fondness for sports metaphors was thought to have contributed to the "Watergate mentality," i.e., that the political world is a game of winners and losers locked in relentless strife, and since the "other side" are rogues and will do anything to win, we are justified in being just as nasty as them in order to win. The famous "Plumbers" office in the basement of the Nixon White House, consisting of those assigned to conduct break-ins, dirty tricks, and the like, had a sign that paraphrased Lombardi: "Winning in politics isn't everything, it's the only thing."

The sportsmanship theme is explicitly stated in political rhetoric, but the winning theme, by emphasis, implicitly suggests to us the necessity of aggressiveness, cunning, and even violence. In areas such as business and politics, the sports metaphor reflects the tension we feel about these two values. In business, for example, we believe that pursuit of material goals all should be bound by the competitive rules of capitalism and moral rules derived from, say, religion; but we also recognize and even admire the business sharpie who makes lots of money by circumventing the rules, participating in underhanded and even illegal deals, and perhaps even using intimidation and violence. Our fascination with the super-rich, instant millionaires, and gangsters stems in part from the popular belief that one cannot make it without being a scoundrel. Similarly, it has been widely believed since Machiavelli that one cannot acquire and use power unless you are not bound by moral rules. Since politics, like sports, is a mean and competitive world, the winners have to be equal to the task. Getting the "material" of power and prestige in politics requires violating morality. Like the Godfather, you have to make people offers they can't refuse.

In American culture, our attitudes toward the conflicting values have roots in the worldview termed social Darwinism. As a metaphor drawn from the theory of evolution, the Social Darwinists argued that business and politics were hard struggles in which the fittest survived and dominated. For this viewpoint, sports offers evidence that life is like that, and thus politics is by necessity that way. Therefore, we want people in charge who use power less bound by moral restraints. But if we take the more "civilized" view of this sportsmanship motif, business and politics, like sports, should be tamed and made fair. For the political rhetorician, sports offers analogies of both motifs, although the "winning" ethic is usually not blatantly said. In any case, it is an indication of a tension in our attitude toward American politics as to which sports metaphor we think most applicable to politics.

Sports as a Dramatic Microcosm of Political Conflicts

The old saw has it that sports reflect society. If sports is a mirror of our conflicts, certainly when our divisions are politicized, sports become a dramatic microcosm of political conflicts. If groups experience material or moral lapses, they may be dramatized on the playing field. We have already mentioned how the post-World War II civil rights revolution was reflected in sports. Many other domestic conflicts work their way into sports. For example, it is nowadays popularly thought that America is a society of litigants eternally suing each other. Certainly this is reflected in sports, which involves a great deal of litigation over the status of players, franchises, fans, the media, and so on. If Americans think that as a people we spend a great deal of time in court, they certainly are reinforced in that view by reading the sports page.

Perhaps the most spectacular way in which sports come to be infested with politics involves international political conflicts. It is no secret that international sports — the Olympics, international track and field meets, even professional sports — often become embroiled in political controversies between nations.

The quadrennial Olympic games are the most important dramatic forum with political overtones. Nations are interested in "proving" the superiority of their political values by success at the Olympic games. The Nazis tried to prove the superiority of the "Aryan race" at the 1936 Olympics, but the dramatic scenario backfired somewhat by the success of American black runners.

But the most memorable recent incident involving the United States occurred at the 1980 Winter Olympics. In late 1979, in an already volatile Middle East following the Iranian Revolution and the hostage crisis, the Soviet Union invaded Afghanistan. This was the culmination of a complex series of political events that signified the crisis of "détente" between the United States and the Soviet Union, and brought the world into one of those periods of international tension. Further, it was an election year in the United States, which made the role of American public opinion all the more crucial in the crisis. It became politically important for President Carter to respond to these developments, given the chauvinistic and retributive mood of the country. So he dispatched the fleet, agitated for Persian Gulf resistance to Soviet expansion, and cut off the shipment of some trade materials to the Russians.

An international sporting event conducted in the midst of a political crisis, can take on an intensely patriotic flavor, and, if victorious, people can feel as if through play they have "won" some sort of political victory. It focuses political emotion onto the drama of the game, and thus gives us deep patriotic pride. Politicians and the news media recognized the political significance of the event, and gave it great play.

Sports as a Political Resource

Since sports are valued popular play-activities, it is common for politicians to use sports and sports figures for a wide variety of political purposes. Like religion and show business, sports offer the politician association with something non-political that large numbers of people are attracted to. Not only do politicians use the rhetoric of sports for political purposes, they also express their interest in sports to dramatize their commonality. Candidates campaigning for office attend sporting events, mention the local team, and seek the endorsement of famous athletes. Endorsement-seeking illustrates how politics seeks out popular culture. The endorsement of a famous athlete somehow gives the aspiring politician a kind of popular status and humanity he might not earn otherwise. The athlete is an embodiment of both material and moral success on the playing field, and the politician seems to think that with the association some of the heroic magic might rub off. All this is nothing new: both Al Smith and Herbert Hoover sought the endorsement of Babe Ruth in 1928! But it doesn't always work. Gerald Ford had an endless list of athletes who endorsed him in 1976, but he lost the election anyway. Ford and other politicians have been accused of being "jocksniffers," zealously exploiting their relationship to athletes and athletics, but the transfer of magic is not guaranteed.

President Carter did not appear to be a jocksniffer, but he was aware of the political uses of participation in sports. He cultivated his Southern regional tie, including hunting, fishing, and wading in hip-boots for bait. He reigned over slow-pitch softball games between the White House staff and the press. He became the First Jogger, and was photographed jogging in long distance races with troops in Korea. President Reagan liked to ride, and professed himself a sports fan. (Many older Americans associated him with sports through his depiction of "The Gipper," since he played Notre Dame's famous George Gipp in *Knute Rockne of Notre Dame* as well as baseball pitcher Grover Cleveland Alexander in *The Winning Team*.) It is always difficult to tell the extent to which sports participation by politicians stems from their desire to stay healthy and enjoy strenuous activity, or from their awareness that such activities are popular, and by participating they communicate to the public their common human interest. In any case, most recent Presidents have cultivated some form of popular leisure activity—golf, touch-football, sailing, etc. However, if some of the recent revelations about President John Kennedy's "favorite leisure activity" are true, then it must be said that although golf and jogging have their virtues as sports, so does his, although the former type is most politically acceptable and performable in public.

Since sports figures do become popular embodiments of heroic success, the celebrity status they enjoy can become a resource for successful political recruitment. Having played college football or even some professional sport seems to have helped a wide variety of political figures, ranging from Ford to Supreme Court Justice Byron "Whizzer" White (a former All-American) and former baseball pitcher and House member Wilmer "Vinegar Bend" Mizell. Former NBA star Bill Bradley became Senator from New Jersey at least partially on his sports celebrity. Congressman Jack Kemp of New York ran for Congress in the city he was an NFL quarterback, stressed how quarterbacking gave him leadership qualities, and used the rhetoric of football for political purposes. It may be the case in the future that more politicians will be drawn from the ranks of well-known sports figures.

Conclusion

We have not exhausted the complex relationships between popular sports and political culture, but the above should give the reader the idea of some of the major linkages. As long as Americans are sports crazy, we should expect that sports will have political relevance, and that "the game of politics" will be conducted in a culture that includes sports as a value.

Notes

1. **General Patton:** George Smith Patton Jr. (1885—1945) was a General of the United States Army who commanded the US Seventh Army in the Mediterranean theater of World War II, and the US Third Army in France and Germany following the Allied invasion of Normandy in June 1944.
2. "We won **letters**, were cheerleaders and pompom girls, went to the school games." (Para. 4) letter: *n.* an emblem in the shape of the initial of a school awarded for outstanding performance, especially in varsity athletics.
3. **The Pledge of Allegiance:** The Pledge of Allegiance of the United States is an expression of allegiance to the flag of the United States and the republic of the United States of America.
4. **School spirit** (Para.7): emotional support for one's educational institution. Members of a school can manifest spirit in the exhibition of school colors in dress and decoration, in attendance at athletic events, or verbally in the form of chants or cheers. This definition of school spirit is closely associated with good sportsmanship among students and their families at sporting events and is loosely based upon encouraging each other.

Unit 9 Jockpop: Popular Sports and Politics

5. **Color guard:** found in most American colleges, universities, high schools, and independent drum corps. Color guard uses props, such as flags and rifles, along with movement, to express dynamic passages in the music accompanying the marching band show. Usually marching bands and color guards perform during football games at halftime, out of tradition. During marching band competitions, the guard adds to the overall score of the band and is also judged in a category usually called auxiliary.

6. **Green Berets:** In the US armed forces, the green beret may be worn only by soldiers awarded the Special Forces Tab, signifying they have been qualified as Special Forces (SF) soldiers. US Special Forces wear the green beret as a distinction of excellence and uniqueness within the Army.

7. **Frank Merriwell:** a fictional character appearing in a series of novels and short stories by Gilbert Patten, who wrote under the pseudonym Burt L. Standish. The model for all later American juvenile sports fiction, Merriwell excelled at football, baseball, basketball, crew and track at Yale while solving mysteries and righting wrongs. He played with great strength and received traumatic blows without injury.

8. **Lambardi:** Vincent Thomas Lombardi (1913—1970) was an American football player, coach, and executive in the National Football League (NFL).

9. **Durocher:** Leo Ernest Durocher (1905—1991), was an American professional baseball player, manager and coach. A controversial and outspoken character, Durocher had a stormy career dogged by clashes with authority, the baseball commissioner, umpires and the press.

10. **Machivalli:** Niccolò di Bernardo dei Machiavelli (1469—1527) was an Italian diplomat, politician, historian, philosopher, humanist, writer, playwright and poet of the Renaissance period. He has often been called the father of modern political science.

11. **Al Smith** (1873—1944)**:** an American statesman who was elected Governor of New York four times and was the Democratic US presidential candidate in 1928. Smith lost in a landslide to Republican Herbert Hoover.

12. **Herbert Hoover** (1874—1964)**:** the 31st President of the United States (1929—1933).

13. **Babe Ruth:** George Herman Ruth Jr. (1895—1948) was an American professional baseball player. Ruth is regarded as one of the greatest sports heroes in American culture and is considered by many to be the greatest baseball player of all time. He was one of the first five inductees into the National Baseball Hall of Fame in 1936.

14. **Gerald Ford** (1913—2006)**:** an American politician who served as the 38th President of the United States from 1974 to 1977. Prior to this he was the 37th Vice President of the United States, serving from 1973 until President Richard Nixon's resignation in

Readings on American Culture and Society

1974. He was the first person appointed to the vice presidency under the terms of the 25th Amendment, following the resignation of Vice President Spiro Agnew on October 10, 1973. Becoming president upon Richard Nixon's departure on August 9, 1974, he claimed the distinction as the first and to date the only person to have served as both Vice President and President of the United States without being elected to either office.

15. **George Gipp** (1895—1920)**:** nicknamed "The Gipper", was a college football player at the University of Notre Dame under head coach Knute Rockne. Gipp was selected as Notre Dame's first Walter Camp All-American, and played several positions, particularly halfback, quarterback, and punter. Gipp died at age 25 of a streptococcal throat infection and pneumonia, three weeks after a win over Northwestern in his senior season, and was the subject of Rockne's "Win just one for the Gipper" speech. In the 1940 film *Knute Rockne, All American*, he was portrayed by Ronald Reagan.

16. **Knute Rockne:** Knute Kenneth Rockne (1888—1931) was a Norwegian-American football player and coach at the University of Notre Dame. Rockne is regarded as one of the greatest coaches in college football history.

17. *Knute Rockne, All American* is a 1940 American biographical film which tells the story of Knute Rockne, Notre Dame football coach. It stars Pat O'Brien portraying the role of Rockne and Ronald Reagan as player George Gipp, a.k.a. "The Gipper."

18. *The Winning Team*: It is a 1952 biographical film directed by Lewis Seiler. It is a fictionalized biography of the life of major league pitcher Grover Cleveland Alexander (1887—1950) starring Ronald Reagan as Alexander.

19. **All-American:** players selected for an All-America sports team. An All-America team is a hypothetical American sports team composed of outstanding amateur players. These players are broadly considered by media and other relevant commentators as the best players in a particular sport, of a specific season, for each team position. Such athletes at the high school and college level are given the honorific title and typically referred to as "All-American athletes" or simply "All-Americans."

Vocabulary

1. microcosm ['maɪkrokɑzəm]: *n.* a small group, society, or place that has the same qualities as a much larger one 缩影；微观世界
2. color guard: *n.* a group of people who carry flags in an official ceremony 护旗队
3. invocation [ˌɪnvə(ʊ)'keɪʃ(ə)n]: *n.* a speech or prayer at the beginning of a ceremony or meeting 祈祷

Unit 9 Jockpop: Popular Sports and Politics

4. deference ['def(ə)r(ə)ns]: *n.* polite behaviour that shows that you respect someone and are therefore willing to accept their opinions or judgment   遵从；尊重

5. ensue [ɪn'sjuː; en-]: *v.* to happen after or as a result of something   跟着发生

6. pageantry ['pædʒ(ə)ntrɪ]: *n.* impressive and colorful events and ceremonies involving a lot of people wearing special clothes   壮观的场面；重大的仪式

7. skit [skɪt]: *n.* a short humorous performance or piece of writing   小品

8. permeate ['pɜːmɪeɪt]: *vt.* (of an idea, an influence, a feeling, etc.) to affect every part of   （思想、影响、感情等）感染；传播

9. repository [rɪ'pɒzɪt(ə)rɪ]: *n.* a place or container in which large quantities of something are stored   知识库

10. analogy [ə'nælədʒɪ]: *n.* something that seems similar between two situations, processes etc.   类比

11. allegory ['ælɪg(ə)rɪ]: *n.* a story, painting etc. in which the events and characters represent ideas or teach a moral lesson   寓言

12. parable ['pærəb(ə)l]: *n.* a short simple story that teaches a moral or religious lesson, especially one of the stories told by Jesus in the Bible   格言，寓言

13. tenet ['tɛnɪt]: *n.* one of the principles or beliefs that a theory or larger set of beliefs is based on   原则；信条

14. magnanimity [ˌmægnə'nɪmɪti]: *n.* being kind, generous and forgiving, especially towards an enemy or a rival   宽宏；大度

15. smack [smæk]: *vi.* to give an indication; be suggestive. Often used with *of*   暗示

16. motif [mɔː'tiəuf]: *n.* a subject, an idea or a phrase that is repeated and developed in a work of literature or a piece of music   （文学作品或音乐的）主题，主旨

17. circumvent [sɜːkəm'vent]: *vt.* to avoid a problem or rule that restricts you, especially in a clever or dishonest way   避开

18. saw [sɔː]: *n.* a short phrase or sentence that states a general truth about life or gives advice   谚语；格言

19. lapse [læps]: *n.* an example or period of bad behavior from somebody who normally behave well   行为失检

20. infest [ɪn'fɛst]: *vt.* to exist in large numbers in a particular place   大批出没于

21. embroil [ɪm'brɔɪl]: *vt.* to involve in an argument or a difficult situation   使陷入纠纷或困境

22. chauvinistic [ˌʃəʊvɪ'nɪstɪk]: *adj.* holding an aggressive and unreasonable belief that one's country is better than others   沙文主义者的

23. dispatch [dɪ'spætʃ]: *vt.* to send somebody/something somewhere, especially for a special purpose 派遣
24. accord [ə'kɔːd]: *vt.* to give someone or something special attention or a particular type of treatment 给与
25. recruit [rɪ'kruːt]: *vt.* to persuade someone to do something for you. recruitment: *n.* 鼓动
26. cultivate ['kʌltɪveɪt]: *vt.* to try hard to develop an attitude, image or skill and make it stronger or better 磨练；陶冶

Expressions

1. I would<u>n't give a hoot</u> in hell for a man who lost and laughed.
   don't give a hoot/don't care two hoots: to not care at all about someone or something 对……全然漠视

2. One may wonder what sorts of feelings playing the national anthem before a game <u>conjures up</u> in our breasts.
   conjure something up: to bring a thought, picture, idea, or memory to someone's mind. 使呈现于脑际

3. Politicians like to <u>draw upon</u> familiar symbols to illustrate some political point, and sports offer familiar and widely used metaphors.
   draw upon/on something: to make use of one's skill or experience in order to do something. 利用；凭借

4. It is no secret that international sports—the Olympics, international track and field meets, even professional sports—often <u>become embroiled in</u> political controversies between nations.
   be/become embroiled in: to cause (oneself or another) to join in an argument or other difficult situation 使（自己或他人）卷入纠纷

5. The athlete is an embodiment of both material and moral success on the playing field, and the politician seems to think that with the association some of the heroic magic might <u>rub off</u>.
   rub off: If a feeling, quality, or habit rubs off on you, you start to have it because you are with another person who has it. 因相处而对……产生影响

Comprehension

I. Discuss the Main Point and the Meanings.

1. How important is sports in our life? Why isn't popular sports "just a game"?

2. How can sports dramatize our life?

3. What are the political meanings and uses of sports in American life?

4. What is the ideal of sportsmanship?

II. Fill in the blanks with the appropriate words or expressions from the box below.

enactment	fair	finish	participate
non-political	orient	the only thing	identify
quit	the bounds of rules		

1. Quitters never win, and winners never _____.

2. The "lessons of sports" help to _____ us to the world and give us much learning about life, and even politics.

3. The game becomes a public arena for the _____ of the more interesting aspects of human life—competition, teamwork, risk-taking, aggression and defense, winning and losing.

4. Sports, like popular drama, dramatizes exemplary situations with which we can _____.

5. Sports involve the affirmation of cultural myths, since sports "_____" in the social order.

6. The ideal of sportsmanship has persisted in political rhetoric as a norm by which the game is supposed to be played, i.e., that one plays _____, enjoys the contest, and accepts victory with magnanimity and defeat with grace.

7. Sportsmanship, on the field or in politics, consists of such attitudes as tolerating and honoring the opposition; being a gracious winner and loser; and playing "the game of politics" within _____ and fair play.

8. Winning isn't everything, goes Lombardi's Law, it's _____.

9. Nice guys, Durocher's Dictum has it, _____ last.

10. Like religion and show business, sports offer the politician association with something _____ that large numbers of people are attracted to.

Structure

I. Find out how the words and expressions in bold are used in the following sentences.

1. And what effect did it all have on us? **Specifically** here, what impact does the play-world of sports have on politics?

2. Sports is a form of play which we **early on** learn is important, come to value, and link to "real life."

3. The root of this **may well** be in the fact that sports *are* dramatic.

4. Whether consciously or not, the "lessons of sports" help to **orient** us to the world.

5. We will consider this **in turn**.

6. Remember that we have **stressed** the ways that popular culture is a political teacher.

7. We all **recall** the invocations given before games, the players all praying in the huddle, and singing "God Bless America."

8. Such rituals may **ring** hollow for many people.

9. Politicians like to **draw upon** familiar symbols to **illustrate** some political point.

10. **In particular**, sports can illustrate the "truth" of either moralistic or materialistic myths.

11. However, such virtues can be **variously** interpreted.

12. The ideal of sportsmanship has **persisted in** political rhetoric as a norm by which the game is supposed to be played.

13. The famous "Plumbers" office in the basement of the Nixon White House, consists of those assigned to conduct break-ins, dirty tricks, **and the like**.

14. Our fascination with the super-rich, instant millionaires, and gangsters **stems** in part **from** the popular belief that one cannot make it without being a scoundrel.

15. Since politics, like sports, is a mean and competitive world, the winners have to **be equal to** the task.

16. We want people **in charge** who use power less bound by moral restraints.

17. So he dispatched the fleet, agitated for Persian Gulf resistance to Soviet expansion, and **cut off** the shipment of some trade materials to the Russians.

18. The endorsement of a famous athlete somehow gives the aspiring politician a kind of popular status and humanity he might not earn **otherwise**.

19. Ford and other politicians **have been accused of** being "jocksniffers."

20. We have not **exhausted** the complex relationships between popular sports and political culture, but the above should give the reader the idea of some of the major linkages.

II. Complete the following sentences with some of the above words or expressions in bold.

1. Soldiers, policemen, _____ were all called in to help with the emergency.

2. You know what this is about. Why pretend _____.

3. Our students _____ toward science subjects.

4. Her confession _____ be a lie, but her original story certainly is.

5. Now do you _____ that song I taught you?

Unit 9   Jockpop: Popular Sports and Politics

6. This is one reason why bad habits need to be stopped as _____ as possible, before they have been repeated too many times.

7. *The Reagans* condemned the book, which was _____ believed and disbelieved by critics and insiders.

8. Mary had to give a speech in front of all the staff, but she proved quite _____ the situation.

9. The newspaper, or more _____, the editor, was taken to court for publishing the photographs.

10. The children call out their names _____.

11. The novelist _____ heavily _____ her personal experiences.

12. She directed the question at no one _____.

13. Don't give up until you _____ all the possibilities.

14. He asked to speak to the person _____.

15. The government has threatened to _____ economic and military aid to this region.

→ Sports in the United States

According to different surveys (including ESPN's survey, the Nielson TV ratings), football is the most popular sport in the United States. But baseball used to be king. Baseball has been replaced by football as America's national pastime. It shows a change in the American national character, states Jeffrey Schrank in his article "Sport and the American Dream." Professor John Finlay of the University of Manitoba, writing in Queen's Quarterly, compares baseball to an acting out of the robber baron stage of capitalism, whereas football more clearly reflects a more mature capitalism. According to Jeffrey Schrank, they reflect different national characters because of their different characteristics. Baseball is a pastoral sport, timeless and highly ritualized. It is a game in which less action is needed, and aggression is subservient to finesse. It is a more leisurely world. Football is a game in which men are engaged in constant frenzied action to gain territory. Time is crucial in that game. American football is passionately concerned with the gain and loss of territory.

Not only do sports reflect national character, national values and wishes, different sports carry different class connotations. Certain sports — especially golf, tennis, swimming, sailing, and collegiate football — were regarded as the recreational prerogatives of upper-class life, leisure-time activities for a leisure class, while professional boxing has offered a way out of poverty for generations of working-class immigrant-athletes. For the inhering class, to play for money was déclassé, something that the lower orders might do. It was everything that the upper-class amateur ideal might sought to avoid.

But the cultural significance of sports has changed dramatically over the years. American sport now has become the commercial entertainment. Professional athletes have become highly paid entertainers who perform for passive, nonparticipating audiences. The amateur ideal only "lingers on today in the realm of collegiate athletics, where, while it is not defended along social class lines, it has still kindled a firestorm of controversy at a time when every other athletic venue—from the Olympics to Wimbledon—has opened its gates to professional athletes.

Baseball

For generations, baseball has been called "America's national pastime". Baseball has come to be seen as a defining part of the American culture, an enduring tie born from a diverse and sprawling young country. Baseball is considered part of the American spirit. Books, songs, movies, plays, poems and lots of baseball terms have become part of the American experience.

Baseball is the second most popular sport in the USA now and it has a completely different atmosphere than football. It is a game of intense concentration and the near perfect execution of playing skill. Attending a baseball game might start with a tailgate party that resembles a family picnic followed by several hours of relaxed socializing with friends while watching the game. And it is a fantastic way to meet the locals and experience American sports culture.

Baseball is a bat-and-ball game played between two opposing teams who take turns batting and fielding. The game proceeds when a player on the fielding team, called the pitcher, throws a ball which a player on the batting team tries to hit with a bat. The objectives of the offensive team (batting team) are to hit the ball into the field of play, and to run the bases—having its runners advance counter-clockwise around four bases to score what are called "runs". The objective of the defensive team (fielding team) is to prevent batters from becoming runners, and to prevent runners' advance around the bases. A run is scored when a runner legally advances around the bases in order and touches home plate (the place where the player started as a batter). The team that scores the most runs by the end of the game is the winner.

The first objective of the batting team is to have a player reach first base safely. A player on the batting team who reaches first base without being called "out" can attempt to advance to subsequent bases as a runner, either immediately or during teammates' turns batting. The fielding team tries to prevent runs by getting batters or runners "out," which forces them out of the field of play. Both the pitcher and fielders have methods of getting the batting team's players out. The opposing teams switch back and forth between batting and fielding; the batting team's turn to bat is over once the fielding team records three outs. One turn batting for each team constitutes an inning. A game is usually composed of nine innings, and the team with the greater number of runs at the end of the game wins. If scores are tied at the end of nine innings, extra innings are usually played. Baseball has no game clock, although most games end in the ninth inning.

The number of players on a baseball roster, or *squad*, varies by league and by the level of organized play. A Major League Baseball team has a roster of 25 players with specific roles. A typical roster features the following players:

- Eight position players: the catcher, four infielders, and three outfielders—all of whom play on a regular basis
- Five starting pitchers who constitute the team's pitching rotation or starting rotation
- Six relief pitchers, including one closer, who constitute the team's bullpen (named for the off-field area where pitchers warm up)
- One backup, or substitute, catcher
- Two backup infielders
- Two backup outfielders
- One pinch hitter, or a second backup catcher, or a seventh reliever

MLB

Major League Baseball is the highest level of baseball played in the US and the richest professional baseball league in the world. There are 30 Major League baseball teams divided into the National League and the American League, each of which is further divided into three divisions: East, Central, and West. Thirty major-league teams are spread across the US in twenty-seven cities. Each team plays about 160 games on weekday evenings or weekend afternoons between early spring and late fall. The regular season begins at the beginning of April, and ends in October.

World Series

Every October, the leaders of each of the three divisions plus a Wild Card team (the best second-place team in the league) from each league will compete to play in the World Series championship. The World Series pits the winner of the National League playoffs against the winner of the American League playoffs.

Football

American football is the most popular spectator sport in the United States. It is a combat game where highly trained athletes skillfully and brutally execute strategic plans. Attending a football game often begins with a "tailgate party" in the parking lot of the stadium followed by several hours of rowdy, emotionally charged excitement. Most fans watch football while gathered in a local bar or at a friend's home in front of a big-screen TV. It also has the most participants of any sport at both high school and college levels.

The objective of the game is to score points by advancing the ball into the opposing team's end zone. The ball can be advanced by running with it or throwing it to a teammate. Points can be scored by carrying the ball over the opponent's goal line, catching a pass thrown over that goal line, kicking the ball through the opponent's goal posts or tackling an opposing ball carrier in his own end zone.

A football game is played between two teams of 11 players each. Playing with more on the field is punishable by a penalty. Teams may substitute any number of their players between downs; this "platoon" system replaced the original system, which featured limited substitution rules, and has resulted in teams utilizing specialized offensive, defensive and special teams squads.

Individual players in a football game must be designated with a uniform number between 1 and 99. NFL teams are required to number their players by a league-approved numbering system, and any exceptions must be approved by the Commissioner. NCAA and NFHS teams are "strongly advised" to number their offensive players according to a league-suggested numbering scheme.

Offensive unit

The role of the offensive unit is to advance the football down the field with the ultimate goal of scoring a touchdown.

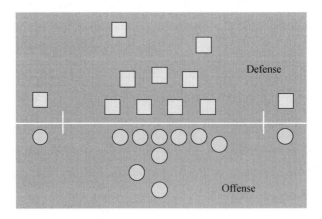

Above is a diagram of a typical pre-snap formation. The offense is lined up in a variation of the I formation, while the defense is lined up in the 4—3 defense. Both formations are legal.

The offensive team must line up in a legal formation before they can snap the ball. An offensive formation is considered illegal if there are more than four players in the backfield or fewer than five players numbered 50—79 on the offensive line. Players can temporarily line up in a position whose eligibility is different from what their number permits as long as they immediately report the change to the referee, who then informs the defensive team of the change. Neither team's players, with the exception of the snapper, are allowed to line up in or cross the neutral zone until the ball is snapped. Interior offensive linemen are not allowed to move until the snap of the ball.

The following is the I-formation of the offense:

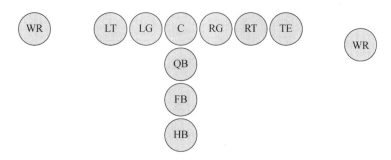

The main backfield positions are the quarterback (QB), halfback/tailback (HB/TB) and fullback (FB). The quarterback is the leader of the offense. Either the quarterback or a coach calls the plays. Quarterbacks typically inform the rest of the offense of the play in the huddle before the team lines up. The quarterback lines up behind the center to take the snap and then hands the ball off, throws it or runs with it.

The primary role of the halfback, also known as the running back or tailback, is to carry the ball on running plays. Halfbacks may also serve as receivers. Fullbacks tend to be larger than halfbacks and function primarily as blockers, but they are sometimes used as runners in short-yardage situations and are seldom used in passing situations.

The offensive line (OL) consists of several players whose primary function is to block members of the defensive line from tackling the ball carrier on running plays or sacking the quarterback on passing plays. The leader of the offensive line is the center (C), who is responsible for snapping the ball to the quarterback, blocking, and for making sure that the other linemen do their jobs during the play. On either side of the center are the guards (G), while tackles (T) line up outside the guards.

The principal receivers are the wide receivers (WR) and the tight ends (TE). Wide receivers line up on or near the line of scrimmage, split outside the line. The main goal of the wide receiver is to catch passes thrown by the quarterback, but they may also function as decoys or as blockers during running plays. Tight ends line up outside the tackles and function both as receivers and as blockers.

Defensive unit

The role of the defense is to prevent the offense from scoring by tackling the ball carrier or by forcing turnovers (interceptions or fumbles).

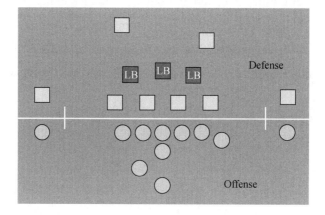

The defensive line (DL) consists of defensive ends (DE) and defensive tackles (DT). Defensive ends line up on the ends of the line, while defensive tackles line up inside, between the defensive ends. The primary responsibilities of defensive ends and defensive tackles is to stop running plays on the outside and inside, respectively, to pressure the quarterback on passing plays, and to occupy the line so that the linebackers can break through.

Linebackers line up behind the defensive line but in front of the defensive backfield. They are divided into two types: middle linebackers (MLB) and outside linebackers (OLB). Linebackers are the defensive leaders and call the defensive plays. Their diverse roles include defending the run, pressuring the quarterback, and guarding backs, wide receivers and tight ends in the passing game.

The defensive backfield, often called the secondary, consists of cornerbacks (CB) and safeties (S). Safeties are themselves divided into free safeties (FS) and strong safeties (SS). Cornerbacks line up outside the defensive formation, typically opposite of a receiver so as to be able to cover him, while safeties line up between the cornerbacks but farther back in the secondary. Safeties are the last line of defense, and are responsible for stopping deep passing plays as well as running plays.

Special teams unit

The special teams unit is responsible for all kicking plays. The special teams unit of the team in control of the ball will try to execute field goal (FG) attempts, punts and kickoffs, while the opposing team's unit will aim to block or return them.

Unit 9 Jockpop: Popular Sports and Politics

Three positions are specific to the field goal and PAT (point-after-touchdown) unit: the placekicker (K or PK), holder (H) and long snapper (LS). The long snapper's job is to snap the football to the holder, who will catch and position it for the placekicker. There is not usually a holder on kickoffs, because the ball is kicked off of a tee; however, a holder may be used in certain situations, such as if wind is preventing the ball from remaining upright on the tee. The player on the receiving team who catches the ball is known as the kickoff returner (KR).

The positions specific to punt plays are the punter (P), long snapper, upback and gunner. The long snapper snaps the football directly to the punter, who then drops and kicks it before it hits the ground. Gunners line up split outside the line and race down the field, aiming to tackle the punt returner (PR) — the player that catches the punt. Upbacks line up a short distance behind the line of scrimmage, providing additional protection to the punter.

The violence of football has always been a matter of concern and the sport has seen periodic attempts at safety and reform. For Buzz Bissinger, *"Violence is not only embedded in football; it is the very celebration of it. It is why we like it. Take it away, continue efforts to curtail the savagery, and the game will be nothing, regardless of age or skill."* He declared in his Daily Beast column in 1988, with a strong sense that the priorities of football culture were warped. Tiki Barber, the former Giants running back, and a man who boasted, in his playing days, of listening to the BBC, voiced a surprisingly similar sentiment. "They can't try to do more," he said. *"They can't afford to change what it is: an aggressively fast, physically brutal game."*

NFL

The National Football League (NFL) is the preeminent professional league in the United States. The NFL consists of 32 teams that are divided into two conferences: the American Football Conference (AFC) and the National Football Conference (NFC), each of which has four divisions. The NFL season is played during the late summer, through autumn, and into January. Professional teams play 4 exhibition games, followed by 16 regular-season games. Teams play one game each week, using the time between games to recover, practice, and prepare for the next game. Each team receives one week without a game, known as a bye, during the season.

At the end of the regular season, each conference holds separate playoff games to determine the conference champion. The top team in each division automatically qualifies for the conference playoffs. Two additional teams in each conference, called wild cards, also qualify for playoff berths based on their win-loss record in the conference. During the first round of the playoffs, the wild-card teams play the lowest-ranked division champions. The top two division winners in each league have byes during the first round. The losers are eliminated and the winners advance to play one of the remaining division champions in the semifinals. Semifinal winners advance to the conference finals, and the winner of that game is declared the conference champion.

Super Bowl

The Super Bowl is the championship game of the National Football League where the champion of the National Football Conference competes against the champion of the American Football Conference. The Super Bowl uses Roman numerals to identify each game, rather than the year in which it is held. For example, Super Bowl I was played in 1967 to determine the championship of the regular season played in 1966.

The day on which the Super Bowl is played is now considered a *de facto* American national holiday, called "Super Bowl Sunday." It is the second-largest day for US food consumption, after Thanksgiving Day. In most years, the Super Bowl is the most-watched American television broadcast. The Super Bowl final is among the most watched sporting events in the world, primarily due to mostly North American audiences, and is second to the UEFA Champions League final as the most watched annual sporting event worldwide.

Because of its high viewership, commercial airtime during the Super Bowl broadcast is the most expensive of the year. Due to the high cost of investing in advertising on the Super Bowl, companies regularly develop their most expensive advertisements for this broadcast. As a result, watching and discussing the broadcast's commercials has become a significant aspect of the event. In addition, many popular singers and musicians have performed during the event's pre-game and halftime ceremonies because of the exposure.

Basketball

Basketball is a pastime of the urban poor. The current generation of black athletes are heirs to a tradition half a century old: In a neighborhood without the money for bats, gloves, hockey sticks, tennis rackets, or shoulder pads, basketball is accessible. That is why American professional basketball is dominated by black athletes. Two-thirds of the players are black. The Most Valuable Player award of the National Basketball Association often goes to the black athletes.

And the mark on basketball of today's players is a question of style. Most simply (remembering we are talking about culture, not chromosomes,) "black" basketball is the use of superb athletic skill to adapt to the limits of space imposed by the game. "White" ball is the pulverization of that space by sheer intensity. "White" ball, then, is the basketball of patience and method. "Black" ball is the basketball of electric self-expression.

Unit 9 Jockpop: Popular Sports and Politics

Basketball is a team sport in which two teams, most commonly of five players each, opposing one another on a rectangular court, compete with the primary objective of shooting a basketball through the defender's hoop while preventing the opposing team from shooting through their own hoop. A field goal is worth two points, unless made from behind the three-point line, when it is worth three. After a foul, timed play stops and the player fouled or designated to shoot a technical foul is given one or more one-point free throws. The team with the most points at the end of the game wins, but if regulation play expires with the score tied, an additional period of play (overtime) is mandated.

Players advance the ball by bouncing it while walking or running (dribbling) or by passing it to a teammate, both of which require considerable skill. On offense, players may use a variety of shots—the lay-up, the jump shot, or a dunk; on defense, they may steal the ball from a dribbler, intercept passes, or block shots; either offense or defense may collect a rebound, that is, a missed shot that bounces from rim or backboard. It is a violation to lift or drag one's pivot foot without dribbling the ball, to carry it, or to hold the ball with both hands then resume dribbling.

The five players on each side at a time fall into five playing positions: the tallest player is usually the center, the tallest and strongest is the power forward, a slightly shorter but more agile big man is the small forward, and the shortest players or the best ball handlers are the shooting guard and the point guard, who implements the coach's game plan by managing the execution of offensive and defensive plays (player positioning). Informally, players may play three-on-three, two-on-two, and one-on-one.

NBA

The National Basketball Association, more popularly known as the NBA, is the world's premier men's professional basketball league and one of the major professional sports leagues of North America. It contains 30 teams (29 teams in the US and 1 in Canada) that play an 82-game season from November to April. After the regular season, eight teams from each conference compete in the playoffs for the Larry O'Brien Championship Trophy.

......

The extent in the United States to which sports are associated with secondary and tertiary education is rare among nations. Millions of students participate in athletics programs operated by high schools and colleges. Especially in basketball and football, high school and particularly college sports are followed with a fervor equaling or exceeding that felt for professional sports. Student-athletes often receive scholarships to colleges in recognition of their athletic potential.

Currently, the largest governing body of collegiate sports is the National Collegiate Athletic Association (NCAA). High school and college sports fill the development role that in many other countries would be the place of youth teams associated with clubs.

All American sports leagues use the same type of schedule. After the regular season, the 8—16 teams with the best records enter a playoff tournament leading to a championship series or game.

International competition is not as important in American sports as it is in the sporting culture of most other countries, although Olympic ice-hockey and basketball tournaments do generate attention.

Sports have been a major part of American broadcasting since the early days of radio. Today, television networks pay millions of dollars for the rights to broadcast sporting events. Contracts between leagues and broadcasters stipulate how often games must be interrupted for commercials. Because of all of the advertisements, broadcasting contracts are very lucrative and account for the biggest chunk of pro teams' revenues.

The advent of cable and satellite television has greatly expanded sports offerings on American TV. ESPN, the first all-sports cable network in the US, went on the air in 1979. It has been followed by several sister networks and competitors. There are also many American sports magazines, the best-known being *Sports Illustrated*.

Vocabulary of Sports

1. **The Little League** gave us an opportunity to play.

2. We attempted to **bat**, or **dribble**, or **pass** like them, even to act like them.

3. If we hung around **locker rooms** or played, we heard the slogans: "**Quitters never win, and winners never quit**."

4. We won letters, were **cheerleaders** and pompom girls, went to the school **games**.

5. The game becomes a public arena for the enactment of the more interesting aspects of human life—**competition**, **teamwork**, risk-taking, **aggression** and **defense**, **winning** and **losing**.

6. Both **coaches** and political figures seem to believe in the necessity of inspiration.

7. Let us illustrate this by reference to two often competing aspects of the sports creed: **sportsmanship** and winning.

8. Sports are good because they promote "**fair play**".

9. **Winning isn't everything, it's the only thing. Nice guys finish last.**

10. It is no secret that international sports—the **Olympics**, international track and field **meets**, even professional sports—often become embroiled in political controversies between nations.

11. The hockey **match** and the national outburst it caused was a dramatic microcosm of a political crisis.

12. Being a "**good sport**" was a trait admirable in all areas of life.

13. The "truth" of sports was not whether one won or lost, but how you **played the game**.

14. The **amateur** ideal only "lingers on today in the realm of **collegiate athletics**, where, while it is not defended along social class lines, it has still kindled a firestorm of controversy at a time when every other **athletic venue**—from the Olympics to Wimbledon—has opened its gates to **professional athletes**.

15. American football is the most popular **spectator sport** in the United States.

16. The role of the **offensive** unit is to advance the football down the field with the ultimate goal of scoring a **touchdown**.

17. The ball can be advanced by running with it or throwing it to a **teammate**. **Points** can be **scored** by carrying the ball over the **opponent's goal line**, catching a pass thrown over that goal line, kicking the ball through the opponent's **goal posts** or **tackling** an opposing ball carrier in his own **end zone**.

18. The main backfield positions are the **quarterback, halfback/tailback** and **fullback**.

19. On either side of the center are the **guards**, while **tackles** line up outside the guards.

20. The principal receivers are the **wide receivers** and the **tight ends**.

21. **Linebackers** are the **defensive** leaders and call the defensive plays.

22. The objective of the defensive team (fielding team) is to prevent **batters** from becoming **runners**, and to prevent runners' advance around the **bases**. A **run** is scored when a runner legally advances around the bases in order and touches home plate.

23. A typical roster features eight position players: the **catcher**, four **infielders** and three **outfielders**. It also has five starting **pitchers**.

24. The batting team's turn to bat is over once the fielding team records three **outs**. One turn batting for each team constitutes an **inning**.

25. The primary objective is to shoot a basketball through the defender's **hoop**.

26. A **field goal** is worth two points, unless made from behind the **three-point line**, when it is worth three.

27. Players advance the ball by bouncing it while walking or running (**dribbling**) or by **passing** it to a teammate.

28. On offense, players may use a variety of shots—the **lay-up**, the **jump shot**, or a **dunk**.

29. The five players on each side at a time fall into five playing positions: the center, the **power forward**, the **small forward**, the **shooting guard** and the **point guard**.

30. Professional teams **play 4 exhibition games**, followed by 16 **regular-season** games.

31. The **losers** are eliminated and the **winners** advance to play one of the remaining **division** champions in the **semifinals**. Semifinal winners advance to the **conference finals**, and the winner of that game is declared the conference **champion**.

32. In a neighborhood without the money for **bats**, **gloves**, **hockey sticks**, **tennis rackets**, or **shoulder pads**, basketball is accessible.

33. After the **regular season**, eight **teams** from each conference **compete** in the **playoffs** for the Larry O'Brien **Championship Trophy**.

Unit 10 The Way We Are

Sydney Pollack

Six weeks ago, I thought I was going to be happy to be a part of this conference, which shows how naïve I am. The agenda—for me at least—is a mine field. Normally, I spend my time worrying about specific problems and not reflecting, as many of you on these panels do. So I've really thought about this, and I've talked to anyone who would listen. My colleagues are sick and tired of it, my wife has left for the country and even my agents—and these are people I pay—don't return my phone calls. By turn, I have felt myself stupid, unethical, a philistine, unpatriotic, a panderer, a cultural polluter, and stupid. And I've completely failed to solve your problems, except in one small way. You have delayed at least six weeks the possibility of my contributing further to the problems you see.

I know your concerns have to do with American values and whether those values are being upheld or assaulted by American entertainment—by what I and others like me do. But which values exactly?

In the thirties, forties, and fifties, six men in the Valley, immigrants really, ran the movie industry. Our society was vastly different. The language of the movies was a language of shared values. If you put forward a virtuousness on the part of your hero, everybody responded to it.

When Sergeant York, played by Gary Cooper, refused to endorse a breakfast cereal, knowing he'd been asked because he'd won the Medal of Honor, he said: "I ain't proud of what I've done. You don't make money off of killing people. That there is wrong." We expected him to behave that way.

But society's values have changed. That kind of scrupulous, ethical concern for the sanctity of human life doesn't exist in the same way, and that fact is reflected in the movies. There's a nostalgia now for some of the old values, but so many people embrace other expressions of values that it's hard to say these other expressions aren't reality.

Their idea of love, for example, is a different idea of love. It's a much less chaste, much less idealized love than was depicted in the earlier films. We are seeing some sort of return to the ideal of marriage. There was a decade or two when marriage really lost its popularity, and while young people are swinging toward it again, I don't believe one could say that values have not changed significantly since the thirties, forties, and fifties.

Morality, the definitions of virtue, justice, and injustice, the sanctity of the individual, have been fairly fluid for American audiences in terms of what they chose to embrace or not embrace.

Take a picture like *Dances with Wolves*. You could not have made it in the thirties or forties. It calls into question every value that existed in traditional Westerns. It may not reflect what everybody thinks now, but it expresses a lot of guilty re-evaluation of what happened in the West, the very things shown in the old Westerns that celebrated the frontiers.

If we got the movies to assert or talk about better values, would that fix our society? Well, let me quote Sam Goldwyn. When he was told by his staff how poorly his studio's new—and very expensive—film was doing, Sam thought a minute, shrugged, and said, "Listen, if they don't want to come, you can't stop them."

Now that's as close to a first principle of Hollywood as I can come. It informs everything that we're here to discuss and it controls every solution that we may propose.

Out of Hollywood

Before they can be anything else, American movies are a product. This is not good or bad, this is what we've got. A very few may become art, but all of them, whatever their ambition, are first financed as commodities. They're the work of craftsmen and artists, but they're soon offered for sale.

Whether we say that we're "creating a film" or merely "making a movie," the enterprise itself is sufficiently expensive and risky that it cannot be and it will not be, undertaken without the hope of reward. We have no Medicis here. It takes two distinct entities, the financiers and the makers, to produce movies, and there is a tension between them. Their goals are sometimes similar, but they do different things. Financiers are not in the business of philanthropy. They've got to answer to stockholders.

Of course, the controlling influence in filmmaking hasn't changed in 50 years: it still belongs to the consumer. That's the dilemma and, in my view, what we're finally talking about. What do you do about culture in a society that celebrates the common man but doesn't always like his taste?

If you operate in a democracy and you're market-supported and—driven, the spectrum of what you will get is going to be very wide indeed. It will range from trash to gems. There are 53,000 books published in this country every year. How many of them are really good? Tired as I may be of fast-food-recipe, conscienceless, simple-minded books, films, TV, and music, the question remains, Who is to be society's moral policeman?

Over the course of their first 30 or 40 years, the movies were a cottage industry, and the morality that was reflected in them was the morality of the early film pioneers. Now, film studios are tiny divisions of multinational corporations, and they feel the pressure for profits that happens in any other repeatable-product business. They look for a formula. Say you get the recipe for a soft drink and perfect it; once customers like it, you just repeat it and it will sell. More fortunes have been lost than made in the movie business pursuing such a formula, but unfortunately today, more junk than anything else is being made pursuing it. And film companies are folding like crazy. Since we are in the democracy business, we can't tell people what they should or shouldn't hear, or support, or see, so they make their choices. The market tries to cater to those choices, and we have what we have.

Making Films

Are American films bad? A lot of them surely are, and so are a lot of everybody else's, the way a lot of anything produced is bad—breakfast cereals, music, most chairs, architecture, mail-order shirts. There probably hasn't been a really beautiful rake since the Shakers stopped making farm implements. But that is no excuse.

I realize that I am a prime suspect here, but I'm not sure that you really understand how odd and unpredictable a business the making of films actually is. It just doesn't conform to the logic or rules of any other business. It's always been an uneasy merger of two antithetical things: some form of art and sheer commerce.

If the people who make films get the money that is invested in them back to the people who finance them, then they'll get to make more. We know that the business of films is to reach as many people as possible. That works two ways; it's not just a market discipline. You have to remember that most of us who are doing this got into it for the romance, the glory, the applause, the chance to tell stories, even to learn, but rarely for the money. The more people you reach, the greater your sense of success. Given the choice, I'd rather make the whole world cry than 17 intellectuals in a classroom.

But, paradoxically, if you are the actual maker of the film—not the financier—you can't make films and worry about whether they'll reach a large audience or make money, first, because nobody really knows a formula for what will make money. If they did, I promise you we would have heard about it, and studios would not be going broke. Second, and much more practically, if you spent your time while you were making the film consciously thinking about what was commercial, then the real mechanism of choice—the mechanism that is your own unconscious, your own taste and imagination, your fantasy—would be replaced by constant reference to this formula that we know doesn't work.

So the only practical approach a filmmaker can take is to make a film that he or she would want to see. This sounds arrogant, but you try to make a movie for yourself, and you hope that as many people as possible will like it too. If that happens, it's because you've done something in the telling of the story that makes people care. One of the things that makes a film distinct from other American business products is this emotional involvement of the maker. A producer of auto parts can become pretty emotional about a sales slump, but it isn't the same thing. His product hasn't come from his history; it isn't somehow in the image of his life; and it lacks mystery. It is entirely measurable and concrete, which is certainly appropriate in the manufacture of auto parts. I wouldn't want to buy a carburetor from a neurotic, mixed-up auto manufacturer.

Fortunately for those of us in film, no such standards apply. Quite the contrary, in fact. No matter what his conscious intentions are, the best part of what the filmmaker does—the part, when it works, that makes you want to see the film—doesn't come from a rational, consciously controllable process. It comes from somewhere inside the filmmaker's unconscious. It comes from making unlikely connections seem inevitable from a kind of free association that jumps to odd or surprising places, conclusions that cause delights, something that creates goose pimples or awe.

This conference has suggested a question: While you're actually making the movie, do you think about whether it will be doing the world any good? I can't answer it for filmmakers in general. For myself, candidly, no, I don't.

I try to discover and tell the truth and not be dull about it. In that sense, the question has no significance for me. I assume that trying to discover the truth is in itself a good and virtuous aim. By truth I don't mean some grand, pretentious axiom to live by; I just mean the truth of a character from moment to moment. I try to discover and describe things like the motives that are hidden in day-to-day life. And the truth is rarely dull. If I can find it, I will have fulfilled my primary obligation as a filmmaker, which is not to bore the pants off you.

Most of us in this business have enormous sympathy for Scheherazade—we're terrified we're going to be murdered if we're boring. So our first obligation is to not bore people; it isn't to teach.

I'm sure that you think the person in whose hands the process actually rests, the filmmaker, could exert an enormous amount of control over the film's final business. The question usually goes like this: Should filmmakers pander to the public, or should they try to elevate public taste to something that many at this conference would find more acceptable? Is the job of an American filmmaker to give the public what it wants or what the filmmaker thinks the public should have? This doesn't leave much doubt as to what you think is the right answer.

But framing your question this way not only betrays a misunderstanding of how the filmmaking process works but also is just plain wishful thinking about how to improve society. I share your nostalgia for some of those lost traditionally values, but attempting to reinstall them by arbitrarily putting them into movies when they don't exist in everyday life will not get people to go to the movies or put those values back into life. I wish it were that simple.

Engaging an Audience

This conference is concerned with something called popular culture and its effect on society, but I am concerned with one film at a time and its effect. You are debating whether movies corrupt our souls or elevate them, and I'm concerned with whether a film will touch a soul. As a filmmaker, I never set out to create popular culture, and I don't know a single other filmmaker who does.

Maybe it's tempting to think Hollywood as some collective behemoth grinding out the same stories and pushing the same values, but it's not that simple. Hollywood, whatever that means, is Oliver Stone castigating war in *Born on the Fourth of July* and John Milius celebrating it in *The Wind and the Lion*. It's Walt Disney and Martin Scorcese. It's Steven Spielberg and Milos Foreman. It's *Amadeus* and *Terminator* and hundreds of choices in between.

I don't want to defend Hollywood, because I don't represent Hollywood—I can't, any more than one particular writer can represent literature or one painter art. For the most part, the impulse toward all art, entertainment, culture, pop culture, comes from the same place within the makers of it. The level of talent and the soul, if you'll forgive the word again, is what finally limits it.

At the risk of telling you more than you need to know about my own work, I make the movies I make because there is in each film some argument that fascinates me, an issue I want to work through. I call this a spine or an armature because it functions for me like an armature in sculpture—something I can cover up and it will support the whole structure. I can test the scenes against it. For me, the film, when properly dramatized, adds up to this idea, this argument.

But there are lots of other ways to go about making a film, and lots of other filmmakers who do it differently. Some filmmakers begin knowing exactly what they want to say and then craft a vehicle that contains that statement. Some are interested in pure escape. Here's the catch. The effectiveness and the success of all our films is determined by exactly the same standards—

unfortunately, not by the particular validity of their message but by their ability to engage the concentration and emotions of the audience.

Citizen Kane is an attack on acquisition, but that's not why people go to see it. I don't have any idea if the audience that saw *Tootsie* thought at any conscious level that it could be about a guy who became a better man for having been a woman; or that *The Way We Were*, a film I made 20 years ago, may have been about the tension between passion, often of the moment, and wisdom, often part of a longer view; or that *Out of Africa* might be about the inability to possess another individual and even the inability of one country to possess another. That's intellectual and stuffy. I just hope the audiences were entertained.

I may choose the movies I make because there's an issue I want to explore, but the how—the framing of that issue, the process of finding the best way to explore it—is a much more mysterious, elusive, and messy process. I can't tell you that I understand it; if I did, I would have a pep talk with myself and go out and make a terrific movie every time.

I would not make a film that ethically, or morally, or politically trashed what I believe is fair. But by the same token, I feel an obligation—and this is more complicated and personal—to do films about arguments. I try hard to give each side a strong argument—not because I'm a fair guy but because I believe it's more interesting. Both things are going on.

I do the same thing on every movie I make. I find an argument, a couple of characters I would like to have dinner with, and try to find the most fascinating way to explore it. I work as hard as I can to tell the story in the way I'd like it told to me.

What is really good is also entertaining and interesting because it's closer to a newer way to look at the truth. You can't do that consciously. You can't start out by saying, "I am now going to make a great film."

The virtue in making a film, if there is any, is in making it well. If there's any morality that's going to come out, it will develop as you begin to construct, at every moment you have a choice to make. You can do it the honest way or you can bend it, and the collection of those moments of choice is what makes the work good or not good and is what reveals morality or the lack of it.

I've made 16 films. I've had some enormous successes and I've had some colossal failures, but I can't tell you what the difference is in terms of what I did.

An American Aesthetic?

In some circles, American films suffer by comparison with European films precisely because a lot of our movies seem to be the product of little deliberation and much instinct. It's been said of European movies that essence precedes existence, which is just a fancy way of saying that European movies exist in order to say something. Certainly one never doubts with a European film that it's saying something, and often it just comes right out and says it.

American films work by indirection, they work by action and movement, either internal or external, but almost always movement. Our films are more narratively driven than others, which has a lot to do with the American character and the way we look at our lives. We see ourselves and our lives as being part of a story.

Most of our movies have been pro the underdog, concerned with injustice, relatively anti-authority. There's usually a system—or a bureaucracy—to triumph over.

More often than not, American movies have been affirmative and hopeful about destiny. They're usually about individuals who control their own lives and their fate. In Europe, the system was so class-bound and steeped in tradition that there was no democratization of that process.

There's no prior education required to assimilate American movies or American culture. American culture is general, as opposed to the specificity of Japanese or Indian culture. America has the most easily digestible culture.

Our movies seem artless. The best of them keep us interested without seeming to engage our minds. The very thing that makes movies so popular here and abroad is one of the primary things that drives their critics to apoplexy, but seeming artlessness isn't necessarily mindlessness. There's a deliberate kind of artlessness in American movies that has come from a discipline or aesthetic long ago imposed by the marketplace. Our movies began as immigrants' dreams that would appeal to the dreams of other immigrants, and this aesthetic has led American films to transcend languages and cultures and communicate to every country in the world.

The Filmmakers' Responsibility

It has been suggested to some extent in this conference that I ought to study my own and American filmmakers' responsibilities to the public and to the world. I realize I have responsibilities as a filmmaker, but I don't believe that they are a moralist, a preacher, or a purveyor of values. I know it's tempting to use filmmaking as such, but utility is a poor standard to use in art.

My responsibility is to try to make good films, but "good" is a subjective word. To me at any rate, "good" doesn't necessarily mean "good for us" in the narrow sense that they must elevate our spirits and send us out of the theater singing, or even that they must promote only those values that some think are worth promoting.

Good movies challenge us, they provoke us, they make us angry sometimes. They present points of view we don't agree with. They force us to clarify our positions in opposition to them, and they do this best when they provide us with an experience and not a polemic.

Somebody gave the okay to pay for *One Flew Over the Cuckoo's Nest*, *Driving Miss Daisy*, *Stand By Me*, *Moonstruck*, *Terms of Endearment*, and *Amadeus*, and despite conventional wisdom that said those films could not be successful, those decisions paid off handsomely because there are no rules. Studio executives and other financiers do exceed themselves. They take chances. They have to, and we have to hope that they'll do it more often.

What we see in movie theaters today is not a simple reflection of today's economics or politics in this country but is a sense of the people who make the movies, and they vary as individuals vary. So what we really want is for this very privileged process to be in the best hands possible, but I know of no force that can regulate this except the moral climate and appetites of our society.

What we're exporting now is largely a youth culture. It's full of adolescent values; it's full of adolescent rage, love, rebelliousness, and a desire to shock. If you're unhappy with their taste—and this is a free market—then an appetite has to be created for something better. How do we do that? Well, we're back to square one: the supplier or the consumer, the chicken or the egg? Let's not even ask the question: the answer is both.

Of course filmmakers ought to be encouraged toward excellence, and audiences ought to be encouraged to demand it. How? That's for thinkers and social scientists to figure out. I have no idea. But if I had to play this scene out as an imaginary dialogue, I might say that you must educate the consumer first, and the best places to start are at school and at home. And then you would say that is my job, that popular entertainment must participate in this education. And I would say, ideally, perhaps, but I do not think that will happen within a system that operates so fundamentally from an economic point of view. On an individual basis, yes, one filmmaker at a time; as an industry, no. An appetite or market will have to exist first.

That's not as bad as it sounds, because in the best of all possible worlds, we do try to satisfy both needs; entertain people and be reasonably intelligent about it. It can be done, and it is done more often than you think. It's just very difficult.

It's like two Oxford dons who were sitting at the Boar's head. They were playwrights, grousing because neither one of them could get produced, neither one could get performed. One turned to the other and said, "Oh, the hell with it. Let's just do what Shakespeare did—give them entertainment."

Notes

1. **Sydney Pollack:** a director of sixteen films—including *The Way We Were*, *Tootsie*, *Out of Africa*, and *The Firm*. The above article is a transcript of an address Pollack delivered at a conference about the influence of the popular media on American values.

2. **Gary Cooper** (1901—1961): an American actor. He was a major movie star from the end of the silent film era through to the end of the golden age of Classical Hollywood.
3. **The Medal of Honor:** the United States of America's highest and most prestigious personal military decoration that may be awarded to recognize U.S. military service members who have distinguished themselves by acts of valor.
4. *Dances with Wolves*: a 1990 American epic Western film . The film is credited as a leading influence for the revitalization of the Western genre of filmmaking in Hollywood.
5. **Sam Goldwyn** (1879—1974): a Polish-American film producer. He was most well known for being the founding contributor and executive of several motion picture studios in Hollywood.
6. **Medicis:** The House of Medici was an Italian banking family and political dynasty that first began to gather prominence in the Republic of Florence during the first half of the 15th century. The family originated in the Mugello region of Tuscany, and prospered gradually until it was able to fund the Medici Bank. This bank was the largest in Europe during the 15th century, and it facilitated the Medicis' rise to political power in Florence, although they officially remained citizens rather than monarchs until the 16th century. The family played an important role in the Renaissance.
7. **Scheherazade:** a major female character and the storyteller in the Middle Eastern literature *One Thousand and One Nights*.
8. **Martin Scorcese:** Martin Charles Scorcese (1942—) is an Italian-American filmmaker and historian, whose career spans more than 50 years. Scorsese's body of work addresses such themes as Sicilian-American identity, Roman Catholic concepts of guilt and redemption, faith, machismo, modern crime, and gang conflict. Many of his films are also known for their depiction of violence and liberal use of profanity.
9. **Steven Spielberg:** Steven Allan Spielberg (1946—) is an American filmmaker. He is considered one of the founding pioneers of the New Hollywood era and one of the American film industry's most critically successful filmmakers, with praise for his directing talent and versatility, and has won the Academy Award for Best Director twice. Some of his movies are also among the highest-grossing movies of all-time, while his total work, unadjusted for ticket-price inflation, makes him the highest-grossing film director in history.
10. **Milos Foreman** (1932—2018): a Czech-American film director, screenwriter, actor and professor who, until 1968, lived and worked primarily in the former Czechoslovakia. Two of his films, *One Flew Over the Cuckoo's Nest* (1975) and *Amadeus* (1984) gained him an Academy Award for Best Director.

11. ***Amadeus***: a 1984 American drama film directed by Milos Forman. The story, set in Vienna, Austria, during the latter half of the 18th century, is a fictionalized biography of Wolfgang Amadeus Mozart. Mozart's music is heard extensively in the soundtrack of the film. The film follows Italian composer Antonio Salieri's rivalry with Mozart at the court of Emperor Joseph II. Considered one of the best films of all time, *Amadeus* was nominated for 53 awards and received 40, which included eight Academy Awards (including Best Picture), four BAFTA Awards, four Golden Globes, and a Directors Guild of America (DGA) award.

12. ***Terminator***: a 1984 American science fiction film directed by James Cameron. It stars Arnold Schwarzenegger as the Terminator, a cyborg assassin sent back in time from 2029 to 1984 to kill Sarah Connor (Linda Hamilton), whose son will one day become a savior against machines in a post-apocalyptic future.

13. ***Citizen Kane***: a 1941 American drama movie. Many have called *Citizen Kane* the best movie of all time. In 1998, it was number one on the American Film Institute's list of 100 Years... 100 Movies.

14. ***At the Boar's Head***: an opera in one act by the English composer Gustav Holst. The libretto is based on Shakespeare's Henry IV, Part I and Part II.

Vocabulary

1. philistine ['fɪlɪstin]: *n.* a person who does not like or understand art, literature, music, etc. 对艺术文化无知的人

2. panderer ['pændərər]: *n.* a person who serves or caters to the vulgar passions or plans of others (especially in order to make money) 淫媒者

3. scrupulous ['skrupjələs]: *adj.* careful to be honest and do what is right 恪守道德规范的

4. sanctity ['sæŋktəti]: *n.* the state of being very important and worth protecting and preserving 神圣性

5. fluid ['fluɪd]: *adj.* (of a situation) likely to change; not fixed 易变的；不稳定的

6. carburetor [ˌkɑːbjʊ'retə]: *n.* the part of an engine, for example in a car, where petrol and air are mixed together and burn to provide power 化油器

7. behemoth [bɪ'hiːmɔθ]: *n.* someone or something that is abnormally large or powerful 巨兽

8. castigate ['kæstɪɡeɪt]: *vt.* to express strong disapproval of (a person, behavior, or ideas) 谴责，强烈反对

9. spine [spaɪn]: *n.* the center of the back of human beings and certain animals that supports the body 脊椎

10. armature ['ɑrmətʃər]: *n.* a frame on which clay or other soft material can be put to make a figure or model （支撑塑像的）骨架

11. aesthetic [es'θetɪk; ɛs'θɛtɪk]: *n.* the ideas concerned with beauty and art and the understanding of beautiful things 审美观

12. apoplexy ['æpəplɛksi]: *n.* the sudden loss of the ability to move, feel, think 中风

13. purveyor [pə'veɪə(r); pɜː'veɪə(r)]: *n.* a person who supply (food or other goods) as a trade （食物或其他货物）供应商

14. polemic [pə'lɛmɪk]: *n.* a controversy (especially over a belief or dogma) 争论

15. don [dɒn]: *n.* a university teacher, esp. at Oxford and Cambridge （尤指牛津大学和剑桥大学的）大学教师

16. grouse [ɡraʊs]: *vi.* to complain 发牢骚

Expressions

1. Maybe it's tempting to think Hollywood as some collective behemoth <u>grinding out</u> the same stories and pushing the same values.

   grind out: to produce something in large quantities, often something that is not good or interesting 大量生产；（尤指）粗制滥造

2. But there are lots of other ways to <u>go about</u> making a film.

   go about: to start working on something 着手做某事

3. I can't tell you that I understand it; if I did, I would have a <u>pep talk</u> with myself and go out and make a terrific movie every time.

   pep talk: a short speech intended to encourage somebody to work harder, try to win, have more confidence, etc. 激励的话

4. In Europe, the system <u>was</u> so class-bound and <u>steeped in</u> tradition that there was no democratization of that process.

   be steeped in something: to spend a lot of time thinking or learning about something 沉浸于

Comprehension

I. Discuss the Main Point and the Meanings.

1. What is the first principle of Hollywood for Pollack?

2. According to Pollack, how have American values changed since the thirties, forties and fifties?

3. Who is the controlling influence in filmmaking?

4. When making films, what does Pollack try to do?

5. What motivated Pollack to make a movie?

6. For Pollack, what is the filmmaker's responsibility?

7. What is the function of movies?

II. Fill in the blanks with the appropriate words or expressions in the box.

a product	an issue	art
commerce	entertain people	general
makes people care	some argument	soul
reflected	talent	the concentration and emotions
the moral climate and appetites	the truth	unconscious

1. Society's values have changed. That kind of scrupulous, ethical concern for the sanctity of human life doesn't exist in the same way, and that fact is _____ in the movies.

2. Before they can be anything else, American movies are _____. The consumers make their choices.

3. Filmmaking has always been an uneasy merger of two antithetical things: some form of _____ and sheer _____.

4. The only practical approach a filmmaker can take is to make a film that he or she would want to see, and you hope that as many people as possible will like it too. If that happens, it's because you've done something in the telling of the story that _____.

5. The best part of what the filmmaker does—the part, when it works, that makes you want to see the film—doesn't come from a rational, consciously controllable process. It comes from somewhere inside the filmmaker's _____.

6. When making films, Pollack tries to discover and tell _____ and not be dull about it. He tries to discover and describe things like the motives that are hidden in day-to-day life.

7. For the most part, the impulse toward all art, entertainment, culture, pop culture, comes from the same place within the makers of it. The level of _____ and the _____, is what finally limits it.

8. Pollack makes the movies because there is in each film _____ that fascinates him, _____ he wants to work through.

9. The effectiveness and the success of all our films is determined by their ability to engage _____ of the audience.

Unit 10　The Way We Are

10. American culture is _____. America has the most easily digestible culture.

11. No force except _____ of our society can regulate the filmmaking.

12. In the best of all possible worlds, filmmakers do try to satisfy both needs; _____ and be reasonably intelligent about it.

Structure

I. Find out how words and expression in bold are used in the following sentences.

1. If you **put forward** a virtuousness on the part of your hero, everybody responded to it.

2. Morality, the definitions of virtue, justice, and injustice, the sanctity of the individual, have been fairly **fluid** for American audiences **in terms of** what they chose to embrace or not embrace.

3. The market tries to **cater to** those choices, and we have what we have.

4. Filmmaking just doesn't **conform to** the logic or rules of any other business.

5. I can't answer it for filmmakers **in general**.

6. By truth I don't mean some grand, pretentious axiom to **live by**.

7. Fortunately for those of us in film, no such standards **apply**.

8. For me, the film, when properly dramatized, **adds up to** this idea, this argument.

9. But there are lots of other ways to **go about** making a film.

10. There's usually a system—or a bureaucracy—to **triumph over**.

11. Despite conventional wisdom that said those films could not be successful, those decisions **paid off** handsomely because there are no rules.

12. Studio executives and other financiers do exceed themselves. They **take chances**.

13. How? That's for thinkers and social scientists to **figure out**.

14. But if I had to **play** this scene **out** as an imaginary dialogue, I might say that you must educate the consumer first.

15. On an individual basis, yes, one filmmaker **at a time**.

II. Complete the following sentences with some of the above words or expressions in bold.

1. We had to go and see the president one _____.

2. Mary was determined to become a doctor and her persistence _____.

3. You _____ (not) the job in the right way.

4. The committee _____ new peace proposals.

5. Special conditions _____ if you are under 18.

201

6. This conversation _____ a difference of opinion between us.

7. As is usual in this kind of movie, good _____ evil in the end.

8. John is not a man to _____.

9. It took him one hour to _____ how to start the machine.

10. The film has eerie parallel with the drama _____ in real life.

Entertainment Media

The US media today is frequently known as the Fourth Estate, an appellation that suggests the press shares equal stature with the other branches of government created by the Constitution. The US media is supposed to be the guardian of US democracy.

There is no formal censorship of media in the USA, but there is what some call "Market Censorship" — that is, the mainstream media do not want to run stories that will offend their advertisers and owners. In this way, the media ends up censoring themselves and not reporting on many important issues, including corporate practices.

Another effect of these so-called market forces at work is that mainstream media will go for what will sell and news coverage becomes all about attracting viewers. Yet the fear of losing viewers from competition seems so high that many report exactly the same story at the very same time! Objective coverage gets a back seat.

In 1934, Congress set up the current oversight agency of the broadcasting industry, the Federal Communications Commission (FCC). The law vested in the FCC not only "watchdog" functions, but licensing and rulemaking powers, subject to "public interest, convenience, and necessity." Acting on this mandate, the FCC has sought to promote diversity in content and ownership in the broadcasting industry.

In recent years Broadcast TV was deregulated, and cable and satellite TV arose in a wholly post-regulation era. Deregulation and convergence are under way, leading to mega-mergers, further concentration of media ownership and the emergence of multinational media conglomerates. Critics allege that localism, local news and other content at the community level, media spending and coverage of news, and diversity of ownership and views have suffered as a result of these process of media concentration.

TV Network

Television is one of the major mass media of the United States. As a whole, the television networks of the United States are the largest and most syndicated in the world. There are three basic types of television in the United States: broadcast, or "over-the-air" television, which is freely available to anyone with a TV in the broadcast area, cable television, and satellite television, both of which require a subscription to receive.

Broadcast television

The United States has a decentralized, market-oriented television system. Unlike many other countries, the United States has no national broadcast programming service. Instead, local media markets have their own television stations, which may be affiliated or owned and operated by a TV network. Stations may sign affiliation agreements with one of the national networks. Except in very small markets with few stations, affiliation agreements are usually exclusive: If a station is an NBC affiliate, the station would not air programs from ABC, CBS or other networks.

However, to ensure local presences in television broadcasting, federal law restricts the amount of network programming local stations can run. Until the 1970s and '80s, local stations supplemented network programming with a good deal of their own produced shows. Today many stations produce only local news shows. They fill the rest of their schedule with syndicated shows, or material produced independently and sold to individual stations in each local market.

Non-commercial television

Public television has a far smaller role than in most other countries. There is no federal state-owned broadcasting authority. The federal government does subsidize non-commercial educational television stations through the Corporation for Public Broadcasting. The income received from the government is insufficient to cover expenses and stations rely on corporate sponsorships and viewer contributions.

American public television stations air programming that commercial stations do not offer, such as educational, including cultural, and public affairs programming. Most public TV stations are affiliates of the Public Broadcasting Service, sharing programs like *Sesame Street* and *Masterpiece Theatre*. Unlike the commercial networks, PBS does not produce its own programming; instead, individual PBS stations create programming and provide these to other affiliates.

Major Broadcast Networks

Other than the non-commercial educational PBS, five major US broadcast television networks are the National Broadcasting Company (NBC), the Columbia Broadcasting System (CBS), the American Broadcasting Company (ABC), the Fox Broadcasting Company (Fox) and the CW Television Network.

Major-network affiliates run very similar schedules. Typically, they begin weekdays with an early-morning locally produced news show, followed by a network morning show, such as NBC's *Today*, which mixes news, weather, interviews and music. Syndicated programming, especially talk shows, fill the late morning, followed often by local news at noon. Soap operas dominate the early afternoon, while syndicated talk shows appear in the late afternoon. Local news comes on again in the early evening, followed by the national network's news program at 6:30 or 5:30 pm, followed by more news. More syndication occupies the next hour (or ½ hour in the Central time zone, called prime access slot) before the networks take over for prime time, the most-watched three hours of television. Typically, family-oriented comedy programs led in the early part of prime time, although in recent years, reality television programs (such as *Dancing with the Stars* and *American Idol*), and more adult-oriented scripted programs — both comedies and dramas — have largely replaced them. Later in the evening, drama series of various types (such as *NCIS*, *Law & Order: Special Victims Unit* and *Grey's Anatomy*) air.

At the end of prime time, another local news program is broadcasted, usually followed by late-night interview shows (such as *The Late Show with Stephen Colbert* or *The Tonight Show*). Rather than sign off for the early hours of the morning (as was standard practice until the early 1970s in larger markets and until the mid 1980's in smaller ones), TV stations now fill the time with syndicated programming, reruns of prime time television shows and/or the local 10 or 11 o'clock news, or 30-minute advertisements, known as infomercials, and in the case of CBS and ABC, overnight network news programs.

Cable television

Today, most American households receive cable TV, and cable networks collectively have greater viewership than broadcast networks. Unlike broadcast networks, most cable networks air the same programming nationwide. Top cable networks include USA Network (which maintains a general entertainment format), ESPN and Fox Sports 1 (which focus on sports programming), MTV (which originally focused on music videos when launched in April 1981, but now largely features music-related, original scripted and reality television programming), CNN, MSNBC and Fox News Channel (which are dedicated news channels with some opinion and other feature-driven programming), Syfy (which focuses on science fiction and fantasy programming), Freeform (which was launched in September 1977 as the CBN Satellite Service, a religious-based cable arm of the Christian Broadcasting Network, before refocusing on secular family-oriented programming, and since 2001 has also featured shows aimed mainly at teenagers and young adults), Disney Channel, Nickelodeon and Cartoon Network (which focus on children's programming, although the latter two run nighttime blocks aimed at a teen and adult audience,

Nick at Nite and *Adult Swim*), Discovery Channel and Animal Planet (which focus on reality and documentary programs), TBS (a general entertainment network with a principal focus on comedy), TNT and FX (also general entertainment networks, with some focus on drama) and Lifetime (which targets at a female audience, with a mix of television films, and original and acquired comedy, reality and drama series).

In recent years, some basic cable networks have begun to relax their self-imposed restrictions, particularly late at night. Programs like Comedy Central's *South Park* often contain content deemed unsuitable for broadcast television.

Premium channels — cable networks that subscribers have to pay an additional fee to their provider to receive — began launching in the 1970s and initially grew in popularity as it allowed subscribers to watch movies without time or content editing common with over-the-air television broadcasts of theatrically released feature films and without interruptions by advertising. The most well known as well as the oldest-existing pay service is Home Box Office (HBO), which launched on November 8, 1972 with a mix of movies, music and concert specials; by the late 1990s, HBO began to be known for groundbreaking first-run series (such as *The Larry Sanders Show*, *The Sopranos* and *Sex and the City*) that were edgier and more risque in content than those allowed to air on broadcast networks.

Emmy Awards

Emmy Awards are statuettes awarded annually in the United States to honor excellence in the television industry. The name Emmy is a derivative of Immy, the nickname of the image orthicon tube, an integral part of early television cameras. The Emmy Awards were first presented in 1949. They are administered by the Academy of Television Arts and Sciences (ATAS) and the National Academy of Television Arts and Sciences (NATAS), nonprofit organizations best known for their supervision of the Emmys. ATAS oversees the awards for shows broadcast between the hours of 6 pm and 2 am, and NATAS supervises awards for daytime, sports, and news and documentary programming. Award categories include those for programs, performers, directors, and writers, as well as those for technical work, such as art direction, costume design, editing, and sound mixing.

The best known of these ceremonies are the Primetime Emmy Awards, honoring excellence in American primetime television programming (excluding sports), and the Daytime Emmy Awards, honoring excellence in American daytime television programming.

Movie Industry

Since the early twentieth century, the US film industry has largely been based in and around Hollywood. Hollywood (informally Tinseltown) is an ethnically diverse, densely populated neighborhood in the central region of Los Angeles, California. It includes several of its historic studios, and its name has come to be a shorthand reference for the industry and the people in it.

In the early 1900s, most motion picture patents were held by Thomas Edison's Motion Picture Patents Company in New Jersey, and filmmakers were often sued to stop their productions. To escape this, filmmakers began moving out west, where Edison's patents could not be enforced. Also, the weather was ideal and there was quick access to various settings. Los Angeles became the capital of the film industry.

Director D. W. Griffith was the first to make a motion picture in Hollywood and he was central to the development of film grammar. The first film by a Hollywood studio, Nestor Motion Picture Company, was shot on October 26, 1911. Four major film companies — Paramount, Warner Bros., RKO, and Columbia — had studios in Hollywood, as did several minor companies and rental studios. In the 1920s, Hollywood was the fifth-largest industry in the nation. Hollywood has since become a major center for film study in the United States.

Golden Age of Hollywood

The period from the end of the silent era in American cinema in the late 1920s to the late 1950s was called the Golden Age of Hollywood. During that period, thousands of movies were issued from the Hollywood studios.

Most Hollywood pictures adhered closely to a formula — Western, slapstick comedy, musical, animated cartoon, biopic (biographical picture) — and the same creative teams often worked on films made by the same studio. For example, Cedric Gibbons and Herbert Stothart always worked on MGM films, Alfred Newman worked at 20th Century Fox for twenty years, Cecil B. De Mille's films were almost all made at Paramount, and director Henry King's films were mostly made for 20th Century Fox.

At the same time, one could usually guess which studio made which film, largely because of the actors who appeared in it; MGM, for example, claimed it had contracted "more stars than there are in heaven." Each studio had its own style and characteristic touches which made it possible to know this — a trait that does not exist today. Yet each movie was a little different, and, unlike the craftsmen who made cars, many of the people who made movies were artists.

Throughout the 1930s, as well as most of the golden age, MGM dominated the film screen and had the top stars in Hollywood, and was also credited for creating the Hollywood star system altogether. Some MGM stars included "King of Hollywood" Clark Gable, Lionel Barrymore, Jean Harlow, Norma Shearer, Greta Garbo, Jeanette MacDonald and husband Gene Raymond, Spencer Tracy, Judy Garland, and Gene Kelly.

Another great achievement of US cinema during this era came through Walt Disney's animation company. In 1937, Disney created the most successful film of its time, *Snow White and the Seven Dwarfs*. Also in 1939, MGM would create what is still, when adjusted for inflation, the most successful film of all time, *Gone with the Wind*.

Many film historians have remarked upon the many great works of cinema that emerged from this period of highly regimented film-making. One reason this was possible is that, with so many movies being made, not every one had to be a big hit. A studio could gamble on a medium-budget feature with a good script and relatively unknown actors: *Citizen Kane*, directed by Orson Welles (1915—1985) and often regarded as the greatest film of all time, fits that description. In other cases, strong-willed directors like Howard Hawks (1896—1977), Alfred Hitchcock (1899—1980) and Frank Capra (1897—1991) battled the studios in order to achieve their artistic visions. The apogee of the studio system may have been the year 1939, which saw the release of such classics as *The Wizard of Oz*, *Gone with the Wind*, *Stagecoach*, *Mr. Smith Goes to Washington*, *Wuthering Heights*, *Only Angels Have Wings*, *Ninotchka*, and *Midnight*. Among the other films from the Golden Age period that are now considered to be classics: *Casablanca*, *It's a Wonderful Life*, *It Happened One Night*, the original *King Kong*, *Mutiny on the Bounty*, *City Lights*, *Red River* and *Top Hat*.

Modern Cinema

The drive to produce a spectacle on the movie screen has largely shaped American cinema ever since. Spectacular epics which took advantage of new widescreen processes had been increasingly popular from the 1950s onwards. Since then, American films have become increasingly divided into two categories: blockbusters and independent films. Studios have focused on relying on a handful of extremely expensive releases every year in order to remain profitable. Such blockbusters emphasize spectacle, star power, and high production value, all of which entail an enormous budget. Blockbusters typically rely upon star power and massive advertising to attract a huge audience. A successful blockbuster will attract an audience large enough to offset production costs and reap considerable profits. Such productions carry a substantial risk of failure, and most studios release blockbusters that both over- and underperform in a year.

Studios supplement these movies with independent productions, made with small budgets and often independently of the studio corporation. Movies made in this manner typically emphasize high professional quality in terms of acting, directing, screenwriting, and other elements associated with production, and also upon creativity and innovation. These movies usually rely upon critical praise or niche marketing to garner an audience.

Golden Globe Awards

Golden Globe Awards are motion-picture and television awards, given annually and administered by the Hollywood Foreign Press Association, a group of international journalists who work in Hollywood, California. The awards were first given in 1944 for films only; awards for television were added in 1956. Golden Globe statuettes are awarded annually in several categories, including best dramatic and comedic motion pictures, best foreign-language film, best director, best actor and actress, best supporting actor and actress, and best dramatic and comedic television series. In addition, the Cecil B. DeMille Award is given for lifetime achievement in motion pictures.

Academy Awards — The Oscars

The Academy Awards (informally known as the Oscars) are prizes given annually in the United States by the Academy of Motion Picture Arts and Sciences for excellence in the creation and production of motion pictures. The formal ceremony at which the awards are presented is one of the most prominent award ceremonies in the world and is televised live in more than 200 countries annually. The Academy of Motion Picture Arts and Sciences itself was conceived by the Metro-Goldwyn-Mayer studio boss Louis B. Mayer.

First presented in 1929 for films shown in 1927 and 1928, the Academy Awards, are among the film industry's most coveted prizes. Academy Award categories include those for Best Picture, Best Director, Best Actor, Best Actress, Best Supporting Actor, Best Supporting Actress, Best Animated Feature Film, Best Animated Short Film, Best Cinematography, Best Costume Design, Best Documentary Feature, Best Documentary Short Subject, Best Film Editing, Best Foreign Language Film, Best Live Action Short Film, Best Makeup and Hairstyling, Best Original Score, Best Original Song, Best Production Design, Best Sound Editing, Best Sound Mixing, Best Visual Effects, Best Adapted Screenplay, Best Original Screenplay.

Vocabulary of Entertainment Media

1. In the thirties, forties, and fifties, six men in the Valley, immigrants really, ran **the movie industry**.

2. If you put forward a virtuousness on the part of your **hero**, everybody responded to it.

3. Sergeant York was **played** by Gary Cooper.

4. We say that we're "creating a film" or merely "**making a movie**."

5. So the only practical approach a **filmmaker** can take is to make a film that he or she would want to see.

Unit 10 The Way We Are

6. The effectiveness and the success of all our films is determined by their ability to engage the concentration and emotions of the **audience**.

7. There is no formal **censorship** in the USA, but there is what some call "Market Censorship".

8. News coverage becomes all about attracting **viewers**.

9. In 1934, Congress set up the current **oversight** agency of the broadcasting industry, the Federal Communications Commission (FCC).

10. **Broadcast**, or **"over-the-air" television**, is freely available to anyone with a TV in the broadcast area.

11. Local media markets have their own television stations, which may be **affiliated** or owned and operated by a **TV network**.

12. Typically, family-oriented **comedy** programs led in the early part of prime time, in recent years, **reality television** programs and more adult-oriented scripted programs — both comedies and **dramas** — have largely replaced them.

13. Later in the evening, drama series of various types **air**.

14. At the end of **prime time**, another local news program is **broadcast**.

15. **Syndicated** programming, especially **talk shows**, fill the late morning, followed often by local news at noon. **Soap operas** dominate the early afternoon.

16. Rather than sign off for the early hours of the morning, TV stations now fill the time with syndicated programming, **reruns** of prime time television shows and/or the local 10 or 11 o'clock news, or 30-minute advertisements, known as **infomercials**.

17. **Premium channels** allow subscribers to watch movies without time or content editing common with over-the-air television broadcasts of theatrically released **feature films** and without interruptions by advertising.

18. The most well known pay service is HBO, which was **launched** in 1972, began to be known for groundbreaking first-run **series**.

19. The Sopranos **premiered** on HBO on January 10, 1999 and ended its original run of six **seasons** and 56 **episodes** on June 10, 2007.

20. The Wire **debuted** on June 2, 2002.

21. Emmy Award categories include those for programs, **performers**, **directors**, and writers, as well as those for technical work, such as art direction, **costume design**, **editing**, and **sound mixing**.

22. **Hollywood** (informally **Tinseltown**) is an ethnically diverse, densely populated neighborhood in the central region of Los Angeles, California.

23. The first film by a Hollywood **studio** was **shot** on October 26, 1911.

24. Most Hollywood pictures adhered closely to a formula — **Western**, **slapstick comedy**, **musical**, **animated cartoon**, **biopic** (biographical picture).

25. One reason this was possible is that, with so many movies being made, not every one had to be a big **hit**.

26. A studio could gamble on a medium-**budget** feature with a good **script** and relatively unknown **actors**.

27. Since then, American films have become increasingly divided into two categories: **blockbusters** and **independent films**.

28. Golden Globe statuettes are awarded annually in several categories, including best dramatic and comedic motion pictures, best foreign-language film, best director, best actor and actress, best **supporting actor** and actress, and best dramatic and comedic television series.

Unit 11 Music

Karl Paulnack

One of my parents' deepest fears, I suspect, is that society would not properly value me as a musician, that I wouldn't be appreciated. I had very good grades in high school, I was good in science and math, and they imagined that as a doctor or a research chemist or an engineer, I might be more appreciated than I would be as a musician. I still remember my mother's remark when I announced my decision to apply to music school — she said, "you're WASTING your SAT scores." On some level, I think, my parents were not sure themselves what the value of music was, what its purpose was. And they LOVED music, they listened to classical music all the time. They just weren't really clear about its function. So let me talk about that a little bit, because we live in a society that puts music in the "arts and entertainment" section of the newspaper, and serious music, the kind your kids are about to engage in, has absolutely nothing whatsoever to do with entertainment; in fact it's the opposite of entertainment. Let me talk a little bit about music, and how it works.

The first people to understand how music really works were the ancient Greeks. And this is going to fascinate you; the Greeks said that music and astronomy were two sides of the same coin. Astronomy was seen as the study of relationships between observable, permanent, external objects, and music was seen as the study of relationships between invisible, internal, hidden objects. Music has a way of finding the big, invisible moving pieces inside our hearts and souls and helping us figure out the position of things inside us. Let me give you some examples of how this works.

One of the most profound musical compositions of all time is the *Quartet for the End of Time* written by French composer Olivier Messiaen in 1940. Messiaen was 31 years old when France entered the war against Nazi Germany. He was captured by the Germans in June of 1940, sent across Germany in a cattle car and imprisoned in a concentration camp.

He was fortunate to find a sympathetic prison guard who gave him paper and a place to compose. There were three other musicians in the camp, a cellist, a violinist, and a clarinetist, and Messiaen wrote his quartet with these specific players in mind. It was performed in January 1941 for four thousand prisoners and guards in the prison camp. Today it is one of the most famous masterworks in the repertoire.

Given what we have since learned about life in the concentration camps, why would anyone in his right mind waste time and energy writing or playing music? There was barely enough energy on a good day to find food and water, to avoid a beating, to stay warm, to escape torture — why would anyone bother with music? And yet — from the camps, we have poetry, we have music, we have visual art; it wasn't just this one fanatic Messiaen; many, many people created art. Why? Well, in a place where people are only focused on survival, on the bare necessities, the obvious conclusion is that art must be, somehow, essential for life. The camps were without money, without hope, without commerce, without recreation, without basic respect, but they were not without art. Art is part of survival; art is part of the human spirit, an unquenchable expression of who we are. Art is one of the ways in which we say, "I am alive, and my life has meaning."

In September 2001 I was a resident of Manhattan. That morning I reached a new understanding of my art and its relationship to the world. I sat down at the piano that morning at 10 am to practice as was my daily routine; I did it by force of habit, without thinking about it. I lifted the cover on the keyboard, and opened my music, and put my hands on the keys and took my hands off the keys. And I sat there and thought, does this even matter? Isn't this completely irrelevant? Playing the piano right now, given what happened in this city yesterday, seems silly, absurd, irreverent, pointless. Why am I here? What place has a musician in this moment in time? Who needs a piano player right now? I was completely lost.

And then I, along with the rest of New York, went through the journey of getting through that week. I did not play the piano that day, and in fact, I contemplated briefly whether I would ever want to play the piano again. And then I observed how we got through the day.

At least in my neighborhood, we didn't shoot hoops or play Scrabble. We didn't play cards to pass the time, we didn't watch TV, we didn't shop, we most certainly did not go to the mall. The first organized activity that I saw in New York, that same day, was singing. People sang. People sang around fire houses, people sang "We Shall Overcome." Lots of people sang "America the Beautiful." The first organized public event that I remember was the Brahms Requiem, later that week, at Lincoln Center, with the New York Philharmonic. The first organized public expression of grief, our first communal response to that historic event, was a concert. That was the beginning of a sense that life might go on. The US Military secured the airspace, but recovery was led by the arts, and by music in particular, that very night.

From these two experiences, I have come to understand that music is not part of "arts and entertainment" as the newspaper section would have us believe. It's not a luxury, a lavish thing that we fund from leftovers of our budgets, not a plaything or an amusement or a pass time. Music is a basic need of human survival. Music is one of the ways we make sense of our lives, one of the ways in which we express feelings when we have no words, a way for us to understand things with our hearts when we can't with our minds.

Some of you may know Samuel Barber's heart wrenchingly beautiful piece *Adagio for Strings*. If you don't know it by that name, then some of you may know it as the background music which accompanied the Oliver Stone movie "Platoon," a film about the Vietnam War. If you know that piece of music either way, you know it has the ability to crack your heart open like a walnut; it can make you cry over sadness you didn't know you had. Music can slip beneath our conscious reality to get at what's really going on inside us the way a good therapist does.

I bet that you have never been to a wedding where there was absolutely no music. There might have been only a little music, there might have been some really bad music, but I bet you there was some music. And something very predictable happens at weddings—people get all pent up with all kinds of emotions, and then there's some musical moment where the action of the wedding stops and someone sings or plays the flute or something. And even if the music is lame, even if the quality isn't good, predictably 30 or 40 percent of the people who are going to cry at a wedding cry a couple of moments after the music starts. Why? The Greeks. Music allows us to move around those big invisible pieces of ourselves and rearrange our insides so that we can express what we feel even when we can't talk about it. Can you imagine watching *Indiana Jones* or *Superman* or *Star Wars* with the dialogue but no music? What is it about the music swelling up at just the right moment in *ET* so that all the softies in the audience start crying at exactly the same moment? I guarantee you if you showed the movie with the music stripped out, it wouldn't happen that way. The Greeks: Music is the understanding of the relationship between invisible internal objects.

I'll give you one more example, the story of the most important concert of my life. I must tell you I have played a little less than a thousand concerts in my life so far. I have played in places that I thought were important. I like playing in Carnegie Hall; I enjoyed playing in Paris; it made me very happy to please the critics in St. Petersburg. I have played for people I thought were important; music critics of major newspapers, foreign heads of state. The most important concert of my entire life took place in a nursing home in Fargo, ND, about 4 years ago.

I was playing with a very dear friend of mine who is a violinist. We began, as we often do, with Aaron Copland's *Sonata*, which was written during World War II and dedicated to a young friend of Copland's, a young pilot who was shot down during the war. Now we often talk to our audiences about the pieces we are going to play rather than providing them with written program notes. But in this case, because we began the concert with this piece, we decided to talk about the piece later in the program and to just come out and play the music without explanation.

Midway through the piece, an elderly man seated in a wheelchair near the front of the concert hall began to weep. This man, whom I later met, was clearly a soldier — even in his 70's, it was clear from his buzz-cut hair, square jaw and general demeanor that he had spent a good deal of his life in the military. I thought it a little bit odd that someone would be moved to tears by that particular movement of that particular piece, but it wasn't the first time I've heard crying in a concert and we went on with the concert and finished the piece.

When we came out to play the next piece on the program, we decided to talk about both the first and second pieces, and we described the circumstances in which the Copland piece was written and mentioned its dedication to a downed pilot. The man in the front of the audience became so disturbed that he had to leave the auditorium. I honestly figured that we would not see him again, but he did come backstage afterwards, tears and all, to explain himself.

What he told us was this: "During World War II, I was a pilot, and I was in an aerial combat situation where one of my team's planes was hit. I watched my friend bail out, and watched his parachute open, but the Japanese planes which had engaged us returned and machine gunned across the parachute chords so as to separate the parachute from the pilot, and I watched my friend drop away into the ocean, realizing that he was lost. I have not thought about this for many years, but during that first piece of music you played, this memory returned to me so vividly that it was as though I was reliving it. I didn't understand why this was happening, why now, but then when you came out to explain that this piece of music was written to commemorate a lost pilot, it was a little more than I could handle. How does the music do that? How did it find those feelings and those memories in me?"

Remember the Greeks: music is the study of invisible relationships between internal objects. This concert in Fargo was the most important work I have ever done. For me to play for this old soldier and help him connect, somehow, with Aaron Copland, and to connect their memories of their lost friends, to help him remember and mourn his friend, this is my work. This is why music matters.

What follows is part of the talk I will give to this year's freshman class when I welcome them a few days from now. The responsibility I will charge your sons and daughters with is this:

"If we were a medical school, and you were here as a med student practicing appendectomies, you'd take your work very seriously because you would imagine that some night at 2 am someone is going to waltz into your emergency room and you're going to have to save their life.

Well, my friends, someday at 8 pm someone is going to walk into your concert hall and bring you a mind that is confused, a heart that is overwhelmed, a soul that is weary. Whether they go out whole again will depend partly on how well you do your craft.

"You're not here to become an entertainer, and you don't have to sell yourself. The truth is you don't have anything to sell; being a musician isn't about dispensing a product, like selling used Chevies. I'm not an entertainer; I'm a lot closer to a paramedic, a firefighter, a rescue worker. You're here to become a sort of therapist for the human soul, a spiritual version of a chiropractor, physical therapist, someone who works with our insides to see if they get things to line up, to see if we can come into harmony with ourselves and be healthy and happy and well.

"Frankly, ladies and gentlemen, I expect you not only to master music; I expect you to save the planet. If there is a future wave of wellness on this planet, of harmony, of peace, of an end to war, of mutual understanding, of equality, of fairness, I don't expect it will come from a government, a military force or a corporation. I no longer even expect it to come from the religions of the world, which together seem to have brought us as much war as they have peace. If there is a future of peace for humankind, if there is to be an understanding of how these invisible, internal things should fit together, I expect it will come from the artists, because that's what we do. As in the concentration camp and the evening of 9/11, the artists are the ones who might be able to help us with our internal, invisible lives."

Notes

1. **SAT:** the Scholastic Assessment Test. It's a standardized test widely used for college admissions in the United States.
2. **Olivier Messiaen** (1908—1992): a French composer, organist, and ornithologist, one of the major composers of the 20th century.
3. **"We Shall Overcome":** a gospel song which became a protest song and a key anthem of the Civil Rights Movement.
4. **"America the Beautiful":** one of the most popular of the many U.S. patriotic songs.
5. **Johannes Brahms** (1833—1897): a German composer and pianist.
6. **New York Philharmonic:** one of the leading American orchestras. It is based in New York city.
7. **Lincoln Center:** a complex of buildings in the Lincoln Square neighborhood of the borough of Manhattan in New York City. It hosts many notable performing arts organizations, which are nationally and internationally renowned, including the New York Philharmonic, the Metropolitan Opera, the New York City Ballet and the New York City Opera.

8. **Samuel Barber** (1910—1981): an American composer of orchestral, opera, choral, and piano music. He is one of the most celebrated composers of the twentieth century. His *Adagio for Strings* (1936) has earned a permanent place in the concert repertory of orchestras.

9. **Oliver Stone:** (1946—   ): an American writer and filmmaker.

10. *Platoon*: a 1986 American anti-war film written and directed by Oliver Stone. *Platoon* was the first Hollywood film to be written and directed by a veteran of the Vietnam War.

11. *Indiana Jones*: an American media franchise based on the adventures of Dr. Henry Walton "Indiana" Jones, Jr., a fictional professor of archaeology.

12. *Superman*: a superhero film. It was an international co-production between the United Kingdom, Switzerland, Panama and the United States.

13. *Star Wars*: an American epic space opera franchise, created by George Lucas and centered around a film series that began with the 1977 movie. The saga quickly became a worldwide pop culture phenomenon.

14. *ET*: a 1982 American science fiction film produced and directed by Steven Spielberg.

15. **Carnegie Hall:** a concert venue in Midtown Manhattan in New York City. It is one of the most prestigious venues in the world for both classical music and popular music.

16. **Aaron Copland** (1900—1990): an American composer, composition teacher, writer, and later a conductor of his own and other American music. Copland was referred to by his peers and critics as "the Dean of American Composers."

17. **Chevy:** Chevrolet colloquially referred to as Chevy and formally the Chevrolet Division of General Motors Company, is an American automobile division of the American manufacturer General Motors (GM).

Vocabulary

1. conservatory [kən'sɜvətɔri]: *n.* a school or college at which people are trained in music and theatre　音乐学院
2. astronomy [ə'strɑnəmi]: *n.* the scientific study of the sun, moon, stars, planets, etc.　天文学
3. quartet [kwɔr'tɛt]: *n.* a piece of music for four musicians or singers　四重奏
4. cellist ['tʃɛlɪst]: *n.* a person who plays the cello　大提琴演奏者
5. clarinetist [klærə'nɛtəst]: *n.* a person who plays the clarinet　单簧管演奏者
6. repertoire ['rɛpə:'twɑr]: *n.* all the plays, songs, pieces of music, etc. that a performer knows and can perform　可表演项目

7. Scrabble ['skræbl]: *n.* a board game in which players try to make words from letters printed on small plastic blocks and connect them to words that have already been placed on the board 拼字游戏

8. requiem ['rɛkwɪəm]: *n.* Christian ceremony for a person who has recently died, at which people say prayers for his or her soul （基督教）追思弥撒

9. lavish ['lævɪʃ]: *adj.* large in amount, or impressive, and usually costing a lot of money 耗资巨大的

10. lame [lem]: *adj.* poor or weak; not good 不太好的

11. sonata [sə'nɑtə]: *n.* a piece of music for one instrument and piano, usually divided into three or four parts 奏鸣曲

12. demeanor [di'miːnə]: *n.* the way what somebody looks or behaves 行为举止

13. auditorium [ˌɔdɪ'tɔrɪəm]: *n.* the part of a concert hall, etc. in which the audience sits 听众席

14. appendectomy [ˌæp(ə)n'dektəmɪ]: *n.* the removal of the appendix by surgery 阑尾切除术

15. dispense [dɪ'spɛns]: *vt.* to give out something to people 分发

16. paramedic [ˌpærə'mɛdɪk]: *n.* a person whose job is to help people who are sick or injured, but who is not a doctor or a nurse 护理人员

17. chiropractor ['kaɪəropræktəː]: *n.* a person whose job involves treating some diseases and physical problems by pressing and moving the bones in a person's spine or joints 脊椎指压治疗师

➔ *Expressions*

1. …people get all <u>pent up</u> with all kinds of emotions…
   pent up: having feelings that you cannot express 感情抑郁的；难以抒怀的

2. What is it about the music <u>swelling up</u> at just the right moment in "ET" so that all the softies in the audience start crying at exactly the same moment?
   swell up: (of a sound) to become louder 变得更响亮

3. I guarantee you if you showed the movie with the music <u>stripped out</u>, it wouldn't happen that way.
   strip out: to leave all the things from a place and leave it empty （使）空无一物

4. I watched my friend <u>bail out</u>…
   bail out: to jump out of a plane that is going to crash （从即将坠毁的飞机）跳伞

Comprehension

I. Discuss the Main Point and the Meanings.

1. How does music work on us? What is the value of music?
2. Why is art and music important to life according to Paulnack?
3. How could music find the hidden emotions and memories inside us?
4. How can our future sense of wellness and a future of peace come from the artists?

II. Fill in the blanks with the appropriate words or expressions in the box.

essential	harmony	hearts and souls
inside us	internal	make sense of
peace	we have no words	wellness
what we feel	who we are	

1. For the Greeks, music was seen as the study of relationships between invisible, _____, hidden objects. Music has a way of finding the big, invisible moving pieces inside our _____ and helping us figure out the position of things _____.

2. Art is _____ for life. It is part of survival; it is part of the human spirit, an unquenchable expression of _____.

3. Music is one of the ways we _____ our lives, one of the ways in which we express feelings when _____, a way for us to understand things with _____ when we can't with our minds.

4. Music can slip beneath our conscious reality to get at what's really going on _____ the way a good therapist does.

5. Music allows us to move around those big invisible pieces of ourselves and rearrange our insides so that we can express _____ even when we can't talk about it.

6. Musicians work with our insides to see if they get things to line up, to see if we can come into _____ with ourselves and be healthy and happy and well.

7. If there is a future wave of _____ on this planet, of harmony, of peace, of an end to war, of mutual understanding, of equality, of fairness, it will come from the artists.

8. If there is a future of _____ for humankind, if there is to be an understanding of how these invisible, internal things should fit together, will come from the artists.

Structure

I. Find out how the words and expression in bold are used in the following sentences.

1. I still remember my mother's remark when I announced my decision to **apply to** music school.

2. **Given** what we have since learned about life in the concentration camps, why would anyone in his right mind waste time and energy writing or playing music?

3. Along with the rest of New York, went through the journey of **getting through** that week.

4. From these two experiences, I **have come to** understand that music is not part of "arts and entertainment" as the newspaper section would have us believe.

5. Music can slip beneath our conscious reality to **get at** what's really **going on** inside us.

6. The most important concert of my entire life **took place** in a nursing home in Fargo, ND, about 4 years ago.

7. We **went on with** the concert and finished the piece.

8. Whether they go out whole again will **depend** partly **on** how well you do your craft.

9. Musicians work with our insides to see if they get things to **line up**.

10. If there is a future of peace for humankind, if there is to be an understanding of how these invisible, internal things should **fit together**, I expect it will come from the artists.

II. Complete the following sentences with some of the above words or expressions in bold.

1. Peter had a job _____ when he left college.

2. I'm all right here. _____ your work.

3. No one knows how Jim Crow _____ refer to racial discrimination in the US.

4. It is hard to see how people will _____ this winter.

5. You must _____ the directors for an increase in pay.

6. _____ her interest in children, teaching seems the right job for her.

7. The truth is sometimes difficult to _____.

8. Major changes _____ in that society.

9. The length of time spent exercising _____ the sport you are training for.

10. It is not clear how Jim Crow _____ describe American segregation and discrimination.

American Popular Music

Every aspect of popular music today regarded as American has sprung from imported traditions. These source traditions may be classified into three broad "streams": European-American music, African-American music, and Latin American music. The native American note was struck in the meeting of Afro-American and Euro-American styles. The first truly native American popular songs are the songs of Stephen Foster. Foster was influenced not only by the minstrel mimicry of slave music but also by Negro church music. After Foster's death in 1864, the disruption of the Civil War and Reconstruction in the lives and culture of black men and women kept black music away from the ears of white Americans, and popular music entered a recession that ended in the 1890s when the sounds of ragtime played by young black pianists began to be heard by a white public.

1. Ragtime

Ragtime is most commonly considered the first style of American popular music to be truly black music due to its essentially African American nature. Ragtime was a style of dance music which originated in the 1880s with black musicians in the saloons and brothels of the South and Midwest. It was played strictly for entertainment. Ragtime developed out of the rich tradition of sacred and secular songs through which African-Americans had long eased the burdens of their lives. Inventive, playful, with catchy syncopations and an infectious rhythm in the bass clef, the music displayed a fresh originality that had an appeal of its own. The "wild" and complex rhythms of ragtime, therefore, were widely interpreted to be a freer and more "natural" expression of elemental feelings about love and affection.

Ragtime's best known composer, Scott Joplin, a talented black piano player from St. Louis, introduced his music at Chicago's Columbian Exposition in 1893. "Maple Leaf Rag," published in 1899, earned him a national reputation.

2. Blues

The blues developed in the rural South in the first decade of the 20th century. The most important characteristics of the blues is its use of the blue scale, with a flatted or indeterminate third, as well as the typically lamenting lyrics. The blues is a genre of African American folk music that is the basis for much of modern American popular music. It is a combination of African work songs, field hollers and shouts.

Whether at work and at prayer, slaves liked to sing. Work songs describing slave experiences usually consisted of a leader's chant and a choral response. The songs of the slave represent the sorrows of his heart; and he is relieved by them, only as an aching heart is relieved by its tears.

Beginning in the 1920s and accelerating greatly in the 1940s, the blues began rapidly diversifying into a broad spectrum of new styles. These included an uptempo, energetic style called rhythm and blues (R&B), a merger of blues and Anglo-Celtic song called country music and the fusion of hymns and spirituals with blues structures called gospel music. Later than these other styles, in the 1940s, a blues, R&B and country fusion eventually called rock and roll developed, eventually coming to dominate American popular music by the beginning of the 1960s.

3. Jazz

Jazz emerged in New Orleans, Louisiana, around 1900 from the confluence of New Orleans's diverse musical traditions such as ragtime, marching bands, the rhythms used in Mardi Gras and funerary processions, French and Italian opera, Caribbean and Mexican music, Tin Pan Alley songs and African-American song traditions, both sacred (the spirituals) and secular (the blues).

Jazz is the anthem for the first well-defined American youth culture and one of America's original art forms. Jazz is a kind of music characterized by blue notes, syncopation, swing, call and response, polyrhythms, and improvisation. One of the distinguishing elements of jazz was its fluidity: in live performance, the musicians would almost never play a song the same way twice but would improvise variations on its notes and words. Louis Armstrong and his colleagues were improvisers, capable of creating numerous variations on a single melody.

Neither jazz nor its far-reaching influence on American music and culture ended in the 1930s. Swing grew out of and was strongly influenced by jazz. Beyond swing, every succeeding generation of musicians has defined its own style of jazz, responding to and challenging the aural legacy that began in New Orleans. Bebop, cool jazz, fusion jazz, soul jazz, and acid jazz are just a few of the varieties that have grown from the origin tree of sound.

4. Swing

In 1935, swing music became popular with the public and quickly replaced jazz as the most popular type of music. Swing is the synthesis of jazz and ballroom dance music. Swing music is characterized by a strong rhythm section, usually consisting of a double bass and drums, playing in a medium to fast tempo, and rhythmic devices like the swung note. Swing used bigger bands than other kinds of jazz, leading to bandleaders tightly arranging the material which discouraged improvisation, previously an integral part of jazz. Swing became a major part of African American dance, and came to be accompanied by a popular dance called the swing dance.

The basic ethos of swing music was one of unfettered enjoyment, "swinging," "having a ball."

5. Country Music

Country music is primarily a fusion of African American blues and spirituals with Appalachian folk music, adapted for pop audiences and popularized beginning in the 1920s. Of particular importance was Irish and Scottish tunes, dance music, balladry and vocal styles, as well as Native American, Spanish, German, French and Mexican music. Although country music is typically identified as a "white" style, some of its biggest stars have been black, and the styles of country musicians were strongly influenced by African-American music.

Popular American country music, is a commercial genre designed to "appeal to a working-class identity, whether or not its listeners are actually working class". Country music is also intertwined with geographic identity, and is specifically rural in origin and function; other genres, like R&B and hip hop, are perceived as inherently urban.

Modern country music — original songs about contemporary concerns — developed in the 1920s, roughly coinciding with a mass migration of rural people to big cities in search of work. Country music tends to have a melancholy sound, and many classic songs are about loss or separation — lost homes, parents left behind, lost loves. Country music always tells a story, which perhaps is the very reason for its success. People can relate to the heart inside the lyrics.

6. Rhythm and Blues

Rhythm and blues (R&B) is a style that arose in the 1930s and 1940s, a rhythmic and uptempo form of blues with more complex instrumentation. Author Amiri Baraka described early R&B as "huge rhythm units smashing away behind screaming blues singers (who) had to shout to be heard above the clanging and strumming of the various electrified instruments and the churning rhythm sections." R&B was recorded during this period, but not extensively and was not widely promoted by record companies, who felt it was not suited for most audiences, especially middle-class whites, because of the suggestive lyrics and driving rhythms.

Michael Jackson and Prince have been described as the most influential figures in contemporary R&B and popular music because of their eclectic use of elements from a variety of genres. The use of melisma, a gospel tradition adapted by vocalists Whitney Houston and Mariah Carey would become a cornerstone of contemporary R&B singers beginning in the late 1980s and throughout the 1990s.

7. Gospel

Christian spirituals and rural blues music were the origin of what is now known as gospel music. Beginning in about the 1920s, African American churches featured early gospel in the form of worshipers proclaiming their religious devotion in an improvised, often musical manner. From these early 20th-century churches, gospel music spread across the country. It remained associated almost entirely with African American churches, and usually featured a choir along with one or more virtuoso soloists.

8. Rock and Roll

Rock and roll is a kind of popular music, developed primarily out of country, blues and R&B. The advent of rock 'n' roll music in the mid-1950s brought enormous changes to American popular music. It was an event of great cultural significance. But, rock 'n' roll was neither a "new," nor indeed even a single musical style; and rock 'n' roll era does not mark the first time that music was written specifically to appeal to young people. Growing up with rock 'n' roll music became a defining characteristic of the baby boom generation.

Three prominent African Americans represent the rhythm & blues-based side of rock 'n' roll: Chuck Berry was a songwriter/performer who addressed his songs to teenage America (white and black) in the 1950s; Little Richard cultivated a deliberately outrageous performance style that appealed on the basis of its strangeness, novelty, and sexual ambiguity; and Fats Domino's work embodied the continuity of rhythm & blues with rock 'n' roll. Domino was the earliest performer, but all three crossed over to mainstream success within the first few months following the massive success of the white rocker Bill Haley's "Rock Around the Clock."

The biggest rock 'n' roll star to come from the country side of the music world was Elvis Presley who brought rock and roll to audiences across the world. It was the white performer Elvis Presley who first appealed to mainstream audiences with a black style of music, becoming one of the best-selling musicians in history.

Bob Dylan extended the reach of folk music by writing striking new songs that addressed contemporary social problems, especially the denial of civil rights to black Americans. Dylan led virtually the entire folk movement into a blend of rock and folk. Jimi Hendrix was the most original, inventive, and influential guitarist of the rock era, and the most prominent African-American rock musician of the late 1960s.

Following the turbulent political, social and musical changes of the 1960s and early 1970s, rock music diversified. What was formerly known as *rock and roll*, a reasonably discrete style of music, had evolved into a catchall category called simply *rock music*, an umbrella term which would eventually include diverse styles like heavy metal music, punk rock and, sometimes even hip-hop music.

9. Soul

Soul music (often referred to simply as soul) is a popular music genre that originated in the United States in the late 1950s and early 1960s. It combines elements of African-American gospel music, rhythm and blues and jazz. Soul music became popular for dancing and listening in the United States; where record labels such as Motown, Atlantic and Stax were influential in the civil rights era. Soul also became popular around the world, directly influencing rock music and the music of Africa.

Catchy rhythms, stressed by handclaps and extemporaneous body moves, are an important feature of soul music. Other characteristics are a call and response between the lead vocalist and the chorus and an especially tense vocal sound. The style also occasionally uses improvisational additions, twirls and auxiliary sounds. Soul music reflected the African-American identity and it stressed the importance of an African-American culture. The new-found African-American consciousness led to new styles of music, which boasted pride in being black.

10. Hip-hop

Hip-hop music started in the South Bronx area of New York City in the early 1970s among young African Americans and Latino Americans. Rap's biggest audience is white suburban teenagers who seek the runaway thrills of gangbanging, drugs, guns, and crime without any risk to themselves. Rappers and their audiences, in particular, view rap and rap videos as subversions of the dominant society, just as baby boomers in the 1960s used rock-and-roll in challenging the "Establishment."

There are four main parts of hip-hop: MCing is singing words or what is called rapping. DJing is using records to produce special sounds. Graffiti is writing messages on outdoor surfaces. And breakdancing is a special kind of dance. Rapping could be described as speaking or singing words at a fast speed over music with quick beats. Some reports say rapping came from the West African tradition of Griots. These storytellers would quickly tell a story while someone played music.

11. Pop Music

Pop music refers to music of general appeal to teenagers; a bland watered-down version of rock 'n' roll with more rhythm and harmony and an emphasis on romantic love. It usually consists of relatively short, simple songs utilizing technological innovations to produce new variations on existing themes.

Unit 11   Music

Like other art forms that aim to attract a mass audience (movies, television, Broadway shows), pop music has been and continues to be a melting pot that borrows and assimilates elements and ideas from a wide range of musical styles. Rock, R&B, country, disco, punk, and hip-hop are all specific genres of music that have influenced and been incorporated into pop music in various ways over the past five decades. Most recently, Latin music seems to be impacting pop music more significantly than at any point in the past.

12. Music Industry

The American music industry includes a number of fields, ranging from record companies to radio stations and community orchestras. Record companies may be affiliated with other music media companies, which produce a product related to popular recorded music. These include television channels like MTV, magazines like *Rolling Stone* and radio stations.

Commercial sales of recordings are tracked by *Billboard* magazine, which compiles a number of music charts for various fields of recorded music sales. The Billboard Hot 100 is the top pop music chart for singles, a recording consisting of a handful of songs; longer pop recordings are albums, and are tracked by the Billboard 200.

13. Grammy Awards

Grammy Awards are prizes given annually in the United States by the National Academy of Recording Arts and Sciences (NARAS) for excellence in the recording industry. The name is derived from an early phonograph called a gramophone. The Grammy Awards are presented in February for recordings released during the previous eligibility period, which runs from October 1st to September 30th. They recognize outstanding performances of various types of music, including rock, folk, jazz, country, gospel, rhythm and blues, popular, and classical. In addition, NARAS gives honors for music videos, spoken-word recordings, motion-picture or television scores, album packaging and album notes, and promising new artists, as well as for composition, musical arrangement, engineering, and production. New categories are added and old categories are dropped as the industry changes and grows.

➔ *Vocabulary of Music*

1. They listened to **classical music** all the time.
2. Your kids are about to engage in **serious music**.
3. One of the most profound musical **compositions** of all time is the ***Quartet** for the End of Time* written by French **composer** Olivier Messiaen in 1940.

4. There were three other musicians in the camp, a **cellist**, a **violinist**, and a **clarinetist**.

5. Today it is one of the most famous masterworks in the **repertoire**.

6. Given what we have since learned about life in the concentration camps, why would anyone in his right mind waste time and energy writing or **playing** music?

7. The first organized public event that I remember was the Brahms **Requiem**.

8. The first organized public expression of grief was a **concert**.

9. We began, as we often do, with Aaron Copland's **Sonata**.

10. Music can be divided into many **genres** in many different ways.

11. The blues is a **combination** of African work songs, field hollers and shouts.

12. R & B is a **merger** of blues and country music.

13. Country music is a primarily a **fusion** of African American blues and spirituals with Appalachian folk music.

14. Swing is the **synthesis** of jazz and ballroom dance music.

15. Rock and roll **developed/came/sprang** primarily out of the country, blues and R&B.

16. The "wild" and complex **rhythms** of ragtime were widely interpreted to be a freer and more "natural" expression of elemental feelings about love and affection.

17. It combines a solid, often lively, **beat** with a looser, complex **melody**.

18. A "clear" **tone** is the ideal for the aesthetics of Western art music.

19. The most important characteristics of the blues is its use of the blue scale as well as the typically lamenting **lyrics**.

20. In live performance, the jazz musicians would improvise variations on the **notes** and **words** of a song.

21. The blues **diversified** into a broad spectrum of new styles.

22. Michael Jackson and Prince have been described as the most influential figures in contemporary R&B and popular music because of their **eclectic** use of elements from a variety of genres.

23. The music **brought together** elements from diverse musical traditions.

24. Pop music has **absorbed** influences from most other genres of popular music.

25. Pop music has been and continues to be a melting pot that **borrows** and **assimilates** elements and ideas from a wide range of musical **styles**.

26. Call-and-response forms, in which a **lead singer** and **chorus** alternate, are a hallmark of African-American musical traditions.

27. Gospel usually features a **choir** along with one or more virtuoso **soloists**.

Answer Key

Unit 1

Comprehension

Fill in the blanks with the appropriate words or expressions in the box.

1. The tonal range of the national anthem corresponds to that of the electric guitar, but not to that of the human voice.

2. The lyrics of the national anthem are a reliable source of titles for the type of potboiler novel, but on the whole the words don't convey core American values.

3. Music teachers don't like "The Star-Spangled Banner" because it is too martial, too irritating, too hard to sing.

4. "The Battle Hymn of the Republic" is perhaps the greatest patriotic hymn ever written.

5. "Lift Ev'ry Voice and Sing" conveys good, solid values that are both American and universal.

Structure

Complete the following sentences with some of the above words or expressions in bold.

1. Many local people object to the building of the new airport.

2. We can't get there before two at best.

3. Panic on the stock market set off a wave of selling.

4. The British job of Lecturer corresponds roughly to the US Associate Professor.

5. The women's shoe, like its male counterpart, is specifically designed for the serious tennis player.

227

6. She <u>came up with</u> a brilliant idea to raise the funds.

7. Several houses have to be pulled down to <u>make way for</u> the new theatre.

8. He'd heard her complaints <u>over the years</u> but didn't take them that seriously.

9. He is so brilliant. I <u>cannot but</u> admire him.

10. I'm not a Republican, and I don't drink scotch, so you are wrong <u>on both counts</u>.

11. There's no point complaining now—we're leaving tomorrow <u>in any case</u>.

12. <u>On the whole</u>, I'm in favor of this idea.

Unit 2

Comprehension

Fill in the blanks with the appropriate words or expressions in the box.

1. Borders everywhere attract violence, violence prompts fences, and eventually fences can mutate into <u>walls</u>. Then everyone pays attention because a wall turns <u>a legal distinction</u> into a visual slap in the face.

2. We seem to love walls, but are embarrassed by them because they say something unpleasant about the neighbors — and us. They flow from two sources: <u>fear</u> and <u>the desire for control</u>.

3. Just as our houses have doors and locks, so do <u>borders</u> call forth garrisons, customs officials, and, now and then, big walls.

4. Residents register a hodgepodge of <u>feelings</u> about the wall.

5. A border wall seems to violate a deep sense of identity most Americans cherish. We see ourselves as a nation of <u>immigrants</u> with our own goddess, the Statue of Liberty, a potent symbol as the visual representation of our yearning for freedom.

6. Walls are curious statements of <u>human needs</u>. Sometimes they are built to keep restive population from <u>fleeing</u>. But most walls are for keeping people out.

7. We think of walls as statements of <u>foreign policy</u>, and we forget the intricate lives of the people we wall in and out.

8. What has changed is this physical statement, a big wall lined with bright lights, that says, yes, <u>we are two nations</u>.

9. Everyone realizes the wall is <u>a police solution</u> to an economic problem.

10. <u>Walls</u> come and go, but quinceañeras are forever…

Answer Key

Structure

Complete the following sentences with some of the above words or expressions in bold.

1. She <u>lightened up</u> when she found out it wasn't so bad after all.
2. Voters wish to <u>register</u> their dissatisfaction with the ruling party.
3. They <u>wound up</u> in an unhappy marriage.
4. This company <u>has changed hands</u> many times over the years.
5. His predictions <u>turned out</u> to be quite wrong.
6. The immigrants were able to come and go <u>at will</u> before the wall.
7. You can hear <u>a touch of</u> sarcasm in her voice.
8. It has no industry, and about two-thirds of the population <u>live off</u> the government.
9. A new social class <u>came into being</u> because of this change in the society.
10. His speech <u>called forth</u> an angry response.
11. They <u>insisted upon</u> a refund of the full amount.
12. He <u>put up</u> a fence between his property and his neighbour's.
13. How many new houses have <u>gone up</u> this year?
14. Someone <u>broke into</u> my car and stole my bag.
15. Robert will open the debate and I will <u>sum up</u>.

Unit 3

Comprehension

Fill in the blanks with the appropriate words or expressions in the box.

1. Some scholars think since all historical judgments involve persons and points of view, one is as good as another and there is no "<u>objective</u>" historical truth.

2. History consists of <u>a corpus of ascertained facts</u>. This is what may be called the common-sense view of history.

3. First get your <u>facts</u> straight, then plunge at your peril into the shifting sands of <u>interpretation</u>—that is the ultimate wisdom of the empirical, common-sense school of history.

4. It recalls the favorite dictum of the great liberal journalist C. P. Scott: "<u>Facts</u> are sacred, opinion is free."

5. According to the common-sense view, there are <u>certain basic facts</u> which are the same for all historians and which form, so to speak, the backbone of history.

6. But when points of this kind are raised, I am reminded of Housman's remark that "<u>accuracy</u>

229

is a duty, not a virtue." To praise a historian for his accuracy is like praising an architect for using well-seasoned timber or properly mixed concrete in his building. It is a necessary condition of his work, but not his <u>essential function</u>.

7. These so-called basic facts which are the same for all historians commonly belong to the category of <u>the raw materials</u> of the historian rather than of history itself.

8. It used to be said that facts <u>speak for themselves</u>. This is of course, untrue. The facts speak only when the historian calls on them: It is he who decides to which facts to give the floor, and in what order or context.

9. The historian is necessarily <u>selective</u>. The belief in a hard core of <u>historical facts</u> existing objectively and independently of the interpretation of the historian is a preposterous fallacy, but one which it is very hard to eradicate.

10. The elements of <u>interpretation</u> enters into every fact of history.

Structure

Complete the following sentences with some of the above words or expressions in bold.

1. You have no experience to <u>call on</u>; you have never seen anything like this.

2. Anxiety about climate change may have, <u>so to speak</u>, gone off the boil in Washington, where the Democrats show no appetite to decisive action.

3. It doesn't <u>make sense</u> for you to work for 40 years in a job you hate.

4. College professors are supposed to both teach and <u>undertake</u> research at the same time.

5. I <u>look forward to</u> seeing you again soon.

6. Has it ever <u>occurred to</u> you that he might have lied to you?

7. The painting <u>appeals to</u> all ages and social groups.

8. The situation <u>calls for</u> prompt action.

9. They <u>were about to</u> start when it rained.

10. Their ideas did not quite <u>fit in with</u> our plans.

Unit 4

Comprehension

Fill in the blanks with the appropriate words or expressions in the box.

1. Our picture of fifth-century Greece has been <u>preselected</u> and <u>predetermined</u> by people who were consciously or unconsciously imbued with a particular view.

Answer Key

2. Professor Barraclough writes: "The history we read, though based on <u>facts</u>, is, strictly speaking, not <u>factual</u> at all, but a series of accepted <u>judgments</u>."

3. Lytton Strachey said in his mischievous way, "<u>ignorance</u> is the first requisite of the historian, <u>ignorance</u> which simplifies and clarifies, which selects and omits."

4. The modern historian has the dual task of discovering the few significant facts and turning them into <u>facts of history</u>, and of discarding the many insignificant facts as unhistorical.

5. What had gone wrong was the belief in this untiring and unending accumulation of <u>hard facts</u> as the foundation of history, the belief that <u>facts</u> speak for themselves and that we cannot have too many facts.

6. What really happened in the past would have to be <u>reconstructed</u> in the mind of the historian.

7. Facts and documents are essential to the historian. But they do not by themselves constitute <u>history</u>.

8. The liberal nineteenth-century view of history had a close affinity with the economic doctrine of laissez-faire—also the product of a <u>serene</u> and <u>self-confident</u> outlook on the world.

→ *Structure*

Complete the following sentences with some of the above words or expressions in bold.

1. She doesn't like being around her colleagues because she often feels <u>inferior</u>.
2. The band <u>have</u> just <u>brought out</u> their second album.
3. He had to <u>give up</u> his studies through lack of money.
4. <u>By and large</u>, I enjoyed my time in the United States.
5. With the election out of the way, the government can <u>get down to</u> business.
6. I <u>came upon</u> an irresistible item at the yard sale.
7. The whole argument <u>rests on</u> a false assumption.
8. The government is trying to <u>get on with</u> the job of running the country in spite of impossible difficulties.
9. Even in prison, he continued to <u>engage in</u> criminal activities.
10. All this gloomy news is enough to make you <u>take to</u> drink.

Unit 5

→ Comprehension

Fill in the blanks with the appropriate words or expressions in the box.

1. Croce declared that all history is "contemporary history," meaning that history consists essentially in seeing the past through the eyes of <u>the present</u> and in the light of its problems, and that the main work of the historian is not to record, but to <u>evaluate</u>.

2. The philosophy of history is concerned neither with "the past by itself" nor with "the historian's thought about it by itself," but with "the two things in their <u>mutual relations</u>."

3. "All history is the history of thought," and "history is the re-enactment in the historian's mind of <u>the thought</u> whose history he is studying."

4. The facts of history never come to us "pure," since they are always refracted through <u>the mind of the recorder</u>.

5. Historians need to have <u>imaginative understanding</u> for the minds of the people with whom he is dealing, for the thought behind their act.

6. We can view the past, and achieve our understanding of the past, only through the eyes of <u>the present</u>.

7. The function of the historian is to master and understand the past as the key to <u>the understanding of the present</u>.

8. Either you write scissors-and-paste history without <u>meaning</u> or <u>significance</u>; or you write propaganda or historical fiction, and merely use <u>facts of the past</u> to embroider a kind of writing which has nothing to do with history.

9. The relation between the historian and his facts is one of <u>equality</u>, of give-and-take.

10. History is a continuous process of <u>interaction</u> between the historian and his facts, an unending <u>dialogue</u> between the present and the past.

→ Structure

Complete the following sentences with some of the above words or expressions in bold.

1. Let's form a <u>provisional</u> government until we can hold an election.

2. She hasn't actually refused, but it <u>amounts to</u> the same thing.

3. She <u>was brought up</u> to respect the laws.

4. I wanted to go to the movie with you, but <u>in the light of</u> the changed circumstances, I'd better go to the hospital.

5. The winners are <u>as follows</u>: Johnson, Miller and Smith.

6. The book <u>in itself</u> is not about racism, but the title is misleading.

7. <u>It</u> doesn't necessarily <u>follow that</u> you're going to do well academically even if you are highly intelligent.

8. All citizens <u>are subject to</u> the laws of this country.

9. The couple next door have a <u>reciprocal</u> loathing for each other.

10. We can't <u>rule out</u> the possibility that she lost her passport.

Unit 6

Comprehension

Fill in the blanks with the appropriate words or expressions in the box.

1. Conservatives tend to blame dependence on government assistance on <u>personal irresponsibility</u> aggravated by a swollen welfare apparatus that saps <u>individual initiative</u>.

2. Liberals are more likely to blame the dependence on government assistance on <u>personal misfortune</u> magnified by the harsh lot that falls to losers in our competitive market economy.

3. Both conservatives and liberals believe that "winners" in America make it <u>on their own</u>.

4. Few families in American history have been able to rely solely on <u>their own resources</u>.

5. Historically, one way that government has played a role in the well-being of its citizens is by <u>regulating</u> the way that employers and civic bodies interact with families.

6. Government has always supported families with <u>direct material aid</u> as well.

7. Federal subsidies to suburbia <u>encouraged</u> family formation, residential stability, upward occupational mobility, and rising educational aspirations among youth.

8. As long as we pretend that only poor or single-parent families need outside assistance, while normal families "stand on their own two feet," we will <u>shortchange</u> poor families, <u>overcompensate</u> rich ones, and fail to come up with effective policies for helping out families in the middle.

9. The reforms in America's aid policies to the poor should put welfare in the context of <u>all federal assistance programs</u>.

10. <u>Assisting families</u> is, simply, what government does.

Structure

Complete the following sentences with some of the above words or expressions in bold.

1. It is hard to <u>reconcile</u> her career ambitions <u>with</u> the needs of her children.

2. Some of the things happening now may seem <u>reminiscent of</u> the old cold war.

3. The national government became involved in areas that <u>previously</u> had been the responsibility of the states.

4. The railway <u>opened up</u> the west of the country.

5. The stripes symbolize the 13 colonies that originally <u>comprised</u> the United States.

6. The change of management <u>ushered in</u> fresh ideas and policies.

7. Police are <u>blaming</u> the accident <u>on</u> drunken driving.

8. When are you going to <u>settle down</u> and have a family?

9. Britain <u>is being left behind</u> in the race for new markets.

10. The council <u>set up</u> a committee to look into unemployment.

11. It's hard to <u>make it</u> to the top in show business.

12. The 13 stripes in the American Flag represent the 13 colonies that originally <u>comprised</u> the United States.

13. This agreement will <u>break down</u> the barriers to free trade.

14. <u>In the face of</u> great hardship, she managed to keep her sense of humor.

15. I can't carry out the plan <u>on my own</u>. It's too time-consuming.

Unit 7

Comprehension

Fill in the blanks with the appropriate words or expressions from the text.

1. Practical atheists are <u>disguised nonbelievers</u> who behave during the rest of the week as if God did not exist.

2. Leaving <u>unanswered</u> the question of what to say God is, some theologians are instead concentrating on an exploration of the ultimate and unconditional in modern life.

3. While modern men have rejected God as a solution to life, they cannot evade <u>a questioning anxiety</u> about its meaning.

4. The apparent eclipse of God is merely a sign that the world is experiencing what Jesuit theologian Karl Rahner calls "<u>the anonymous presence</u>" of God, whose word comes to man not on tablets of stone but in the inner murmurings of the heart.

Answer Key

5. Langdon Gilkey argues that the area of life dealing with <u>the ultimate</u> and with mystery points the way toward God.

6. To Oxford theologian Ian Ramsey, the area of ultimate concern offers what he calls "<u>discernment situations</u>"—events that can be the occasion for insight, for awareness of something beyond man.

7. Rudolf Bultmann answers that these human situations of anxiety and discernment represent "<u>transformations of God</u>," and are the only way that secular man is likely to experience any sense of the eternal and unconditional.

8. As always, faith is something of <u>an irrational leap</u> in the dark, a gift of God.

9. God will be seen as <u>the order</u> in which life takes on meaning, as being, as the source of creativity, suggests Langdon Gilkey.

10. Langdon Gilkey argues that Christianity must go on escaping from its too-strictly anthropomorphic past, and still needs to learn that talk of God is largely <u>symbolic</u>.

11. The churches, moreover, will also have to accept the <u>empiricism</u> of the modern outlook and become more <u>secular</u> themselves.

12. To some, this suggests that the church might well need to take a position of <u>reverent agnosticism</u> regarding some doctrines that it had previously proclaimed with excessive conviction.

13. But Christian history allows the possibility of <u>development</u> in doctrine, and even an admission of ignorance in the face of the divine mystery is part of tradition.

14. St. Thomas Aquinas declared that "we cannot know what God is, but rather <u>what he is not</u>."

15. Gabriel Vahanian suggests that there may well be no true faith without <u>a measure of doubt</u>, and thus contemporary Christians worry about God could be a necessary and healthy antidote to centuries in which faith was too confident and sure.

→ *Structure*

Complete the following sentences with some of the above words or expressions in bold.

1. The fall in the number of deaths from heart disease <u>is</u> generally <u>attributed to</u> improvements in diet.

2. The President trusted him so much that he <u>conferred on</u> him the role of "Principal Advisor."

3. What he says is right <u>in a sense</u>.

4. You must <u>put aside</u> your pride and call her.

235

5. He had time to <u>reflect on</u> his successes and failures.

6. Don't worry, we'll <u>get along</u> without you.

7. People thought that the use of robots would <u>do away with</u> boring low-paid factory jobs.

8. He felt he needed to <u>focus</u> more <u>on</u> his career.

9. Here again are today's headlines <u>in brief</u>.

10. The truth, <u>as always</u>, is more complicated.

Unit 8

Comprehension

Fill in the blanks with the appropriate words or expressions in the box.

1. *Commentary* pages and Doonesbury panels alike have lampooned the self-esteem movement as a baleful confluence of <u>1960s liberal indulgence</u> and soft psychology that distracts from schools' central mission of <u>teaching the basics</u>.

2. Indeed, the critics' back-to-basics call to teach just reading and writing will also <u>fail</u> large numbers of children.

3. Instead, educators need to embark on a third path: developing <u>a wide range of intellectual and social skills</u> in children and creating more sustained relationships between children and adults.

4. Self-esteem doesn't lead to greater academic achievement unless a child <u>values such achievement</u>.

5. Too much <u>unconditional praise</u> produces not self-confidence but cynicism about adults and doubts about themselves.

6. No amount of <u>talking</u> about discrimination can substitute for raising nonwhite children's achievements.

7. Cultivating capacities such as self-awareness, control of one's impulses, and persistence needn't detract from <u>teaching academics</u>.

8. Schools should <u>set high expectations of children</u>, cultivate in them a wide range of competencies, coping strategies, and ethical sensibilities and show them the value of these abilities.

9. Persistence, the capacity to handle shame and disappointment, the ability to recognize the needs of others, and to balance them with one's own are the <u>ingredients of maturity</u>.

10. All children need <u>adults</u> who listen to and understand them and regularly reflect their understanding. At certain stages of development, every child needs adults whom he or she <u>idealizes</u>.

→ Structure

Complete the following sentences with some of the above words or expressions in bold.

1. He is a teacher <u>worthy of</u> respect.

2. The Industrial Revolution, <u>among other things</u>, necessarily produced general literacy.

3. The recipe says you can <u>substitute</u> yogurt <u>for</u> the sour cream.

4. The law requires equal treatment for all, <u>regardless of</u> race, religion, or sex.

5. That little girl is interested in writing <u>for its own sake</u>.

6. Most slimmers <u>end up</u> putting weight back on.

7. His reluctance to help could, <u>in part</u>, be explained by his laziness.

8. When women joined the organization, it "took on a new look," <u>as</u> news reports <u>put it</u>.

9. <u>For all</u> her efforts, she didn't succeed.

10. <u>Granted</u>, the music is not perfect, but the flaws are outweighed by the sheer joy of the piece.

Unit 9

→ Comprehension

Fill in the blanks with the appropriate words or expressions from the box.

1. Quitters never win, and winners never <u>quit</u>.

2. The "lessons of sports" help to <u>orient</u> us to the world and give us much learning about life, and even politics.

3. The game becomes a public arena for the <u>enactment</u> of the more interesting aspects of human life—competition, teamwork, risk-taking, aggression and defense, winning and losing.

4. Sports, like popular drama, dramatizes exemplary situations with which we can <u>identify</u>.

5. Sports involve the affirmation of cultural myths, since sports "<u>participate</u>" in the social order.

6. The ideal of sportsmanship has persisted in political rhetoric as a norm by which the game is supposed to be played, i.e., that one plays <u>fair</u>, enjoys the contest, and accepts victory with magnanimity and defeat with grace.

7. Sportsmanship, on the field or in politics, consists of such attitudes as tolerating and honoring the opposition; being a gracious winner and loser; and playing "the game of politics" within <u>the bounds of rules</u> and fair play.

8. Winning isn't everything, goes Lombardi's Law, it's <u>the only thing</u>.

9. Nice guys, Durocher's Dictum has it, <u>finish</u> last.

10. Like religion and show business, sports offer the politician association with something <u>non-political</u> that large numbers of people are attracted to.

→ Structure

Complete the following sentences with some of the above words or expressions in bold.

1. Soldiers, policemen, <u>and the like</u> were all called in to help with the emergency.

2. You know what this is about. Why pretend <u>otherwise</u>.

3. Our students <u>are oriented</u> toward science subjects.

4. Her confession <u>might well</u> be a lie, but her original story certainly is.

5. Now do you <u>recall</u> that song I taught you?

6. This is one reason why bad habits need to be stopped as <u>early on</u> as possible, before they have been repeated too many times.

7. *The Reagans* condemned the book, which was <u>variously</u> believed and disbelieved by critics and insiders.

8. Mary had to give a speech in front of all the staff, but she proved quite <u>equal to</u> the situation.

9. The newspaper, or more <u>specifically</u>, the editor, was taken to court for publishing the photographs.

10. The children call out their names <u>in turn</u>.

11. The novelist <u>draws</u> heavily <u>upon</u> her personal experiences.

12. She directed the question at no one <u>in particular</u>.

13. Don't give up until you <u>have exhausted</u> all the possibilities.

14. He asked to speak to the person <u>in charge</u>.

15. The government has threatened to <u>cut off</u> economic and military aid to this region.

Unit 10

→ Comprehension

Fill in the blanks with the appropriate words or expressions in the box.

1. Society's values have changed. That kind of scrupulous, ethical concern for the sanctity of human life doesn't exist in the same way, and that fact is <u>reflected</u> in the movies.

2. Before they can be anything else, American movies are <u>a product</u>. The consumers make

Answer Key

their choices.

3. Filmmaking has always been an uneasy merger of two antithetical things: some form of <u>art</u> and sheer <u>commerce</u>.

4. The only practical approach a filmmaker can take is to make a film that he or she would want to see, and you hope that as many people as possible will like it too. If that happens, it's because you've done something in the telling of the story that <u>makes people care</u>.

5. The best part of what the filmmaker does—the part, when it works, that makes you want to see the film—doesn't come from a rational, consciously controllable process. It comes from somewhere inside the filmmaker's <u>unconscious</u>.

6. When making films, Pollack tries to discover and tell <u>the truth</u> and not be dull about it. He tries to discover and describe things like the motives that are hidden in day-to-day life.

7. For the most part, the impulse toward all art, entertainment, culture, pop culture, comes from the same place within the makers of it. The level of <u>talent</u> and the <u>soul</u>, is what finally limits it.

8. Pollack makes the movies because there is in each film <u>some argument</u> that fascinates him, <u>an issue</u> he wants to work through.

9. The effectiveness and the success of all our films is determined by their ability to engage <u>the concentration and emotions</u> of the audience.

10. American culture is <u>general</u>. America has the most easily digestible culture.

11. No force except <u>the moral climate and appetites</u> of our society can regulate the filmmaking.

12. In the best of all possible worlds, filmmakers do try to satisfy both needs; <u>entertain people</u> and be reasonably intelligent about it.

Structure

Complete the following sentences with some of the above words or expressions in bold.

1. We had to go and see the president one <u>at a time</u>.
2. Mary was determined to become a doctor and her persistence <u>paid off</u>.
3. You are not <u>going about</u> the job in the right way.
4. The committee <u>has put forward</u> new peace proposals.
5. Special conditions <u>apply</u> if you are under 18.
6. This conversation <u>adds up to</u> a difference of opinion between us.
7. As is usual in this kind of movie, good <u>triumphs over</u> evil in the end.
8. John is not a man to <u>take chances</u>.

9. It took him one hour to <u>figure out</u> how to start the machine.

10. The film has eerie parallel with the drama <u>being played out</u> in real life.

Unit 11

→ Comprehension

Fill in the blanks with the appropriate words or expressions in the box.

1. For the Greeks, music was seen as the study of relationships between invisible, <u>internal</u>, hidden objects. Music has a way of finding the big, invisible moving pieces inside our <u>hearts and souls</u> and helping us figure out the position of things <u>inside us</u>.

2. Art is <u>essential</u> for life. It is part of survival; it is part of the human spirit, an unquenchable expression of <u>who we are</u>.

3. Music is one of the ways we <u>make sense of</u> our lives, one of the ways in which we express feelings when <u>we have no words</u>, a way for us to understand things with <u>our hearts</u> when we can't with our minds.

4. Music can slip beneath our conscious reality to get at what's really going on <u>inside us</u> the way a good therapist does.

5. Music allows us to move around those big invisible pieces of ourselves and rearrange our insides so that we can express <u>what we feel</u> even when we can't talk about it.

6. Musicians work with our insides to see if they get things to line up, to see if we can come into <u>harmony</u> with ourselves and be healthy and happy and well.

7. If there is a future wave of <u>wellness</u> on this planet, of harmony, of peace, of an end to war, of mutual understanding, of equality, of fairness, it will come from the artists.

8. If there is a future of <u>peace</u> for humankind, if there is to be an understanding of how these invisible, internal things should fit together, will come from the artists.

→ Structure

Complete the following sentences with some of the above words or expressions in bold.

1. Peter had a job <u>lined up</u> when he left college.

2. I'm all right here. <u>Go on with</u> your work.

3. No one knows how Jim Crow <u>has come to</u> refer to racial discrimination in the U.S.

4. It is hard to see how people will <u>get through</u> this winter.

5. You must <u>apply to</u> the directors for an increase in pay.

Answer Key

6. <u>Given</u> her interest in children, teaching seems the right job for her.

7. The truth is sometimes difficult to <u>get at</u>.

8. Major changes <u>are taking place</u> in that society.

9. The length of time spent exercising <u>depends on</u> the sport you are training for.

10. It is not clear how Jim Crow <u>came to</u> describe American segregation and discrimination.

读本中的美国文化与社会

尊敬的老师：

您好！

为了方便您更好地使用本教材，我们特向使用该书作为教材的老师赠送本书配套电子课件。如有需要请完整填写"教师联系表"并加盖所在单位系（院）或培训中心公章，免费向出版社索取。谢谢！

北京大学出版社

教 师 联 系 表

教材名称	读本中的美国文化与社会					
姓名：		性别：		职务：		职称：
E-mail:			联系电话：		邮政编码：	
供职学校：			所在院系：			（章）
学校地址：						
教学科目与年级：			班级人数：			
通信地址：						

填写完毕后，请将此表邮寄给我们，我们将为您免费寄送本教材配套课件，谢谢！

北京市海淀区成府路205号
北京大学出版社外语编辑部　　邮 购 部 电 话：010-62752015
邮政编码：100871　　　　　　市场营销部电话：010-62750672
电子邮箱：zln0120@163.com　　外语编辑部电话：010-62759634